Japanese Stitches Unraveled

160+ STITCH PATTERNS TO KNIT TOP DOWN,
BOTTOM UP, BACK AND FORTH,
AND IN THE ROUND

Wendy Bernard

ABRAMS / NEW YORK

Contents

1 Knits & Purls

2 Ribs

3 Fancy & Twisted

4 Cables

From-Scratch Projects   265

5 Lace

Introduction

My grandmother taught me to knit when I was eight years old. I suspect she showed me how to knit in a manner most others are taught: She cast on a number of stitches to a needle, demonstrated the knit stitch, and then handed me the needles and yarn. I struggled at first, and then I began to knit stitch after stitch, producing a swatch, albeit messy, of what we call garter stitch. After a time—maybe weeks or months—she showed me how to purl. This one came easier, since I had mastered the knit stitch, so I combined the two: a knit side following a purl side, or what we call Stockinette stitch. Last, she showed me how to cast on and bind off.

For many of us knitters, learning how to manage these four basic skills—to knit, to purl, to cast on, and to bind off—is a stepping-off point to a whole new world of knitted fabric. Stitch dictionaries, like the one you hold in your hands, provide a peek into what the basic building blocks can do when combined in a multitude of ways. Not only are they a serious resource for hobby knitters and designers, they are also a book of dreams. We page through, look at the swatches, and imagine knitting them, adding the patterns to hats, scarves, afghans, even pillows. We look at some of the more intricate stitch patterns and wonder if we could master them, let alone memorize them. Like cookbooks, we display them on the shelves for when the moment hits us and we crave a new project.

In my knitting journey, the craving for finding new sources of stitches grew steadily over time. I collected stitch dictionary after stitch dictionary, and it didn't matter if some of the stitches presented were the same. I loved browsing through the stitch patterns, looking at the photography, and studying how the stitches were formed. This went on for a number of years, until I came upon a selection of Japanese stitch pattern books while at a large needle arts trade show where I was signing books.

When I opened the books, I couldn't believe my eyes—a whole new world of knitting possibilities opened up to me that day. Until that point, I thought I really understood the ins and outs of knitting stitch patterns. However, as I paged through these volumes, I realized that many of the stitches contained in them were entirely different animals. I had never seen stitch patterns like these before. They were not given names (they were numbered), they were extraordinarily beautiful and unusual, and they appeared to be intricate and carefully thought out. How did someone somewhere come up with these knitting stitches? How could someone conceive, plan, and chart out these amazing patterns, many of them with up to thirty or more rows and with so many stitch multiples? I had known how to work knits, purls, yarnovers, and such, but some of these stitches were so new to me that I began collecting as many of these hard-to-find stitch dictionaries as I could, just to study the unique techniques.

As I collected these volumes, I would talk to my knitting friends and professional colleagues about them. Most had heard of and seen them, but the consensus was that, despite their wonderful appeal, they were elusive and not widely accessible. First, they're entirely in Japanese (I had studied Japanese in college, and I still had trouble understanding most of it). Many of the symbols were difficult to decipher, and the layout tended to be overwhelming. Second, the books themselves can be expensive and difficult to find, as they are imported from Japan. With this in mind, I decided to try my hand at coming up with a new stitch dictionary devoted to making a large selection of these Japanese stitch patterns accessible, easy-to-read and decipher, and charted in a way that was more familiar to a Western audience.

Most of the stitch patterns in this book come from Japanese stitch dictionaries, so many of the patterns in this book will be new to your eyes, and I'm excited to have taken on the business of translating them for you. They are not numbered as they are in traditional Japanese stitch dictionaries. Instead, I have given them names for easy identification and reference. All of them are converted to be worked in the round, and where it is possible, I have converted them to top down as well, so the motifs will look similar when you knit a body of a sweater bottom up and work set-in sleeves from the top down.

Almost all of these 150 stitch patterns are suitable for use in top-down or bottom-up (flat or in the round) garments, accessories, and home projects. For each chapter, I've designed a project to show you how to incorporate the stitch patterns. You can follow the patterns exactly, but you can also swap in another stitch pattern—from that chapter or another—for the one I used. To make it easy,

I've included a stitch multiple index on page 282. If you're feeling like you want to come up with something of your own making, you'll find three do-it-yourself formulas starting on page 265: An any-size blanket, an oversized cowl, and a cocoon shrug.

I love to talk to knitters about how my stitch dictionaries work. When they realize that they no longer have to sit down and figure out how to convert a flat stitch pattern into one that can be worked in the round, I can see a light bulb flash on above their heads. It is so exciting to know that I've already done the work, and the fun of knitting can begin right away without those extra—and sometimes difficult—planning steps that often stand in the way.

Wendy.

Getting Started

Stitch pattern books are wonderful resources to enhance your creativity. All you have to do is thumb through one and find a pattern that strikes your fancy, do a minimal amount of math (yikes!), and cast on. But first things first: The Dreaded Swatch.

WHY SWATCHING IS NECESSARY

When you make a test swatch, not only will you get a chance to get to know your yarn and how it behaves, you'll also get a chance to see if your chosen yarn looks good wearing your stitch pattern. Other things you'll discover? The number of stitches you'll ultimately need to cast on so that your garment or accessory ends up the size you want it to be.

I don't need to tell you a story about a knitter who cast on and happily knit for weeks only to bind off and discover the item was the wrong size and bore no resemblance to the original pattern or intent once it was laundered. It most likely has happened to you too, right? Knitting a swatch and checking and rechecking your gauge will help you to avoid this disaster. Taking this crucial first step will result in the likelihood that your projects will be the size and look that you planned.

Other reasons to swatch: The marriage of yarn and needles can be a little iffy. Have you ever purchased yarn and cast on only to discover that your yarn and needles were so close in color that you have to knit under special lighting so you can knit without dropping stitches? Or have you noticed that "splitty" yarn and pointy needles don't work well together? Swatching isn't just for counting stitches or achieving gauge. Sometimes you have to test out different needles to see which combination works best. Personally, I tend to choose metal needles for most projects unless I'm knitting with super-slippery yarn. In that case, I reach for wood. Of course, every knitter has their preferences, and swatching will help you find yours.

When it comes to other factors, like how yarn behaves before and after laundering, swatching is your friend. Imagine finding a fantastic blue yarn, casting on, and knitting an entire sweater with it, adding on white cuffs at the sleeves and bottom hem for contrast. Imagine also laundering it, only to find that the blue yarn bled into the white. If you had swatched the two yarns together and laundered it, you would have seen that the colors bled together and would have been able to avoid this outcome.

How to Swatch

Knitting patterns will almost always give you a gauge or tension for a 4" (10 cm) square. In a perfect scenario, your swatch will be this size or larger (not counting a ribbed or garter stitch edge of a few stitches), to ensure the most accurate reading.

Start by using the yarn and needles suggested in the pattern or on the ball band of your yarn. Cast on the number of stitches, or more, required to knit a square of at least 4" (10 cm), then add a few stitches on either side for an edging that will keep the sides from rolling.

Most knitting patterns will tell you what your goal gauge should be, and if you should be working it in stockinette, garter, or a stitch that is featured in the pattern. Further, if more than one size needle is used, the pattern should tell you if you should swatch with the smaller or larger needles.

For example, the pattern may say 22 stitches over 4" (10 cm) or 5.5 stitches per inch (2.5 cm), in Stockinette stitch on smaller needles. Sometimes, no stitch pattern is given. If this is the case, default to Stockinette. If you are going it alone and designing "from scratch," choose a stitch pattern and experiment. Just be sure to keep copious notes on yarn, needle size, and type of needle.

Once you've completed your swatch and bound off (make sure to do this loosely), launder and dry the swatch exactly as you intend to launder the project when done. That way, your swatch will give you the most accurate reading.

Whether your swatch is a knit/purl pattern, cable, or lace, you'll treat it the same way. After laundering, squeeze out the water, roll it in a towel to absorb the remaining moisture, and lay it on something soft where it can air dry. Some swatches, like lace, will need to be "blocked." What is blocking? Blocking is meant to set the stitches in place so that they result in an evenly knit fabric. Some people buy special blocking pins or wires to spread the stitches out exactly. Others (like me) tend to spread the knitting out on a towel on top of a table or bed with their hands and let it dry on its own, only using pins if the stitches shrink and distort. Either way, it is your knitting, and you'll want to treat the swatch the same way as you intend to treat your project when it is complete. The goal is to—in your own way—end up with a project that is the size you want it to be. This will allow you to find out ahead of time if your yarn bleeds color or has the drape you want. Ribbed fabric, on the other hand, gets a slightly different treatment. With ribs, you don't want to stretch too much: otherwise you'll end up with columns of stitches that don't do the job

they're meant to do (i.e., stretch). When you handle a swatch made of ribs, just trust your instincts and lay it out in a way that makes sense to you.

Once your swatch is dry, measure the gauge between the non-rolling selvage stitches using a tape measure. If your stitch count is less than the called-for stitch count in your knitting pattern, you'll need to go down a needle size or two. The opposite will be true if you have too many stitches to the inch. For example, if your pattern tells you to use size US 5 (3.75 mm) needles with a DK-weight yarn to obtain a gauge of 24 stitches over a 4" (10 cm) square and you get 26 stitches, you'll have to swatch again with a larger needle.

When it comes to row gauge, there are times when it doesn't really matter (think about a scarf), but other times it really does. When you shape portions of a top-down pullover like sleeves, if you work the decreases and the instructions tell you to decrease every fifth round and your row gauge doesn't match the gauge in the pattern, your sleeves may come out too short or too long. In some cases, you may even reach the wrist ribbing without having completed all your shaping increments. Another example would be if you're following a charted knitting pattern rather than the written instructions and it tells you to knit to a particular length. If you knit each row in the chart and your gauge is off, you might end up with an item that is the wrong length. So, if your row gauge is "off," you may want to swatch with a different size needle or a needle that is made of a different material—or even a needle that is the same size but a different brand. You'd be surprised at how subtle differences can make a difference in gauge. Even your mood can make a difference!

Swatching in the Round

If you're knitting a project in the round, you might want to knit a gauge swatch in the round. Most of us who prefer to knit in the round know ahead of time if our stitch gauge will be different than when we knit flat. In my case, I tend to knit a bit tighter in the round, and although I swatch flat even when I plan on knitting in the round, I automatically round the stitch count up a bit to compensate for my tighter stitch gauge.

One method of knitting an in-the-round gauge swatch is to simply choose your needles and yarn, cast on to three double-pointed needles, and join. Make a reasonably long and wide tube, bind off, and proceed as you would a flat swatch, except you'll be laying the tube flat and measuring across its surface. Another method that works is casting onto a double-pointed needle and instead of turning after your first row as you would a flat swatch, slide the stitches to the right-hand end of the needle and continue working right-side rows only, which will give you a flat, "in-the-round" swatch. As you work in this manner, drape the working yarn loosely across the wrong side after each row (make sure there is quite a bit of slack or it can get too tight, which will affect your resulting gauge). Once the swatch is done, bind off your stitches and cut the strands of yarn in the back so the swatch can lay flat.

Other Swatching Tricks

If you are prone to forgetting to keep track of which needles you used, you can purl a series of stitches to denote the size needle you used on a Stockinette swatch. For example, if you're using a US 7 (4.5 mm) needle, just choose a spot in the background of Stockinette and purl a series of 7 stitches. That way, when you reach for your swatch, all you have to do is count the number of purl stitches and know you used a size US 7 (4.5 mm) needle. If you are using metric measurements only, and are using a 4.5-mm needle, you can purl a series of 4 stitches, knit a couple of stitches, then purl 1 stitch to denote the half millimeter.

There are times when I'm swatching that I realize that the needle size I'm using just isn't up to snuff. Midway through the swatching process I will often swap out one size needle for another. Instead of ripping out the swatch and starting over, I turn to the wrong side, knit a row (so there is a purl ridge on the right-side row) and on the next row, I switch to the different-size needle and work for awhile, remembering to make a series of purl stitches to note the new needle size. After I'm done, I may have a long, rectangular swatch that looks untidy, but this swatch holds a lot of information. Not only can I physically see and feel the difference the fabric makes when made from varying sizes of needles, I can file it away and at a glance know which section was knit with which size needles. I often attach the yarn label to the swatch and file it in a notebook or save it for later.

Another solution is to leave a long tail when casting on or binding off and tying a series of knots in the tail. If I have used a size US 4 (3.5 mm) needle, I will tie four knots in the tail. In the case of a US 10½ (6.5 mm) needle, I will tie ten knots, leave a long space, and then make another knot for the half. In the case of US sizes, this size needle is the only outlier, so whenever there are ten knots it is a tip-off to check for that extra knot.

Following the Charts in This Book

Before you get started, it's a good idea to read through this section so that knitting from the charts in this book is easy and straightforward. The charts vary based on the direction in which you are knitting: top-down, bottom-up, flat, or in the round. In some cases, you'll see that there is one chart for all directions, and in others, there are two or even more. All of them have labels, so just watch for them as you work.

The charts show you what the stitch pattern looks like as you're looking at it from the right side versus the wrong side. I try to use symbols that resemble the actual stitches, so when you look at the chart as you knit, you're able to see where you are in the pattern. The charts are numbered on the edges to help you keep track of what row or round you are on.

If you're working on a flat pattern—back and forth—with a right side and a wrong side, the row numbers on the right-hand edge indicate right-side rows, and the numbers on the left indicate wrong-side rows. Row 1 indicates the first row of the chart that you will work. If Row 1 appears on the left side of the chart, that means the pattern starts with a wrong-side row. You will always work the chart from right to left for right-side rows and left to right for wrong-side rows. For a chart that shows a stitch pattern worked in the round, there will only be round numbers on the right-hand side of the chart. If a chart displays both the flat and in-the-round stitch pattern, as it does for Slipped Zigzag Cable on page 192, you will only have numbers on the right side; the rows that aren't numbered will be wrong-side rows when working flat.

When looking at a wrong-side row, you need to work the stitch so that it will appear correctly on the right side. For example, a blank white square means you need to make a knit stitch. It's obvious that you'll knit the stitch when you're working on the right side, but what would you do when you're on the wrong side? The answer is "purl." But if you're working the wrong-side row and you're presented with a symbol that isn't as obvious, say a knit through the back loop, and you're not sure what to do, there is a key that will tell you how the stitch should be worked. As an example, the decrease that looks just like a k2tog on the right side is a p2tog on the wrong side. So, the key will say "K2tog on RS, p2tog on WS."

Since this book of stitches is heavily based on stitches found in Japanese stitch dictionaries, you'll notice that there are some new-to-you symbols in the charts. When working from them, you'll find that there are explanations for what to do on the right sides and wrong sides of the work. Take a look at the Flower Bud Texture chart (page 107). At the bottom of the chart, there are two explanations (see page 107), one regarding "Wrap 3" and another for "DW" (Decrease Wrap). The Wrap 3 symbol is something that some knitters will recognize, but the DW symbol is more unusual. The explanation under the chart tells you how to work this stitch on both right-side and wrong-side rows. And if you are ever challenged by the chart and want further information, all charts are accompanied by written instructions; refer to them for clarification as needed or use them, if that is your preference.

In each chart, every stitch repeat is indicated on the bottom of each chart, and the row/round repeats are shown to the right. In many cases, the repeat takes up the entire chart (see Waving Wheat, page 203). Sometimes, when working flat, there will be one or more extra stitches on either side (or both sides) of the main pattern repeat (see Lily of the Valley Flat, page 217, and Candelabra Flat, page 207). This is so the end of the stitch pattern mirrors the beginning. In this case, you will work X stitches before the repeat (if there are any), Y stitches in the repeat the appropriate number of times for your pattern, and end with the last Z stitches to balance the pattern. There is no need to balance the stitch pattern when the piece is worked in the round, so you won't find extra stitches on an in-the-round chart.

Occasionally there are one or more set-up rows or rounds at the beginning of a chart that are worked before the main pattern begins (see Butterfly Checkerboard Flat, page 106). You will usually work these rows/rounds just once, then work the pattern repeats as directed. If the repeat (stitch or row/round) doesn't take up the entire chart, you'll find a heavy vertical or horizontal line before and/or after the repeat to help you keep track.

Sometimes, in some patterns, a pattern repeat will shift a few stitches to the right or left to accommodate stitches within the pattern. Example: A decrease worked at the end of a repeat or a cable or other multi-stitch motif that overlaps into the following repeat. In the Syncopated Waves pattern on page 121, the repeat shifts 2 stitches to the right on Rounds 11–13 to accommodate the right-twist cable.

With some stitch patterns that are worked in the round, the pattern might be worked across the beginning-of-the-round marker, beginning or ending one or more stitch(es) before or after the marker (see Wheat Sheaves in the Round, page 211). The symbols and the chart key will tell you how to work these extra stitches. Many times you will need to shift the marker to keep the pattern flowing correctly.

Keeping Track

The first thing to do when presented with a chart is to look at it and notice the stitches—knits, purls, yarnovers, decreases, and increases—and how they line up. Are the purls stacked on top of each other? What about yarnovers? Do they stack diagonally to the right or left? Do the purls form a checkerboard?

Feel free to re-chart the chart. That's right—go ahead and get some graph paper and re-draw your chart. Sometimes re-drawing the chart encourages your brain to make sense of the chart. Also, if a certain symbol doesn't speak to you, change it! Other ideas: Use a highlighter pen to color stitches that you want to stand out. This works great for cable crosses or yarnovers that you find you've been skipping over as you knit.

Use a sticky note to keep track. By placing a sticky note or straight edge (like a ruler) above the row you're working on, your eyes will follow the chart more smoothly. By covering the rows that you haven't yet knit, you'll be able to see how your stitches line up with rows or rounds below it, just like looking at the work on your needles.

Make your stitches match the chart. As you knit, look at your knitting and compare it to the chart. By checking in on your chart often, you'll be less likely to make a mistake, but if you do, you'll be able to fix it quickly before you're stuck un-knitting several rows or rounds.

How the Swatches in This Book Were Made

I made an effort to knit all the swatches in this book in the same manner so they look uniform. Almost every swatch contains one or more repeats of the stitch pattern plus the number of stitches it took to center it on the swatch. In some cases, I added 2 or more pattern rows at the top of the swatch in order to make the top and bottom of the swatch mirror. All swatches begin with a cast-on edge at the bottom, two rows of Garter stitch, and end with two rows of Garter stich and the bound-off edge. They all feature Garter edges of two stitches on each side. Sometimes, especially in the case of cables, the stitch patterns will have repeats that begin and end with panels of Reverse Stockinette stitch. Due to the Garter edges, it will appear as if these swatches have an extended area of Reverse Stockinette or Garter stitch when that is not the case. When you see stitch patterns like this (a good example is Waves and Garter Ridges, page 126), take a look at the stitch pattern chart to gather more information and get a complete picture as to how the stitch pattern will look in your knitting project.

Reversible versus Two-Sided

In this book, you'll find stitch patterns labeled "reversible." When a stitch pattern truly is reversible, the combination of knits and purls are exactly the same on the right side and wrong side. There are times, however, when the stitch pattern looks the same, but upon closer inspection, it is not the same, just similar. There are also some instances where it looks nice on both sides, but the pattern is markedly different. In the first case, the stitch patterns are labeled "fully reversible." In the latter two, they will be labeled as "two-sided," indicating that the right and wrong sides will not be exactly the same. Examples of patterns that look nearly the same on both sides are 4-Stitch Cross Texture on page 159 and Grand Chevron Rib on page 77. Garter stitch on page 18 and many rib patterns are truly reversible; it is nearly impossible to tell the difference between the right and wrong sides.

PLAYING WITH STITCH PATTERNS TO CREATE YOUR OWN

If you have had some experience knitting combinations of stitches in one project, you will have enough skill to play with stitch patterns and make your own. Although the prospect of combining them or taking elements out of them may seem difficult or daunting, with a bit of experimentation and pre-planning, you can definitely master it.

Combining and Mixing Cables and Other Stitches

An Aran sweater is a great example of a garment that contains a mixture of cables and textured stitches. These sweater's or cardigan's main features are the panels of cables that extend down the front of the garment. The sweater or cardigan also often has textured background fabric, which serves to set off the cables and other stitches.

As you page through this book and the Stitch Multiple Index (page 282) looking for stitch patterns that you'd like to mix, take into consideration that patterns with small multiples and row repeats look great when combined with a larger, centered pattern. These small-multiple patterns can form backgrounds for the more elaborate panels. Because the more elaborate panels, such as Knots and Twisted Columns on page 145 and Eyelets and Cables on page 160, are usually worked in Stockinette stitch, the most frequently used background stitch is Reverse Stockinette stitch (purl showing on right side) as it allows the patterns to stand out.

The cable patterns in this book include a wide range of row repeats. Although it isn't absolutely necessary, it is a great idea to select a combination of panels and stitches that are compatible; that is, a stitch pattern in which each of the shorter row repeats will fit equally into the largest row repeat mathematically. If you do this, it will be easier to keep track of the pattern rows or rounds. On the other hand, if you find a stitch pattern that isn't compatible, you can work a practice swatch and alter a cable by working more rows of Stockinette stitch between cabling rows to make it work.

Compatible Row Repeats	Largest Row Repeat
2, 4, 8	8
2, 4, 6, 12	12
2, 4, 8, 16	16
2, 6, 18	18
2, 4, 10, 20	20
2, 4, 6, 8, 12, 24	24
2, 4, 14, 28	28
2, 6, 10, 30	30
2, 4, 8, 16, 32	32
2, 4, 6, 12, 18, 36	36
2, 4, 8, 10, 20, 40	40
2, 4, 22, 44	44
2, 4, 6, 8, 12, 16, 24, 48	48

Positioning Your Stitch Patterns

There are many ways to approach combining and positioning stitch patterns, but here is my preferred method:

1. Using graph paper and a pencil, draw a rough placement of your chosen stitches, making note of the multiple of stitches and rows. If you like, sketch out the basic outline of each panel to see if you like the way they'll look next to each other. Be sure to include placement of the background stitches.
2. Make a gauge swatch in your chosen background stitch. You can choose Reverse Stockinette, Moss, Seed, or Stockinette stitch, depending on the look you're after and whether or not you're using cables.
3. Knit a sample of each chosen panel and make note of the gauge.
4. Using the gauge of the various panels, calculate the width of the combined panels when knitted, and add this number to your sheet. You may decide to add or subtract stitches based on whether you're planning on using this panel in an original design or subbing it into a published design.

CALCULATING HOW MUCH YARN YOU NEED

For each of the projects in this book, I will tell you how much yarn you need to reproduce the results exactly. But when you are personalizing or making up your own patterns, you'll need to have an idea as to how much yarn to buy.

Ask your local yarn shop about the type and size of the item you want to make and the yarn you'll be using. If this is something familiar to them, they should be able to advise you on how much you'll need for your project.

Find a pattern that looks like what you want to make that is in the same gauge. Multiply the number of balls in the yarn requirement in the pattern by the yardage for one ball, then calculate how many balls of your yarn you'll need. Refer to yarn requirement charts, such as Ann Budd's *The Knitter's Handy Guide to Yarn Requirements*, which provide approximate yardage for garments in a broad range of sizes and gauges. Knit a swatch. Your gauge swatch will give you a pretty accurate picture as to how much yarn you'll need, but you'll have to do a little math. Make a swatch that is whole inches on both the top and the side (like 4 × 4"/10 × 10 cm). Multiply the length of two sides to get 16 square inches (100 square cm). Now, cut the swatch off the skein and weigh it on an accurate scale. If it weighs, say, 10 grams, that means that each 10 grams will yield 16 square inches (100 square cm) of knitted fabric. Divide the 10 grams into the total weight of the skein (50 grams, for our example) and you get 5; then multiply that 5 by 16 square inches (100 square cm), and you'll get a total of 80 square inches (500 square cm) of fabric in each skein.

The next step is to figure out the total area you'll be knitting. For example, if you want to knit a blanket like the one on page 266, first determine the number of square inches in the blanket [35" × 33¾" = 1181 square inches (89 × 85.5 cm = 7609 square cm)]. Divide those numbers by the square inches (cm) of fabric that you get out of each skein, and you'll find that you need about 14.8 skeins of yarn (15.2 skeins if you're calculating based on cm rather than inches), rounded up to the nearest whole number. Because 14.8 skeins is so close to 15, I'd suggest buying 16 skeins to be on the safe side.

CHAPTER

1

Knits & Purls

Just about any knitter—beginner to expert—can make what looks like super-intricate stitch patterns out of simple knit and purl stitches without any of the added flair that yarnovers and slipped stitches provide. Simple knit-purl combos like the ones in this chapter can create unique textures. Some are linear, others seem random, and there are some that are pictorial or geometric. When knitting knit-purl patterns, consider using solid, semi-solid, and heathered yarns. If you choose multicolored or hand-painted yarns, your stitch pattern may get lost. Many knit-purl stitch patterns are reversible. A couple examples are Zigzags on page 20 and Mosaic Stitch on page 46.

Stockinette Stitch

FLAT

(any number of sts; 2-row repeat)
Row 1 (RS): Knit.
Row 2: Purl.
Repeat Rows 1 and 2 for Stockinette Stitch Flat.

IN THE ROUND

(any number of sts; 1-rnd repeat)
All Rnds: Knit.

Garter Stitch (FULLY REVERSIBLE)

FLAT

(any number of sts; 1-row repeat)
All Rows: Knit.

IN THE ROUND

(any number of sts; 2-rnd repeat)
Rnd 1: Knit.
Rnd 2: Purl.
Repeat Rnds 1 and 2 for Garter Stitch in the Round.

Arrows (TWO-SIDED)

BOTTOM-UP FLAT

(multiple of 8 sts; 14-row repeat)
Row 1 (RS): Knit.
Row 2: Knit.
Row 3: *K5, p3; repeat from * to end.
Row 4: P1, k3, *p5, k3; repeat from * to last 4 sts, p4.
Row 5: K3, p3, *k5, p3; repeat from * to last 2 sts, k2.
Row 6: P3, k3, *p5, k3; repeat from * to last 2 sts, p2.

Row 7: K1, p3, *k5, p3; repeat from * to last 4 sts, k4.

Row 8: *P5, k3; repeat from * to end.

Row 9: Repeat Row 7.

Row 10: Repeat Row 6.

Row 11: Repeat Row 5.

Row 12: Repeat Row 4.

Row 13: Repeat Row 3.

Row 14: Knit.

Repeat Rows 1–14 for Arrows Bottom-Up Flat.

BOTTOM-UP IN THE ROUND

(multiple of 8 sts; 14-rnd repeat)

Rnd 1: Knit.

Rnd 2: Purl.

Rnd 3: *K5, p3; repeat from * to end.

Rnd 4: K4, p3, *k5, p3; repeat from * to last st, k1.

Rnd 5: K3, p3, *k5, p3; repeat from * to last 2 sts, k2.

Rnd 6: K2, p3, *k5, p3; repeat from * to last 3 sts, k3.

Rnd 7: K1, p3, *k5, p3; repeat from * to last 4 sts, k4.

Rnd 8: *P3, k5; repeat from * to end.

Rnd 9: Repeat Rnd 7.

Rnd 10: Repeat Rnd 6.

Rnd 11: Repeat Rnd 5.

Rnd 12: Repeat Rnd 4.

Rnd 13: Repeat Rnd 3.

Rnd 14: Purl.

Repeat Rnds 1–14 for Arrows Bottom-Up in the Round.

BOTTOM-UP FLAT AND IN THE ROUND

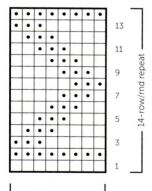

TOP-DOWN FLAT

(multiple of 8 sts; 14-row repeat)

Row 1 (RS): Knit.

Row 2: Knit.

Row 3: *P3, k5; repeat from * to end.

Row 4: P4, k3, *p5, k3; repeat from * to last st, p1.

Row 5: K2, p3, *k5, p3; repeat from * to last 3 sts, k3.

Row 6: P2, k3, *p5, k3; repeat from * to last 3 sts, p3.

Row 7: K4, p3, *k5, p3; repeat from * to last st, k1.

Row 8: *K3, p5; repeat from * to end.

Row 9: Repeat Row 7.

Row 10: Repeat Row 6.

Row 11: Repeat Row 5.

Row 12: Repeat Row 4.

Row 13: Repeat Row 3.

Row 14: Knit.

Repeat Rows 1–14 for Arrows Top-Down Flat.

TOP-DOWN IN THE ROUND

(multiple of 8 sts; 14-rnd repeat)

Rnd 1: Knit.

Rnd 2: Purl.

Rnd 3: *P3, k5; repeat from * to end.

Rnd 4: K1, p3, *k5, p3; repeat from * to last 4 sts, k4.

Rnd 5: K2, p3, *k5, p3; repeat from * to last 3 sts, k3.

Rnd 6: K3, p3, *k5, p3; repeat from * to last 2 sts, k2.

Rnd 7: K4, p3, *k5, p3; repeat from * to last st, k1.

Rnd 8: *K5, p3; repeat from * to end.

Rnd 9: Repeat Rnd 7.

Rnd 10: Repeat Rnd 6.

Rnd 11: Repeat Rnd 5.

Rnd 12: Repeat Rnd 4.

Rnd 13: Repeat Rnd 3.

Rnd 14: Purl.

Repeat Rnds 1–14 for Arrows Top-Down in the Round.

TOP-DOWN FLAT AND IN THE ROUND

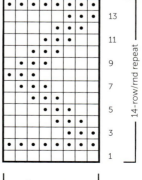

Row 12: K3, p4, *k4, p4; repeat from * to last st, k1.
Row 13: *K2, p1, k2, p3; repeat from * to end.
Row 14: Repeat Row 2.
Row 15: *P3, k2, p1, k2; repeat from * to end.
Row 16: *P5, k3; repeat from * to end.
Repeat Rows 1–16 for Zigzags Flat.

IN THE ROUND

(multiple of 8 sts; 16-rnd repeat)
Rnd 1: *K1, p2, k3, p2; repeat from * to end.
Rnd 2: K1, p2, *k2, p2; repeat from * to last st, k1.
Rnd 3: [K1, p2] twice, *k3, p2, k1, p2; repeat from * to last 2 sts, k2.
Rnd 4: K1, p4, *k4, p4; repeat from * to last 3 sts, k3.
Rnd 5: K1, p3, k2, p1, *k2, p3, k2, p1; repeat from * to last st, k1.
Rnd 6: Repeat Rnd 2.
Rnd 7: K1, p1, k2, p3, *k2, p1, k2, p3; repeat from * to last st, k1.
Rnd 8: K3, p4, *k4, p4; repeat from * to last st, k1.
Rnd 9: K2, p2, k1, p2, *k3, p2, k1, p2; repeat from * to last st, k1.
Rnd 10: Repeat Rnd 2.
Rnd 11: *P2, k3, p2, k1; repeat from * to end.
Rnd 12: P1, k4, *p4, k4; repeat from * to last 3 sts, p3.
Rnd 13: *K2, p1, k2, p3; repeat from * to end.
Rnd 14: Repeat Rnd 2.
Rnd 15: *P3, k2, p1, k2; repeat from * to end.
Rnd 16: *P3, k5; repeat from * to end.
Repeat Rnds 1–16 for Zigzags in the Round.

Zigzags (FULLY REVERSIBLE)
....

FLAT

(multiple of 8 sts; 16-row repeat)
Row 1 (RS): *K1, p2, k3, p2; repeat from * to end.
Row 2: P1, k2, *p2, k2; repeat from * to last st, p1.
Row 3: [K1, p2] twice, *k3, p2, k1, p2; repeat from * to last 2 sts, k2.
Row 4: P3, k4, *p4, k4; repeat from * to last st, p1.
Row 5: K1, p3, k2, p1, *k2, p3, k2, p1; repeat from * to last st, k1.
Row 6: Repeat Row 2.
Row 7: K1, p1, k2, p3, *k2, p1, k2, p3; repeat from * to last st, k1.
Row 8: P1, k4, *p4, k4; repeat from * to last 3 sts, p3.
Row 9: K2, p2, k1, p2, *k3, p2, k1, p2; repeat from * to last st, k1.
Row 10: Repeat Row 2.
Row 11: *P2, k3, p2, k1; repeat from * to end.

FLAT AND IN THE ROUND

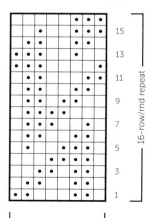

8-st repeat

16-row/rnd repeat

Banded Squares (TWO-SIDED)

FLAT

(multiple of 3 sts + 1; 16-row repeat)

Row 1 (RS): Knit.

Rows 2–5: Knit.

Row 6: Purl.

Row 7: K1, *p2, k1; repeat from * to end.

Rows 8 and 9: P1, *k2, p1; repeat from * to end.

Row 10: Repeat Row 7.

Rows 11–14: Repeat Rows 7–10.

Rows 15 and 16: Repeat Rows 7 and 8.

Repeat Rows 1–16 for Banded Squares Flat.

IN THE ROUND

(multiple of 3 sts; 16-rnd repeat)

Rnd 1: Knit.

Rnd 2: Purl.

Rnds 3 and 4: Repeat Rnds 1 and 2.

Rnds 5 and 6: Knit.

Rnds 7 and 8: *K1, p2; repeat from * to end.

Rnds 9 and 10: *P1, k2; repeat from * to end.

Rnds 11–14: Repeat Rnds 7–10.

Rnds 15 and 16: Repeat Rnds 7 and 8.

Repeat Rnds 1–16 for Banded Squares in the Round.

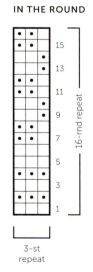

FLAT

IN THE ROUND

Stacked Books (TWO-SIDED)

FLAT

(multiple of 20 sts + 10; 28-row repeat)

Row 1 (RS): P2, [k2, p2] twice, *k10, p2, [k2, p2] twice; repeat from * to end.

Row 2: Knit the knit sts and purl the purl sts as they face you.

Row 3: [P2, k2] twice, *p14, k2, p2, k2; repeat from * to last 2 sts, p2.

Row 4: Repeat Row 2.

Rows 5–12: Repeat Rows 1–4 twice.

Rows 13 and 14: Repeat Rows 1 and 2.

Row 15: K10, *p2, [k2, p2] twice, k10; repeat from * to end.

Row 16: Repeat Row 2.

Row 17: P12, k2, p2, k2, *p14, k2, p2, k2; repeat from * to last 12 sts, p12.

Row 18: Repeat Row 2.

Rows 19–26: Repeat Rows 15–18 twice.

Rows 27 and 28: Repeat Rows 15 and 16.

Repeat Rows 1–28 for Stacked Books Flat.

IN THE ROUND

(multiple of 20 sts; 28-rnd repeat)

Rnds 1 and 2: *P2, [k2, p2] twice, k10; repeat from * to end.

Rnds 3 and 4: [P2, k2] twice, *p14, k2, p2, k2; repeat from * to last 12 sts, p12.

Rnds 5–12: Repeat Rnds 1–4 twice.

Rnds 13 and 14: Repeat Rnds 1 and 2.

Rnds 15 and 16: *K10, p2, [k2, p2] twice; repeat from * to end.

Rnds 17 and 18: P12, k2, p2, k2, *p14, k2, p2, k2; repeat from * to last 2 sts, p2.

Rnds 19–26: Repeat Rnds 15–18 twice.

Rnds 27 and 28: Repeat Rnds 15 and 16.

Repeat Rnds 1–28 for Stacked Books in the Round.

FLAT

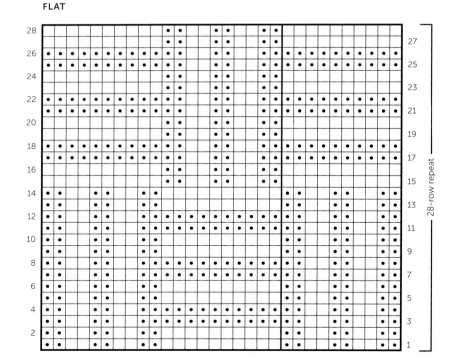

20-st repeat

28-row repeat

IN THE ROUND

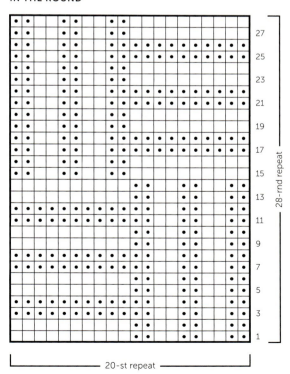

20-st repeat

28-rnd repeat

Ribs and Ridges (TWO-SIDED)

FLAT

(odd number of sts; 10-row repeat)
Row 1 (RS): K1, *p1, k1; repeat from * to end.
Row 2: P1, *k1, p1; repeat from * to end.
Rows 3–6: Repeat Rows 1 and 2 twice.
Rows 7–10: Knit.
Repeat Rows 1–10 for Ribs and Ridges Flat.

IN THE ROUND

(even number of sts; 10-rnd repeat)
Rnds 1–6: *K1, p1; repeat from * to end.
Rnd 7: Knit.
Rnd 8: Purl.
Rnds 9 and 10: Repeat Rnds 7 and 8.
Repeat Rnds 1–10 for Ribs and Ridges in the Round.

FLAT

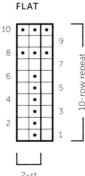

2-st repeat

IN THE ROUND

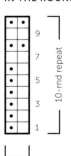

2-st repeat

Stacked Boxes

FLAT

(multiple of 14 sts + 2; 20-row repeat)

Row 1 (RS): Purl.

Row 2: Knit.

Row 3: P2, *k7, [p1, k1] twice, p3; repeat from * to end.

Row 4: K2, *[p1, k1] 3 times, p6, k2; repeat from * to end.

Rows 5–10: Repeat Rows 3 and 4 three times.

Row 11: Repeat Row 3.

Row 12: K2, *[p1, k1] 5 times, p1, k3; repeat from * to end.

Row 13: P2, *[k1, p1] 3 times, k6, p2; repeat from * to end.

Row 14: K2, *p7, [k1, p1] twice, k3; repeat from * to end.

Rows 15–20: Repeat Rows 13 and 14 three times.

Repeat Rows 1–20 for Stacked Boxes Flat.

IN THE ROUND

(multiple of 14 sts; 20-rnd repeat)

Rnds 1 and 2: Purl.

Rnd 3: *P2, k7, p1, [k1, p1] twice; repeat from * to end.

Rnd 4: *P2, k6, [p1, k1] 3 times; repeat from * to end.

Rnds 5–10: Repeat Rnds 3 and 4 three times.

Rnd 11: Repeat Rnd 3.

Rnd 12: *P3, k1, [p1, k1] 5 times; repeat from * to end.

Rnd 13: *P2, [k1, p1] 3 times, k6; repeat from * to end.

Rnd 14: *P3, [k1, p1] twice, k7; repeat from * to end.

Rnds 15–20: Repeat Rnds 13 and 14 three times.

Repeat Rnds 1–20 for Stacked Boxes in the Round.

FLAT

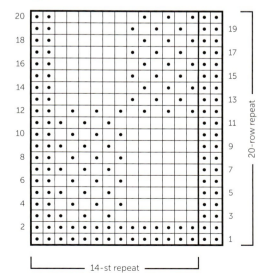

IN THE ROUND

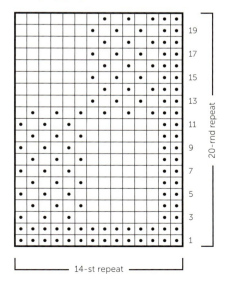

8-Point Stars

FLAT

(multiple of 22 sts + 5; 28-row repeat)

Row 1 (RS): K7, p1, [k5, p1] twice, *k9, p1, [k5, p1] twice; repeat from * to last 7 sts, k7.

Row 2: P8, k1, p3, k1, p1, k1, p3, k1, *p11, k1, p3, k1, p1, k1, p3, k1; repeat from * to last 8 sts, p8.

Row 3: K9, p1, k1, p1, k3, p1, k1, p1, *k13, p1, k1, p1, k3, p1, k1, p1; repeat from * to last 9 sts, k9.

Row 4: P10, k1, p5, k1, *p15, k1, p5, k1; repeat from * to last 10 sts, p10.

Row 5: Repeat Row 3.

Row 6: Repeat Row 2.

Row 7: Repeat Row 1.

Row 8: P6, k1, p13, k1, *p7, k1, p13, k1; repeat from * to last 6 sts, p6.

Row 9: K5, *p1, k3, p1, k7, p1, k3, p1, k5; repeat from * to end.

Row 10: K1, p3, *k1, p4, k2, p5, k2, p4, k1, p3; repeat from * to last st, k1.

Row 11: K1, p1, *k1, p1, k5, p3, k3, p3, k5, p1; repeat from * to last 3 sts, k1, p1, k1.

Row 12: P2, k1, *p6, k4, p1, k4, p6, k1; repeat from * to last 2 sts, p2.

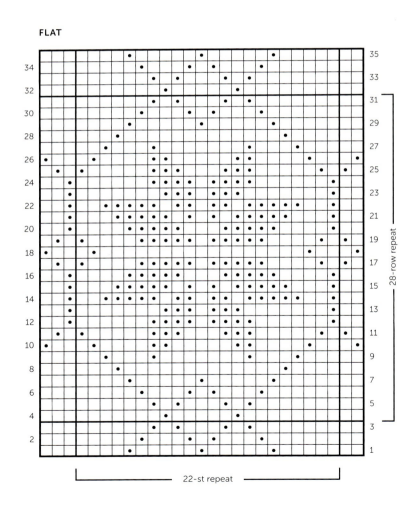

FLAT

22-st repeat

28-row repeat

Row 13: K2, *p1, k7, p3, k1, p3, k7; repeat from * to last 3 sts, p1, k2.

Row 14: P2, k1, *p2, k5, p1, [k2, p1] twice, k5, p2, k1; repeat from * to last 2 sts, p2.

Row 15: K2, *p1, k3, p5, k1, [p1, k1] twice, p5, k3; repeat from * to last 3 sts, p1, k2.

Row 16: P2, k1, *p4, k5, p3, k5, p4, k1; repeat from * to last 2 sts, p2.

Row 17: K1, p1, *k1, p1, k4, p5, k1, p5, k4, p1; repeat from * to last 3 sts, k1, p1, k1.

Row 18: K1, p3, *k1, p17, k1, p3; repeat from * to last st, k1.

Row 19: Repeat Row 17.

Row 20: Repeat Row 16.

Row 21: Repeat Row 15.

Row 22: Repeat Row 14.

Row 23: Repeat Row 13.

Row 24: Repeat Row 12.

Row 25: Repeat Row 11.

Row 26: Repeat Row 10.

Row 27: Repeat Row 9.

Row 28: Repeat Row 8.

Row 29: Repeat Row 7.

Row 30: Repeat Row 6.

Row 31: Repeat Row 5.

Repeat Rows 4–31 as desired for 8-Point Stars Flat.

Row 32: Repeat Row 4.

Row 33: Repeat Row 3.

Row 34: Repeat Row 2.

Row 35: Repeat Row 1.

IN THE ROUND

(multiple of 22 sts; 28-rnd repeat)

Rnd 1: K7, p1, [k5, p1] twice, *k9, p1, [k5, p1] twice; repeat from * to last 2 sts, k2.

Rnd 2: K8, p1, k3, p1, k1, p1, k3, p1, *k11, p1, k3, p1, k1, p1, k3, p1; repeat from * to last 3 sts, k3.

Rnd 3: K9, p1, k1, p1, k3, p1, k1, p1, *k13, p1, k1, p1, k3, p1, k1, p1; repeat from * to last 4 sts, k4.

Rnd 4: K10, p1, k5, p1, *k15, p1, k5, p1; repeat from * to last 5 sts, k5.

Rnd 5: Repeat Rnd 3.

Rnd 6: Repeat Rnd 2.

Rnd 7: Repeat Rnd 1.

Rnd 8: K6, p1, k13, p1, *k7, p1, k13, p1; repeat from * to last st, k1.

Rnd 9: *K5, p1, k3, p1, k7, p1, k3, p1; repeat from * to end.

Rnd 10: *P1, k3, p1, k4, p2, k5, p2, k4; repeat from * to end.

Rnd 11: [K1, p1] twice, k5, p3, k3, p3, *k5, p1, k1, p1, k5, p3, k3, p3; repeat from * to last 4 sts, k4.

Rnd 12: K2, p1, k6, p4, k1, p4, *k6, p1, k6, p4, k1, p4; repeat from * to last 4 sts, k4.

Rnd 13: K2, p1, k7, p3, k1, p3, *k7, p1, k7, p3, k1, p3; repeat from * to last 5 sts, k5.

Rnd 14: *K2, p1, k2, p5, k1, [p2, k1] twice, p5; repeat from * to end.

Rnd 15: K2, p1, k3, p5, k1, [p1, k1] twice, p5, *k3, p1, k3, p5, k1, [p1, k1] twice, p5; repeat from * to last st, k1.

Rnd 16: K2, p1, k4, p5, k3, p5, *k4, p1, k4, p5, k3, p5; repeat from * to last 2 sts, k2.

Rnd 17: [K1, p1] twice, k4, p5, k1, p5, *k4, p1, k1, p1, k4, p5, k1, p5; repeat from * to last 3 sts, k3.

Rnd 18: *P1, k3, p1, k17; repeat from * to end.

Rnd 19: Repeat Rnd 17.

Rnd 20: Repeat Rnd 16.

Rnd 21: Repeat Rnd 15.

Rnd 22: Repeat Rnd 14.

Rnd 23: Repeat Rnd 13.

Rnd 24: Repeat Rnd 12.

Rnd 25: Repeat Rnd 11.

Rnd 26: Repeat Rnd 10.

Rnd 27: Repeat Rnd 9.

Rnd 28: Repeat Rnd 8.

Rnd 29: Repeat Rnd 7.

Rnd 30: Repeat Rnd 6.

Rnd 31: Repeat Rnd 5.

Repeat Rnds 4–31 as desired for 8-Point Stars in the Round.

Rnd 32: Repeat Rnd 4.

Rnd 33: Repeat Rnd 3.

Rnd 34: Repeat Rnd 2.

Rnd 35: Repeat Rnd 1.

IN THE ROUND

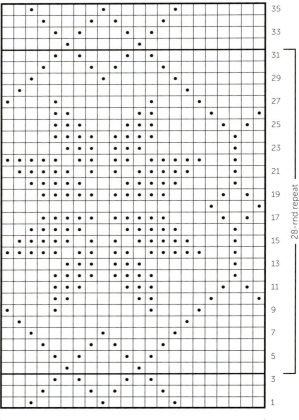

22-st repeat

28-rnd repeat

Diagonals and Crosses

FLAT

(multiple of 8 sts; 16-row repeat)

Row 1 (RS): K2, p1, *k3, p1; repeat from * to last st, k1.

Row 2 and all WS Rows: Knit the knit sts and purl the purl sts as they face you.

Row 3: *K1, p1, k3, p3; repeat from * to end.

Row 5: P1, k3, *p5, k3; repeat from * to last 4 sts, p4.

Row 7: *K3, p1, k1, p3; repeat from * to end.

Row 9: Repeat Row 1.

Row 11: K1, p3, k1, p1, *k3, p3, k1, p1; repeat from * to last 2 sts, k2.

Row 13: *P5, k3; repeat from * to end.

Row 15: *K1, p3, k3, p1; repeat from * to end.

Row 16: Repeat Row 2.

Repeat Rows 1–16 for Diagonals and Crosses Flat.

IN THE ROUND

(multiple of 8 sts; 16-rnd repeat)

Rnds 1 and 2: K2, p1, *k3, p1; repeat from * to last st, k1.

Rnds 3 and 4: *K1, p1, k3, p3; repeat from * to end.

Rnds 5 and 6: P1, k3, *p5, k3; repeat from * to last 4 sts, p4.

Rnds 7 and 8: *K3, p1, k1, p3; repeat from * to end.

Rnds 9 and 10: Repeat Rnd 1.

Rnds 11 and 12: K1, p3, k1, p1, *k3, p3, k1, p1; repeat from * to last 2 sts, k2.

Rnds 13 and 14: *P5, k3; repeat from * to end.

Rnds 15 and 16: *K1, p3, k3, p1; repeat from * to end.

Repeat Rnds 1–16 for Diagonals and Crosses in the Round.

FLAT AND IN THE ROUND

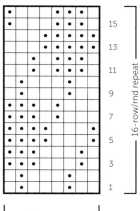

IN THE ROUND

(multiple of 6 sts; 18-rnd repeat)
Rnds 1–4: Knit.
Rnd 5: *P3, k3; repeat from * to end.
Rnd 6: Knit.
Rnds 7–10: Repeat Rnds 5 and 6 twice.
Rnds 11–13: Knit.
Rnd 14: *K3, p3; repeat from * to end.
Rnds 15–18: Repeat Rnds 13 and 14 twice.
Repeat Rnds 1–18 for Lizard Lattice in the Round.

Lizard Lattice

FLAT

(multiple of 6 sts + 3; 18-row repeat)
Row 1 (RS): Knit.
Row 2: Purl.
Rows 3 and 4: Repeat Rows 1 and 2.
Row 5: P3, *k3, p3; repeat from * to end.
Row 6: Purl.
Rows 7–10: Repeat Rows 5 and 6 twice.
Row 11: Knit.
Row 12: Purl.
Row 13: Knit.
Row 14: P3, *k3, p3; repeat from * to end.
Rows 15–18: Repeat Rows 13 and 14 twice.
Repeat Rows 1–18 for Lizard Lattice Flat.

FLAT

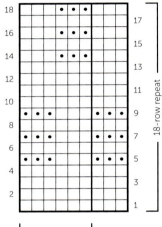

6-st repeat

IN THE ROUND

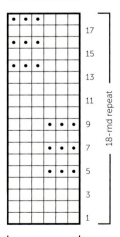

6-st repeat

Seed Stitch Squares

FLAT

(multiple of 12 sts + 3; 14-row repeat)

Row 1 (RS): Knit.

Row 2: Purl.

Row 3: K4, *p1, [k1, p1] 3 times, *k5, p1, [k1, p1] 3 times; repeat from * to last 4 sts, k4.

Row 4: P3, *k1, [p1, k1] 4 times, p3; repeat from * to end.

Row 5: K4, p1, *k5, p1; repeat from * to last 4 sts, k4.

Row 6: P3, *k1, p7, k1, p3; repeat from * to end.

Rows 7–10: Repeat Rows 5 and 6 twice.

Row 11: Repeat Row 5.

Row 12: Repeat Row 4.

Row 13: Repeat Row 3.

Row 14: Purl.

Repeat Rows 1–14 for Seed Stitch Squares Flat.

IN THE ROUND

(multiple of 12 sts; 14-rnd repeat)

Rnds 1 and 2: Knit.

Rnd 3: K4, p1, [k1, p1] 3 times, *k5, p1, [k1, p1] 3 times; repeat from * to last st, k1.

Rnd 4: *K3, p1, [k1, p1] 4 times; repeat from * to end.

Rnd 5: K4, p1, *k5, p1; repeat from * to last st, k1.

Rnd 6: *K3, p1, k7, p1; repeat from * to end.

Rnds 7–10: Repeat Rnds 5 and 6 twice.

Rnd 11: Repeat Rnd 5.

Rnd 12: Repeat Rnd 4.

Rnd 13: Repeat Rnd 3.

Rnd 14: Knit.

Repeat Rnds 1–14 for Seed Stitch Squares in the Round.

FLAT

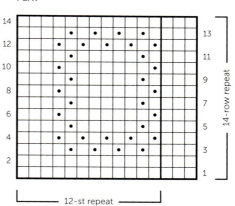

12-st repeat

14-row repeat

IN THE ROUND

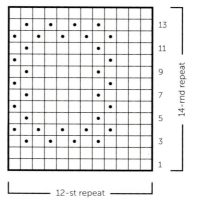

12-st repeat

14-rnd repeat

Cross Motif

FLAT

(multiple of 12 sts + 6; 24-row repeat)

Row 1 (RS): K2, p2, *k10, p2; repeat from * to last 2 sts, k2.

Row 2 and all WS Rows: Knit the knit sts and purl the purl sts as they face you.

Row 3: Repeat Row 1.

Row 5: P6, *k6, p6; repeat from * to end.

Rows 7 and 9: Repeat Row 1.

Row 11: Knit.

Rows 13 and 15: K8, p2, *k10, p2; repeat from * to last 8 sts, k8.

Row 17: K6, *p6, k6; repeat from * to end.

Rows 19 and 21: Repeat Row 13.

Row 23: Knit.

Row 24: Purl.

Repeat Rows 1–24 for Cross Motif Flat.

IN THE ROUND

(multiple of 12 sts; 24-rnd repeat)

Rnds 1–4: K2, p2, *k10, p2; repeat from * to last 8 sts, k8.

Rnds 5 and 6: *P6, k6; repeat from * to end.

Rnds 7–10: Repeat Rnd 1.

Rnds 11 and 12: Knit.

Rnds 13–16: K8, p2, *k10, p2; repeat from * to last 2 sts, k2.

Rnds 17 and 18: *K6, p6; repeat from * to end.

Rnds 19–22: Repeat Rnd 13.

Rnds 23 and 24: Knit.

Repeat Rnds 1–24 for Cross Motif in the Round.

FLAT

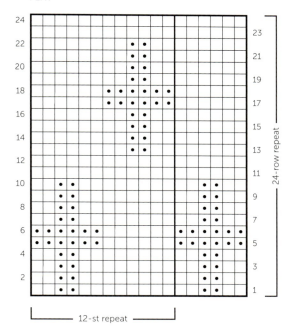

IN THE ROUND

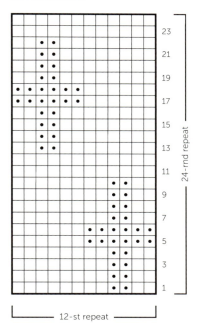

Centipede Stitch

....

FLAT

(multiple of 6 sts + 4; 24-row repeat)

Row 1 and all RS Rows (RS): Knit.

Rows 2, 4, 6, 8, 10, and 12: P1, k2, *p4, k2; repeat from * to last st, p1.

Rows 14, 16, 18, 20, 22, and 24: P4, *k2, p4; repeat from * to end.

Repeat Rows 1–24 for Centipede Stitch Flat.

IN THE ROUND

(multiple of 6 sts; 24-rnd repeat)

Rnd 1 and all Odd-Numbered Rnds: Knit.

Rnds 2, 4, 6, 8, 10, and 12: K1, p2, *k4, p2; repeat from * to last 3 sts, k3.

Rnds 14, 16, 18, 20, 22, and 24: *K4, p2; repeat from * to end.

Repeat Rnds 1–24 for Centipede Stitch in the Round.

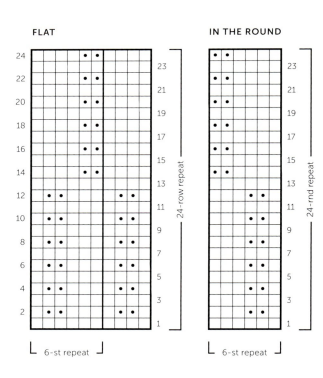

Stripe Pillars

BOTTOM-UP FLAT

(multiple of 6 sts + 3; 12-row repeat)

Row 1 (RS): Knit.

Row 2 and all WS Rows: Knit the knit sts and purl the purl sts as they face you.

Row 3: Knit.

Rows 5 and 7: K1, *p1, k1; repeat from * to end.

Rows 9 and 11: K1, p1, k1, *p3, k1, p1, k1; repeat from * to end.

Row 12: Repeat Row 2.

Repeat Rows 1–12 for Stripe Pillars Bottom-Up Flat.

BOTTOM-UP IN THE ROUND

(multiple of 6 sts; 12-rnd repeat)

Rnds 1–4: Knit.

Rnds 5–8: *K1, p1; repeat from * to end.

Rnds 9–12: *K1, p1, k1, p3; repeat from * to end.

Repeat Rnds 1–12 for Stripe Pillars Bottom-Up in the Round.

TOP-DOWN FLAT

(multiple of 6 sts + 3; 12-row repeat)

Row 1 (RS): K1, p1, k1, *p3, k1, p1, k1; repeat from * to end.

Row 2 and all WS Rows: Knit the knit sts and purl the purl sts as they face you.

Row 3: Repeat Row 2.

Rows 5 and 7: K1, *p1, k1; repeat from * to end.

Rows 9 and 11: Knit.

Row 12: Repeat Row 2.

Repeat Rows 1–12 for Stripe Pillars Top-Down Flat.

TOP-DOWN IN THE ROUND

(multiple of 6 sts; 12-rnd repeat)

Rnds 1–4: *K1, p1, k1, p3; repeat from * to end.

Rnds 5–8: *K1, p1; repeat from * to end.

Rnds 9–12: Knit.

Repeat Rnds 1–12 for Stripe Pillars Top-Down in the Round.

BOTTOM-UP FLAT

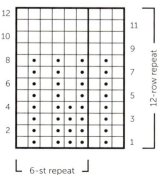

6-st repeat

BOTTOM-UP IN THE ROUND

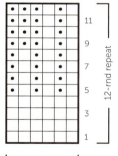

6-st repeat

TOP-DOWN FLAT

6-st repeat

TOP-DOWN IN THE ROUND

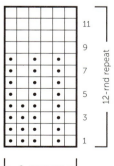

6-st repeat

Intertwined Texture

....

FLAT

(multiple of 15 sts + 2; 18-row repeat)

Row 1 (RS): *P13, k2; repeat from * to last 2 sts, p2.

Rows 2 and 3: Knit the knit sts and purl the purl sts as they face you.

Row 4: Purl.

Row 5: P2, *k2, p1, [k1, p1] 4 times, k2, p2; repeat from * to end.

Row 6: K2, *p3, k1, [p1, k1] 3 times, p3, k2; repeat from * to end.

Rows 7–14: Repeat Rows 5 and 6 four times.

Row 15: P2, *k2, p13; repeat from * to end.

Rows 16 and 17: Repeat Row 2.

Row 18: Purl.

Repeat Rows 1–18 for Intertwined Texture Flat.

IN THE ROUND

(multiple of 15 sts; 18-rnd repeat)

Rnds 1–3: *P13, k2; repeat from * to end.

Rnd 4: Knit.

Rnd 5: *P2, k2, p1, [k1, p1] 4 times, k2; repeat from * to end.

Rnd 6: *P2, k3, p1, [k1, p1] 3 times, k3; repeat from * to end.

Rnds 7–14: Repeat Rnds 5 and 6 four times.

Rnds 15–17: P2, k2, *p13, k2; repeat from * to last 11 sts, p11.

Rnd 18: Knit.

Repeat Rnds 1–18 for Intertwined Texture in the Round.

FLAT

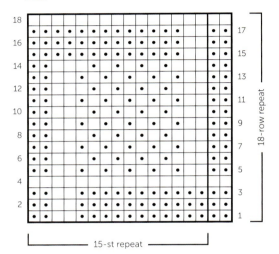

IN THE ROUND

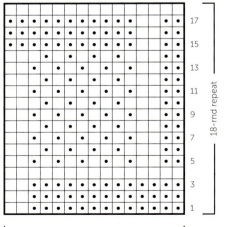

Small Basket Stitch (TWO-SIDED)

···

FLAT

(multiple of 10 sts + 5; 8-row repeat)

Row 1 (RS): [K1, p1] twice, *k7, p1, k1, p1; repeat from * to last st, k1.

Row 2: P1, [k1, p1] twice, *k5, p1, [k1, p1] twice; repeat from * to end.

Rows 3 and 4: Repeat Rows 1 and 2.

Row 5: K6, p1, k1, p1, *k7, p1, k1, p1; repeat from * to last 6 sts, k6.

Rows 6–8: Knit the knit sts and purl the purl sts as they face you.

Repeat Rows 1–8 for Small Basket Stitch Flat.

IN THE ROUND

(multiple of 10 sts; 8-rnd repeat)

Rnd 1: *P1, k1, p1, k7; repeat from * to end.

Rnd 2: *[P1, k1] twice, p5, k1; repeat from * to end.

Rnds 3 and 4: Repeat Rnds 1 and 2.

Rnds 5–8: K5, p1, k1, p1, *k7, p1, k1, p1; repeat from * to last 2 sts, k2.

Repeat Rnds 1–8 for Small Basket Stitch in the Round.

FLAT

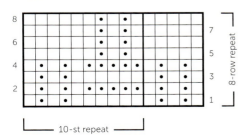

IN THE ROUND

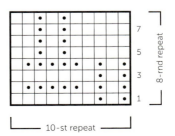

Enlarged Basket Stitch (TWO-SIDED)

FLAT

(multiple of 18 sts + 10; 18-row repeat)

Row 1 (RS): K11, p2, k2, p2, *k12, p2, k2, p2; repeat from * to last 11 sts, k11.

Row 2: P1, k8, *p2, [k2, p2] twice, k8; repeat from * to last st, p1.

Row 3: Knit the knit sts and purl the purl sts as they face you.

Row 4: P11, k2, p2, k2, *p12, k2, p2, k2; repeat from * to last 11 sts, p11.

Rows 5–8: Repeat Rows 1–4.

Row 9: Knit.

Row 10: [P2, k2] twice, *p12, k2, p2, k2; repeat from * to last 2 sts, p2.

Row 11: K2, [p2, k2] twice, *p8, k2, [p2, k2] twice; repeat from * to end.

Row 12: Repeat Row 3.

Row 13: [K2, p2] twice, *k12, p2, k2, p2; repeat from * to last 2 sts, k2.

Rows 14–17: Repeat Rows 10–13.

Row 18: Purl.

Repeat Rows 1–18 for Enlarged Basket Stitch Flat.

IN THE ROUND

(multiple of 18 sts; 18-rnd repeat)

Rnd 1: K10, p2, k2, p2, *k12, p2, k2, p2; repeat from * to last 2 sts, k2.

Rnds 2 and 3: *P8, k2, [p2, k2] twice; repeat from * to end.

Rnds 4 and 5: Repeat Rnd 1.

Rnds 6–8: Repeat Rnds 2–4.

Rnd 9: Knit.

Rnd 10: K1, p2, k2, p2, *k12, p2, k2, p2; repeat from * to last 11 sts, k11.

Rnds 11 and 12: K1, [p2, k2] twice, p8, *k2, [p2, k2] twice, p8; repeat from * to last st, k1.

Rnds 13 and 14: Repeat Rnd 10.

Rnds 15–17: Repeat Rnds 11–13.

Rnd 18: Knit.

Repeat Rnds 1–18 for Enlarged Basket Stitch in the Round.

FLAT

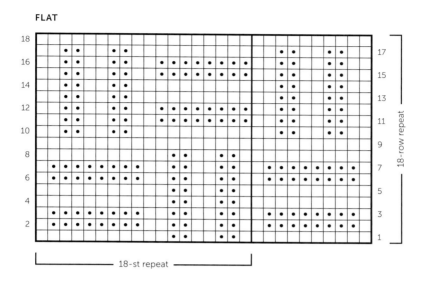

18-row repeat

18-st repeat

IN THE ROUND

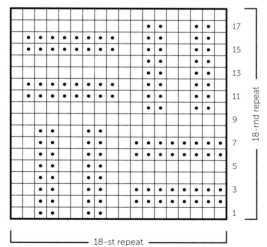

18-rnd repeat

18-st repeat

IN THE ROUND (A)

(multiple of 16 sts + 16; 24-rnd repeat)

Note: Use version A if you must have a fixed location for the beginning-of-rnd marker. Use version B if you are working a piece where the beginning-of-rnd marker can shift with every vertical repeat.

Rnd 1: *K11, p5; repeat from * to end.

Rnds 2 and 3: Knit the knit sts and purl the purl sts as they face you.

Rnds 4–6: Knit.

Rnd 7: K7, p5, *k11, p5; repeat from * to last 4 sts, k4.

Rnds 8–12: Repeat Rnds 2–6.

Rnd 13: K3, p5, *k11, p5; repeat from * to last 8 sts, k8.

Rnds 14–18: Repeat Rnds 2–6.

Rnd 19: P4, *k11, p5; repeat from * to last 12 sts, k11, slip st to right-hand needle, pick up strand between needles from back to front, slip st from right-hand needle back to left-hand needle, p2tog (slipped st together with picked-up strand). *Note: This will minimize the jog in the purl sections at beginning and end of the rnd.*

Rnds 20 and 21: Repeat Rnd 2.

Rnd 22: Slip 1 purlwise wyib, knit to end. *Note: Slipping the first st will minimize the jog in the knit sections at the beginning and end of the rnd.*

Rnds 23 and 24: Knit.

Repeat Rnds 1–24 for Escalator Pattern in the Round (A).

IN THE ROUND (B)

(multiple of 16 sts; 6-rnd repeat)

Note: Use version B if you are working a piece where the beginning-of-rnd marker can shift with every vertical repeat. Use version A if you must have a fixed location for the beginning-of-rnd marker.

Rnds 1–3: *K11, p5; repeat from * to end.

Rnds 4 and 5: Knit.

Rnd 6: Knit to last 4 sts; reposition beginning-of-rnd marker to before these 4 sts. *Note: This will shift beginning of rnd 4 sts to the right every 6 rnds.*

Repeat Rnds 1–6 for Escalator Pattern in the Round (B).

Escalator Pattern

....

FLAT

(multiple of 16 sts + 16; 24-row repeat)

Row 1 (RS): *K11, p5; repeat from * to end.

Rows 2 and 3: Knit the knit sts and purl the purl sts as they face you.

Row 4: Purl.

Row 5: Knit.

Row 6: Purl.

Row 7: K7, p5, *k11, p5; repeat from * to last 4 sts, k4.

Rows 8–12: Repeat Rows 2–6.

Row 13: K3, p5, *k11, p5; repeat from * to last 8 sts, k8.

Rows 14–18: Repeat Rows 2–6.

Row 19: P4, *k11, p5; repeat from * to last 12 sts, k11, p1.

Rows 20–24: Repeat Rows 2–6.

Repeat Rows 1–24 for Escalator Pattern Flat.

FLAT AND IN THE ROUND (A)

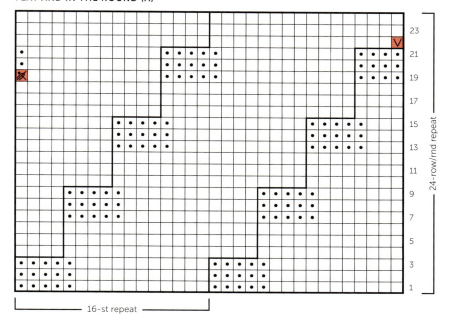

16-st repeat

24-row/rnd repeat

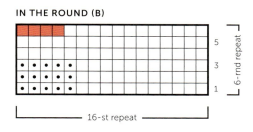 When working flat, purl this st. When working in the rnd, at end of Rnd 19, slip last st purlwise wyib to right-hand needle, pick up strand between needles from back to front, slip st purlwise from right-hand needle back to left-hand needle and purl this st together with picked-up strand; this will minimize the jog in the purl sections at the beginning and end of the rnd.

When working flat, knit this st. When working in the rnd, on first repeat only of Rnd 22, slip first st purlwise wyib; this will minimize the jog in the knit sections at the beginning and end of the rnd. On all following repeats, knit this st.

IN THE ROUND (B)

16-st repeat

6-rnd repeat

On last repeat only of Rnd 6, knit to last 4 sts; reposition beginning-of-rnd marker to before these 4 sts. Work these sts as knit sts for all preceding repeats. **Note:** *Beginning of rnd will shift 4 sts to the right every 6 rnds.*

Banded Insertion

FLAT

(any number of sts; 6-row repeat)
Note: *This pattern requires two pairs of needles, one pair*
4 or 5 sizes larger than the other.
Row 1 (RS): Using smaller needles, knit.
Rows 2–4: Repeat Row 1.
Row 5: Using larger needles, knit.
Row 6: Purl.
Repeat Rows 1–6 for Banded Insertion Flat.

IN THE ROUND

(any number of sts; 6-rnd repeat)
Note: *This pattern requires two circular needles (or two sets*
of dpns), one 4 or 5 sizes larger than the other.
Rnd 1: Using smaller needle(s), knit.
Rnd 2: Purl.
Rnds 3 and 4: Repeat Rnds 1 and 2.
Rnds 5 and 6: Using larger needle(s), knit.
Repeat Rnds 1–6 for Banded Insertion in the Round.

Block Quilting

FLAT

(multiple of 14 sts; 12-row repeat)

Note: Pattern begins with a WS row.

Row 1 (WS): K3, p8, *k6, p8; repeat from * to last 3 sts, k3.

Row 2: Knit.

Rows 3 and 4: Repeat Rows 1 and 2.

Row 5: Repeat Row 1.

Row 6: K2, p2, k6, p2, *k4, p2, k6, p2; repeat from * to last 2 sts, k2.

Row 7: P3, k2, p4, k2, *p6, k2, p4, k2; repeat from * to last 3 sts, p3.

Row 8: K4, p2, k2, p2, *k8, p2, k2, p2; repeat from * to last 4 sts, k4.

Row 9: P5, k4, *p10, k4; repeat from * to last 5 sts, p5.

Row 10: Repeat Row 8.

Row 11: Repeat Row 7.

Row 12: Repeat Row 6.

Repeat Rows 1–12 for Block Quilting Flat.

IN THE ROUND

(multiple of 14 sts; 12-rnd repeat)

Rnd 1: P3, k8, *p6, k8; repeat from * to last 3 sts, p3.

Rnd 2: Knit.

Rnds 3 and 4: Repeat Rnds 1 and 2.

Rnd 5: Repeat Rnd 1.

Rnd 6: K2, p2, k6, p2, *k4, p2, k6, p2; repeat from * to last 2 sts, k2.

Rnd 7: K3, p2, k4, p2, *k6, p2, k4, p2; repeat from * to last 3 sts, k3.

Rnd 8: K4, p2, k2, p2, *k8, p2, k2, p2; repeat from * to last 4 sts, k4.

Rnd 9: K5, p4, *k10, p4; repeat from * to last 5 sts, k5.

Rnd 10: Repeat Rnd 8.

Rnd 11: Repeat Rnd 7.

Rnd 12: Repeat Rnd 6.

Repeat Rnds 1–12 for Block Quilting in the Round.

FLAT AND IN THE ROUND

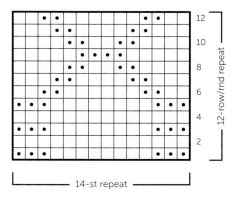

Note: Flat pattern begins with a WS row.

Welted Leaf (TWO-SIDED)

BOTTOM-UP FLAT

(multiple of 8 sts; 14-row repeat)
Row 1 (RS): Knit.
Row 2: Purl.
Row 3: *K4, p4; repeat from * to end.
Row 4: K3, p4, *k4, p4; repeat from * to last st, k1.
Row 5: P2, k4, *p4, k4; repeat from * to last 2 sts, p2.
Row 6: K1, p4, *k4, p4; repeat from * to last 3 sts, k3.
Rows 7–9: Repeat Rows 4–6.
Row 10: *P4, k4; repeat from * to end.
Rows 11–14: Knit.
Repeat Rows 1–14 for Welted Leaf Bottom-Up Flat.

BOTTOM-UP IN THE ROUND

(multiple of 8 sts; 14-rnd repeat)
Rnds 1 and 2: Knit.
Rnd 3: *K4, p4; repeat from * to end.
Rnd 4: P1, k4, *p4, k4; repeat from * to last 3 sts, p3.
Rnd 5: P2, k4, *p4, k4; repeat from * to last 2 sts, p2.
Rnd 6: P3, k4, *p4, k4; repeat from * to last st, p1.
Rnd 7: K3, p4, *k4, p4; repeat from * to last st, k1.
Rnd 8: K2, p4, *k4, p4; repeat from * to last 2 sts, k2.
Rnd 9: K1, p4, *k4, p4; repeat from * to last 3 sts, k3.
Rnd 10: *P4, k4; repeat from * to end.
Rnd 11: Knit.
Rnd 12: Purl.
Rnds 13 and 14: Repeat Rnds 11 and 12.
Repeat Rnds 1–14 for Welted Leaf Bottom-Up in the Round.

TOP-DOWN FLAT

(multiple of 8 sts; 14-row repeat)
Row 1 (RS): Purl.
Rows 2–4: Purl.
Row 5: *K4, p4; repeat from * to end.
Row 6: P1, k4, *p4, k4; repeat from * to last 3 sts, p3.
Row 7: K2, p4, *k4, p4; repeat from * to last 2 sts, k2.
Row 8: P3, k4, *p4, k4; repeat from * to last st, p1.
Rows 9–11: Repeat Rows 6–8.
Row 12: *P4, k4; repeat from * to end.
Row 13: Knit.
Row 14: Purl.
Repeat Rows 1–14 for Welted Leaf Top-Down Flat.

TOP-DOWN IN THE ROUND

(multiple of 8 sts; 14-rnd repeat)
Rnd 1: Purl.
Rnd 2: Knit.
Rnds 3 and 4: Repeat Rnds 1 and 2.
Rnd 5: *K4, p4; repeat from * to end.
Rnd 6: K3, p4, *k4, p4; repeat from * to last st, k1.
Rnd 7: K2, p4, *k4, p4; repeat from * to last 2 sts, k2.
Rnd 8: K1, p4, *k4, p4; repeat from * to last 3 sts, k3.
Rnd 9: P1, k4, *p4, k4; repeat from * to last 3 sts, p3.
Rnd 10: P2, k4, *p4, k4; repeat from * to last 2 sts, p2.
Rnd 11: P3, k4, *p4, k4; repeat from * to last st, p1.
Rnd 12: *P4, k4; repeat from * to end.
Rnds 13 and 14: Knit.
Repeat Rnds 1–14 for Welted Leaf Top-Down in the Round.

BOTTOM-UP FLAT AND IN THE ROUND

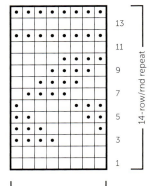

8-st repeat

14-row/rnd repeat

TOP-DOWN FLAT AND IN THE ROUND

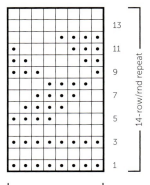

8-st repeat

14-row/rnd repeat

Mosaic Stitch (TWO-SIDED)

FLAT

(multiple of 20 sts + 10; 20-row repeat)

Row 1 (RS): P2, *k2, p2; repeat from * to end.

Row 2: Knit the knit sts and purl the purl sts as they face you.

Row 3: [K2, p2] twice, *k4, p2, k2, p2; repeat from * to last 2 sts, k2.

Row 4: Repeat Row 2.

Rows 5–8: Repeat Rows 1–4.

Rows 9 and 10: Repeat Rows 1 and 2.

Row 11: K2, *p2, k2; repeat from * to end.

Row 12: Repeat Row 2.

Rows 13 and 14: Repeat Rows 3 and 4.

Rows 15–18: Repeat Rows 11–14.

Rows 19 and 20: Repeat Rows 11 and 12.

Repeat Rows 1–20 for Mosaic Stitch Flat.

IN THE ROUND

(multiple of 20 sts; 20-rnd repeat)

Rnds 1 and 2: *P2, k2; repeat from * to end.

Rnds 3 and 4: [K2, p2] twice, *k4, p2, k2, p2; repeat from * to last 2 sts, k2.

Rnds 5–8: Repeat Rnds 1–4.

Rnds 9 and 10: Repeat Rnds 1 and 2.

Rnds 11 and 12: *K2, p2; repeat from * to end.

Rnds 13 and 14: Repeat Rnds 3 and 4.

Rnds 15–18: Repeat Rnds 11–14.

Rnds 19 and 20: Repeat Rnds 11 and 12.

Repeat Rnds 1–20 for Mosaic Stitch in the Round.

FLAT

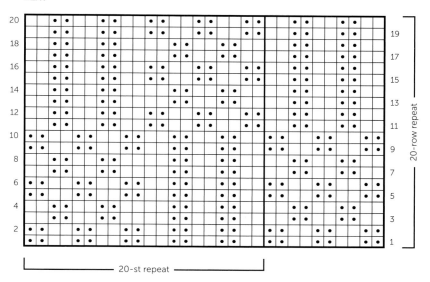

20-st repeat

20-row repeat

IN THE ROUND

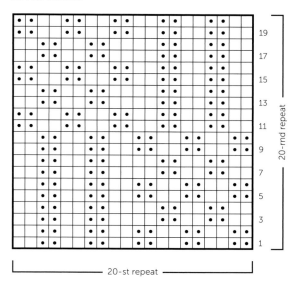

20-st repeat

20-rnd repeat

FINISHED MEASUREMENTS
13" (33 cm) square

YARN
Blue Sky Fibers Organic Cotton (Skinny) [100% certified organic cotton; 150 yards (138 meters) / 2½ ounces (65 grams)]: 1 hank #314 Gravel
Note: You will need to purchase a second hank if you make a double-sided pillow.

NEEDLES
One pair straight needles size US 5 (3.75 mm)
One pair double-pointed needles size US 5 (3.75 mm), for optional I-cord
Change needle size if necessary to obtain correct gauge.

NOTIONS
14" (35.5 cm) square fabric backing (optional), sewing machine or sewing needle (optional), matching thread (optional), 13" (33 cm) square pillow form

GAUGE
17 sts and 32 rows = 4" [10 cm] in Small Basket Stitch, washed and blocked

Common Decorative Pillow Sizes

If you're unsure of what size pillow to knit, the most important thing to remember is that pillow dimensions always refer to the pillow cover's width and length while laying flat, unstuffed. The measurements are always taken along the seams from corner to corner.

Square Shape
16" (40.5 cm)
18" (45.5 cm)
26" (66 cm) Euro or Continental
30" (76 cm) Euro or Continental

Rectangle Shape
10 × 20" (25.5 × 51 cm) Lumbar
12 × 16" (30.5 × 40.5 cm) Boudoir
12 × 24" (30.5 × 61 cm) Lumbar
14 × 36" (35.5 × 91.5 cm) Lumbar
12 × 16" (30.5 × 40.5 cm) Travel

Basket Stitch Pillow

Sometimes it's fun to deviate from garment knitting and work on an item for your home instead. These pillows are quick knits; to make these "your own," all you have to do is select a favorite stitch pattern, make a swatch to find your gauge, and then determine the number of stitches you need to cast on for the width of your pillow form. The next step? Just keep knitting and stretching your knitted piece over your form, bind off when it's the right length, and work another piece for the back (or find a piece of fabric for the back). Then sew the two pieces together, leaving a space to insert your pillow form, and close it up. Add an optional attached I-cord, and you're good to go!

STITCH PATTERN

SMALL BASKET STITCH

(multiple of 10 sts + 5; 8-row repeat)
Set-Up Row (WS): P1, [k1, p1] twice, *k5, p1, [k1, p1] twice; repeat from * to end.
Row 1: [K1, p1] twice, *k7, p1, k1, p1; repeat from * to last st, k1.
Row 2: P1, [k1, p1] twice, *k5, p1, [k1, p1] twice; repeat from * to end.
Rows 3 and 4: Repeat Rows 1 and 2.
Row 5: K6, p1, k1, p1, *k7, p1, k1, p1; repeat from * to last 6 sts, k6.
Rows 6–8: Knit the knit sts and purl the purl sts as they face you.
Repeat Rows 1–8 for Small Basket Stitch.

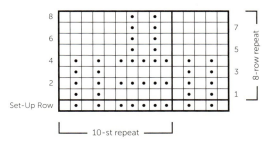

SMALL BASKET STITCH

8-row repeat

10-st repeat

Note: Pattern begins with a WS row.

Front

(For sample knit in taupe, shown opposite.)
CO 57 sts.
Row 1 (WS): P1 (edge st, keep in St st), work in Small Basket Stitch to last st, p1 (edge st, keep in St st).

Work even, working first and last st in St st, until piece measures approximately 13" (33 cm) from the beginning, or until piece is large enough to stretch firmly over pillow form, ending with a WS row. BO all sts.
Note: If you prefer to make a double-sided pillow, work Back panel to match Front and omit fabric backing. If you work a double-sided pillow, you will need to purchase additional yarn.

Finishing

Pillow with Fabric Backing
With RSs of Front and fabric together, using sewing machine or needle and thread, sew 3 sides of Front to 3 sides of fabric backing using ¼" (6 mm) seam allowance. Turn right side out. Insert pillow form; sew last side closed by hand.

Double-Sided Pillow
With RS of Front and Back facing out, using working yarn, sew 3 sides together. Insert pillow form; sew last side closed. If desired, work a 3-st applied I-cord (see Special Techniques, page 278) around entire pillow, beginning and ending at bottom center of pillow. BO all sts. Sew CO edge to BO edge.

The coral pillow was made using 2 hanks of Blue Sky Fibers Organic Cotton (Skinny) (#317 Coral), 13" × 18" (33 cm × 45.5 cm) pillow form, and 14" × 19" (35.5 cm × 48.5 cm) fabric backing. Cast on 79 sts and work in the Butterfly Checkerboard pattern (see page 106) for approximately 13" (33 cm), keeping the first and last st of every row in St st. Finish it as for the Basket Stitch Pillow.

CHAPTER **2** Ribs

When you think of ribs, you probably think of alternating columns of knit and purl stitches. These columns are what give the ribbed patterns the stretch we look for when adding them to the cuffs of a sweater or a cap brim. In addition to adding that needed stretch, ribs offer us a preventative for curling edges. Some rib patterns are not as stretchy as others and can be used for an allover effect or function as a decorative border rather than a snug edging. When knitting things like mittens, you'll want to look for a rib with stretch, like Supple Rib on page 66. If you want a rib that serves as a border, try Charlie Brown Twisted Ribs on page 57. Like the look of a close-knit rib in this chapter but want it to be less stretchy? Try swatching it on larger needles and see what happens.

Chained Eyelet Columns

FLAT

(multiple of 8 sts + 2; 4-row repeat)

Row 1 (RS): P2, *k1, p1, yo, k2tog, p1, k1, p2; repeat from * to end.

Row 2: K2, *p1b, k1, p2, k1, p1b, k2; repeat from * to end.

Row 3: P2, *k1, p1, ssk, yo, p1, k1, p2; repeat from * to end.

Row 4: Repeat Row 2.

Repeat Rows 1–4 for Chained Eyelet Columns Flat.

IN THE ROUND

(multiple of 8 sts; 4-rnd repeat)

Rnd 1: *P2, k1, p1, yo, k2tog, p1, k1; repeat from * to end.

Rnd 2: *P2, k1b, p1, k2, p1, k1b; repeat from * to end.

Rnd 3: *P2, k1, p1, ssk, yo, p1, k1; repeat from * to end.

Rnd 4: Repeat Rnd 2.

Repeat Rnds 1–4 for Chained Eyelet Columns in the Round.

FLAT

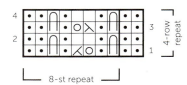

IN THE ROUND

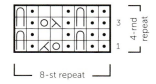

P1b on WS, k1b on RS.
K1

Ribs and Frogs

FLAT

(multiple of 12 sts + 7; 4-row repeat)

Note: Pattern begins with a WS row.

Row 1 (WS): P1-tbl, [k1, p1-tbl] 3 times, *k5, p1-tbl, [k1, p1-tbl] 3 times; repeat from * to end.

Row 2: K1-tbl, [p1, k1-tbl] 3 times, *p1, k3, [p1, k1-tbl] 4 times; repeat from * to end.

Row 3: P1-tbl, [k1, p1-tbl] 3 times, *k1, p3, [k1, p1-tbl] 4 times; repeat from * to end.

Row 4: K1-tbl, [p1, k1-tbl] 3 times, *p1, yo, s2kp2, yo, [p1, k1-tbl] 4 times; repeat from * to end.

Repeat Rows 1–4 for Ribs and Frogs Flat.

FLAT

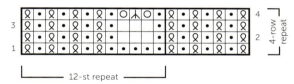

Note: Pattern begins with a WS row.

IN THE ROUND

(multiple of 12 sts; 4-rnd repeat)

Rnd 1: K1-tbl, p1, k1-tbl, p5, *k1-tbl, [p1, k1-tbl] 3 times, p5; repeat from * to last 4 sts, [k1-tbl, p1] twice.

Rnds 2 and 3: [K1-tbl, p1] twice, k3, p1, *[k1-tbl, p1] 4 times, k3, p1; repeat from * to last 4 sts, [k1-tbl, p1] twice.

Rnd 4: [K1-tbl, p1] twice, yo, s2kp2, yo, p1, *[k1-tbl, p1] 4 times, yo, s2kp2, yo, p1; repeat from * to last 4 sts, [k1-tbl, p1] twice.

Repeat Rnds 1–4 for Ribs and Frogs in the Round.

IN THE ROUND

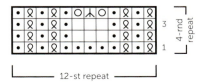

(multiple of 8 sts; 8-rnd repeat)

1/2 RTPC: See key.

1/2 LTPC: See key.

Rnd 1: *P1, 1/2 RTPC, [p1, k1-tbl] twice; repeat from * to end.

Rnd 2 and all Even-Numbered Rnds: *P1, k1-tbl; repeat from * to end.

Rnd 3: *P1, k1-tbl, p1, 1/2 LTPC, p1, k1-tbl; repeat from * to end.

Rnd 5: *P1, [k1-tbl, p1] twice, 1/2 LTPC; repeat from * to end.

Rnd 7: *P1, k1-tbl, p1, 1/2 RTPC, p1, k1-tbl; repeat from * to end.

Rnd 8: Repeat Rnd 2.

Repeat Rnds 1–8 for Bramble Ribs Bottom-Up in the Round.

Bramble Ribs

BOTTOM-UP FLAT

(multiple of 8 sts + 1; 8-row repeat)

1/2 RTPC: See key.

1/2 LTPC: See key.

Row 1 (RS): P1, *1/2 RTPC, p1, [k1-tbl, p1] twice; repeat from * to end.

Row 2 and all WS Rows: K1, *p1-tbl, k1; repeat from * to end.

Row 3: P1, *k1-tbl, p1, 1/2 LTPC, p1, k1-tbl, p1; repeat from * to end.

Row 5: P1, *[k1-tbl, p1] twice, 1/2 LTPC, p1; repeat from * to end.

Row 7: P1, *k1-tbl, p1, 1/2 RTPC, p1, k1-tbl, p1; repeat from * to end.

Row 8: Repeat Row 2.

Repeat Rows 1–8 for Bramble Ribs Bottom-Up Flat.

BOTTOM-UP FLAT

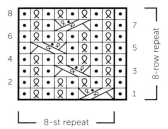

8-st repeat

1/2 RTPC: Slip 2 sts to cn, hold to back, k1-tbl, (p1, k1-tbl) from cn.

1/2 LTPC: Slip 1 st to cn, hold to front, k1-tbl, p1, k1-tbl from cn.

BOTTOM-UP IN THE ROUND

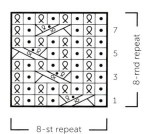

8-st repeat

TOP-DOWN FLAT

(multiple of 8 sts + 1; 8-row repeat)

1/2 RTPC: See key.

1/2 LTPC: See key.

Row 1 (RS): P1, *k1-tbl, p1, 1/2 RTPC, p1, k1-tbl, p1; repeat from * to end.

Row 2 and all WS Rows: K1, *p1-tbl, k1; repeat from * to end.

Row 3: P1, *1/2 LTPC, p1, [k1-tbl, p1] twice; repeat from * to end.

Row 5: P1, *k1-tbl, p1, 1/2 LTPC, p1, k1-tbl, p1; repeat from * to end.

Row 7: P1, *[k1-tbl, p1] twice, 1/2 RTPC, p1; repeat from * to end.

Row 8: Repeat Row 2.

Repeat Rows 1–8 for Bramble Ribs Top-Down Flat.

TOP-DOWN IN THE ROUND

(multiple of 8 sts; 8-rnd repeat)

1/2 RTPC: See key.

1/2 LTPC: See key.

Rnd 1: *K1-tbl, p1, 1/2 RTPC, p1, k1-tbl, p1; repeat from * to end.

Rnd 2 and all Even-Numbered Rnds: *K1-tbl, p1; repeat from * to end.

Rnd 3: *1/2 LTPC, p1, [k1-tbl, p1] twice; repeat from * to end.

Rnd 5: *K1-tbl, p1, 1/2 LTPC, p1, k1-tbl, p1; repeat from * to end.

Rnd 7: *[K1-tbl, p1] twice, 1/2 RTPC, p1; repeat from * to end.

Rnd 8: Repeat Rnd 2.

Repeat Rnds 1–8 for Bramble Ribs Top-Down in the Round.

TOP-DOWN FLAT

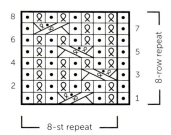

8-st repeat

TOP-DOWN IN THE ROUND

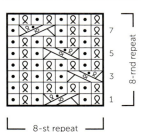

8-st repeat

 1/2 RTPC: Slip 2 sts to cn, hold to back, k1-tbl, (p1, k1-tbl) from cn.

 1/2 LTPC: Slip 1 st to cn, hold to front, k1-tbl, p1, k1-tbl from cn.

Charlie Brown Twisted Ribs

FLAT

(multiple of 20 sts + 3; 26-row repeat)

Wrap 3: See key.

Row 1 (RS): K1-tbl, *p1, k1-tbl; repeat from * to end.

Row 2 and all WS Rows: P1-tbl, *k1, p1-tbl; repeat from * to end.

Rows 3 and 5: Repeat Row 1.

Row 7: Wrap 3, *p1, [k1-tbl, p1] 8 times, wrap 3; repeat from * to end.

Row 9: K1-tbl, p1, wrap 3, p1, [k1-tbl, p1] 6 times, *[wrap 3, p1] twice, [k1-tbl, p1] 6 times; repeat from * to last 5 sts, wrap 3, p1, k1-tbl.

Row 11: [Wrap 3, p1] twice, [k1-tbl, p1] 4 times, *[wrap 3, p1] 3 times, [k1-tbl, p1] 4 times; repeat from * to last 7 sts, wrap 3, p1, wrap 3.

Row 13: K1-tbl, p1, [wrap 3, p1] twice, [k1-tbl, p1] twice, *[wrap 3, p1] 4 times, [k1-tbl, p1] twice; repeat from * to last 9 sts, [wrap 3, p1] twice, k1-tbl.

Row 15: K1-tbl, p1, k1-tbl, *[p1, wrap 3] 4 times, [p1, k1-tbl] twice; repeat from * to end.

Row 17: [K1-tbl, p1] 3 times, [wrap 3, p1] 3 times, *[k1-tbl, p1] 4 times, [wrap 3, p1] 3 times; repeat from * to last 5 sts, k1-tbl, [p1, k1-tbl] twice.

Row 19: [K1-tbl, p1] 4 times, [wrap 3, p1] twice, *[k1-tbl, p1] 6 times, [wrap 3, p1] twice; repeat from * to last 7 sts, k1-tbl, [p1, k1-tbl] 3 times.

Row 21: [K1-tbl, p1] 5 times, wrap 3, *p1, [k1-tbl, p1] 8 times, wrap 3; repeat from * to last 10 sts, [p1, k1-tbl] 5 times.

Rows 23 and 25: Repeat Row 1.

Row 26: Repeat Row 2.

Repeat Rows 1–26 for Charlie Brown Twisted Ribs Flat.

FLAT

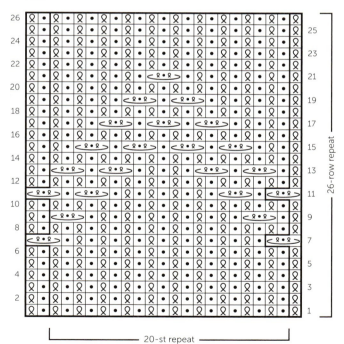

20-st repeat

26-row repeat

Wrap 3: K1-tbl, p1, k1-tbl, slip these 3 sts to cn; bring yarn to front and wrap yarn around these sts twice counterclockwise; slip sts back to right-hand needle.

IN THE ROUND

(multiple of 20 sts; 26-rnd repeat)

Wrap 3: See key.

Rnds 1–5: *K1-tbl, p1; repeat from * to end.

Rnd 6: *K1-tbl, p1; repeat from * to last 2 sts.

Rnd 7: *Wrap 3 (keeping beginning-of-rnd marker in place as you work first repeat), p1, [k1-tbl, p1] 8 times; repeat from * to last 2 sts, k1-tbl, p1.

Rnd 8: Repeat Rnd 1.

Rnd 9: Wrap 3, p1, [k1-tbl, p1] 6 times, *[wrap 3, p1] twice, [k1-tbl, p1] 6 times; repeat from * to last 4 sts, wrap 3, p1.

Rnd 10: Repeat Rnd 6.

Rnd 11: [Wrap 3 (keeping beginning-of-rnd marker in place as you work first repeat), p1] twice, [k1-tbl, p1] 4 times, *[wrap 3, p1] 3 times, [k1-tbl, p1] 4 times; repeat from * to last 6 sts, wrap 3, p1, k1-tbl, p1.

Rnd 12: Repeat Rnd 1.

Rnd 13: [Wrap 3, p1] twice, [k1-tbl, p1] twice, *[wrap 3, p1] 4 times, [k1-tbl, p1] twice; repeat from * to last 8 sts, [wrap 3, p1] twice.

Rnd 14: Repeat Rnd 1.

Rnd 15: K1-tbl, p1, [wrap 3, p1] 4 times, *[k1-tbl, p1] twice, [wrap 3, p1] 4 times; repeat from * to last 2 sts, k1-tbl, p1.

Rnd 16: Repeat Rnd 1.

Rnd 17: [K1-tbl, p1] twice, [wrap 3, p1] 3 times, *[k1-tbl, p1] 4 times, [wrap 3, p1] 3 times; repeat from * to last 4 sts, [k1-tbl, p1] twice.

Rnd 18: Repeat Rnd 1.

Rnd 19: [K1-tbl, p1] 3 times, [wrap 3, p1] twice, *[k1-tbl, p1] 6 times, [wrap 3, p1] twice; repeat from * to last 6 sts, [k1-tbl, p1] 3 times.

Rnd 20: Repeat Rnd 1.

Rnd 21: [K1-tbl, p1] 4 times, wrap 3, *p1, [k1-tbl, p1] 8 times, wrap 3; repeat from * to last 9 sts, p1, [k1-tbl, p1] 4 times.

Rnds 22–26: Repeat Rnd 1.

Repeat Rnds 1–26 for Charlie Brown Twisted Ribs in the Round.

IN THE ROUND

20-st repeat

26-rnd repeat

Wrap 3: K1-tbl, p1, k1-tbl, slip these 3 sts to cn; bring yarn to front and wrap yarn around these sts twice counterclockwise; slip sts back to right-hand needle.

On final repeat only of Rnds 6 and 10, end 2 sts before beginning-of-rnd marker; the last 2 sts will be worked with the first wrap 3 of Rnds 7 and 11. On all preceding repeats, work these sts as k1-tbl, p1.

On first repeat only of Rnds 7 and 11, work wrap 3 on last 2 sts of Rnds 6 and 10 and first st of Rnds 7 and 11, leaving beginning-of-rnd marker in place as you work. On remaining repeats, work wrap 3 as before.

Work as indicated after final repeat of Rnds 7 and 11 are complete.

Bobble in a Basket

FLAT

(multiple of 8 sts + 1; 12-row repeat)

Row 1 (RS): P1, *k1, p1; repeat from * to end.

Row 2 and all WS Rows: Knit the knit sts and purl the purl sts as they face you; purl all yos.

Row 3: P1, *LPC, k1, p1, k1, RPC, p1; repeat from * to end.

Row 5: P2, k2tog, yo, p1, yo, ssk, *p3, k2tog, yo, p1, yo, ssk; repeat from * to last 2 sts, p2.

Row 7: P2, k2, MB, k2, *p3, k2, MB, k2; repeat from * to last 2 sts, p2.

Row 9: Repeat Row 5.

Row 11: P1, *RPC, k1, p1, k1, LPC, p1; repeat from * to end.

Row 12: Repeat Row 2.

Repeat Rows 1–12 for Bobble in a Basket Flat.

IN THE ROUND

(multiple of 8 sts; 12-rnd repeat)

Rnd 1: *P1, k1; repeat from * to end.

Rnd 2 and all Even-Numbered Rnds: Knit the knit sts and purl the purl sts as they face you; knit all yos.

Rnd 3: *P1, LPC, k1, p1, k1, RPC; repeat from * to end.

Rnd 5: P2, k2tog, yo, p1, yo, ssk, *p3, k2tog, yo, p1, yo, ssk; repeat from * to last st, p1.

Rnd 7: P2, k2, MB, k2, *p3, k2, MB, k2; repeat from * to last st, p1.

Rnd 9: Repeat Rnd 5.

Rnd 11: *P1, RPC, k1, p1, k1, LPC; repeat from * to end.

Rnd 12: Repeat Rnd 2.

Repeat Rnds 1–12 for Bobble in a Basket in the Round.

FLAT

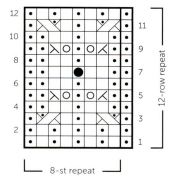

IN THE ROUND

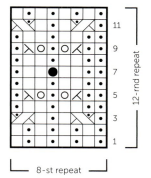

 MB: Make Bobble.

Rnd 9: P3, RC, LC, *p4, RC, LC; repeat from * to last st, p1.
Rnd 10: Repeat Rnd 2.
Rnd 11: P3, LC, RC, *p4, LC, RC; repeat from * to last st, p1.
Rnd 12: Repeat Rnd 2.
Rnd 13: *P2, 2/1 RPC, 2/1 LPC; repeat from * to end.
Rnds 14–16: Repeat Rnd 2.
Repeat Rnds 1–16 for Prosperity Ribs in the Round.

Prosperity Ribs

....

FLAT

(multiple of 8 sts + 2; 16-row repeat)
Row 1 (RS): P2, *k2, p2; repeat from * to end.
Row 2 and all WS Rows: Knit the knit sts and purl the purl sts as they face you.
Rows 3 and 5: Repeat Row 1.
Row 7: P2, *2/1 LPC, 2/1 RPC, p2; repeat from * to end.
Row 9: P3, RC, LC, *p4, RC, LC; repeat from * to last 3 sts, p3.
Row 11: P3, LC, RC, *p4, LC, RC; repeat from * to last 3 sts, p3.
Row 13: P2, *2/1 RPC, 2/1 LPC, p2; repeat from * to end.
Rows 15 and 16: Repeat Rows 1 and 2.
Repeat Rows 1–16 for Prosperity Ribs Flat.

IN THE ROUND

(multiple of 8 sts; 16-rnd repeat)
Rnd 1: *P2, k2; repeat from * to end.
Rnds 2–6: Knit the knit sts and purl the purl sts as they face you.
Rnd 7: *P2, 2/1 LPC, 2/1 RPC; repeat from * to end.
Rnd 8: Repeat Rnd 2.

FLAT

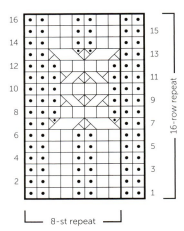

IN THE ROUND

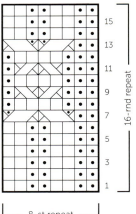

Wrapped Columns
....

FLAT

(multiple of 13 sts + 6; 4-row repeat)

Wrap 3: See key.

Row 1 (RS): K2, p2, k2, *p2, wrap 3, [p2, k2] twice; repeat from * to end.

Rows 2–4: Knit the knit sts and purl the purl sts as they face you; do not twist the sts.

Repeat Rows 1–4 for Wrapped Columns Flat.

IN THE ROUND

(multiple of 13 sts; 4-rnd repeat)

Wrap 3: See key.

Rnd 1: *[K2, p2] twice, wrap 3, p2; repeat from * to end.

Rnds 2–4: Knit the knit sts and purl the purl sts as they face you; do not twist the sts.

Repeat Rnds 1–4 for Wrapped Columns in the Round.

FLAT

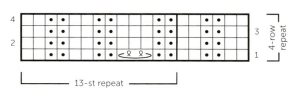

IN THE ROUND

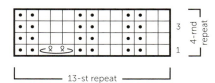

Wrap 3: K1-tbl, k1, k1-tbl, slip these 3 sts to cn; bring yarn to front and wrap yarn around these sts twice counterclockwise; slip sts back to right-hand needle.

Twists and Chains

FLAT

(multiple of 7 sts + 5; 2-row repeat)
Row 1 (RS): P2, k1, p2, *RC, p2, k1, p2; repeat from * to end.
Row 2: K2, p1b, k2, *p2, k2, p1b, k2; repeat from * to end.
Repeat Rows 1 and 2 for Twists and Chains Flat.

IN THE ROUND

(multiple of 7 sts; 2-rnd repeat)
Rnd 1: *RC, p2, k1, p2; repeat from * to end.
Rnd 2: *K2, p2, k1b, p2; repeat from * to end.
Repeat Rnds 1 and 2 for Twists and Chains in the Round.

FLAT

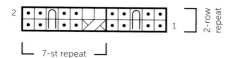

IN THE ROUND

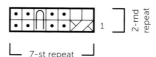

 K1b on RS, p1b on WS.
K1

Chained Ribs (TWO-SIDED)

FLAT

(multiple of 5 sts + 2; 2-row repeat)
Row 1 (RS): K2, *p3, k2; repeat from * to end.
Row 2: P2, *k1b, k1, k1b, p2; repeat from * to end.
Row 3: K2, *p1, p1b, p1, k2; repeat from * to end.
Row 4: Repeat Row 2.
Repeat Rows 3 and 4 for Chained Ribs Flat.

IN THE ROUND

(multiple of 5 sts; 2-rnd repeat)
Rnd 1: *K2, p3; repeat from * to end.
Rnd 2: *K2, p1b, p1, p1b; repeat from * to end.
Rnd 3: *K2, p1, p1b, p1; repeat from * to end.
Rnd 4: Repeat Rnd 2.
Repeat Rnds 3 and 4 for Chained Ribs in the Round.

FLAT

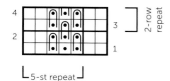

IN THE ROUND

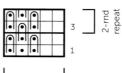

P1b on RS, k1b on WS.
P1 on RS, k1 on WS.

Oblique Rib Left (TWO-SIDED)

FLAT

(multiple of 4 sts; 4-row repeat)

Row 1 (RS): *K2, p2; repeat from * to end.
Row 2: K1, p2, *k2, p2; repeat from * to last st, k1.
Row 3: *P2, k2; repeat from * to end.
Row 4: P1, k2, *p2, k2; repeat from * to last st, p1.
Repeat Rows 1–4 for Oblique Rib Left Flat.

IN THE ROUND

(multiple of 4 sts; 4-rnd repeat)

Rnd 1: *K2, p2; repeat from * to end.
Rnd 2: P1, k2, *p2, k2; repeat from * to last st, p1.
Rnd 3: *P2, k2; repeat from * to end.
Rnd 4: K1, p2, *k2, p2; repeat from * to last st, k1.
Repeat Rnds 1–4 for Oblique Rib Left in the Round.

Oblique Rib Right (TWO-SIDED)

FLAT

(multiple of 4 sts; 4-row repeat)

Row 1 (RS): *P2, k2; repeat from * to end.
Row 2: K1, p2, *k2, p2; repeat from * to last st, k1.
Row 3: *K2, p2; repeat from * to end.
Row 4: P1, k2, *p2, k2; repeat from * to last st, p1.
Repeat Rows 1–4 for Oblique Rib Right Flat.

IN THE ROUND

(multiple of 4 sts; 4-rnd repeat)

Rnd 1: *P2, k2; repeat from * to end.
Rnd 2: P1, k2, *p2, k2; repeat from * to last st, p1.
Rnd 3: *K2, p2; repeat from * to end.
Rnd 4: K1, p2, *k2, p2; repeat from * to last st, k1.
Repeat Rnds 1–4 for Oblique Rib Right in the Round.

FLAT AND IN THE ROUND

FLAT AND IN THE ROUND

Ridged Rib (TWO-SIDED)

FLAT

(odd number of sts; 4-row repeat)
Row 1 (RS): Knit.
Row 2: Knit.
Row 3: K1, *p1, k1; repeat from * to end.
Row 4: P1, *k1, p1; repeat from * to end.
Repeat Rows 1–4 for Ridged Rib Flat.

IN THE ROUND

(even number of sts; 4-rnd repeat)
Rnd 1: Knit.
Rnd 2: Purl.
Rnds 3 and 4: *K1, p1; repeat from * to end.
Repeat Rnds 1–4 for Ridged Rib in the Round.

Lacy Chevron Rib

FLAT

(multiple of 7 sts; 4-row repeat)
Row 1 (RS): K1, k2tog, yo, k1, yo, ssk, *k2, k2tog, yo, k1, yo, ssk; repeat from * to last st, k1.
Row 2: Purl.
Row 3: *K2tog, yo, k3, yo, ssk; repeat from * to end.
Row 4: Purl.
Repeat Rows 1–4 for Lacy Chevron Rib Flat.

IN THE ROUND

(multiple of 7 sts; 4-rnd repeat)
Rnd 1: K1, k2tog, yo, k1, yo, ssk, *k2, k2tog, yo, k1, yo, ssk; repeat from * to last st, k1.
Rnd 2: Knit.
Rnd 3: *K2tog, yo, k3, yo, ssk; repeat from * to end.
Rnd 4: Knit.
Repeat Rnds 1–4 for Lacy Chevron Rib in the Round.

FLAT

IN THE ROUND

FLAT AND IN THE ROUND

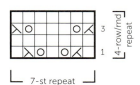

Supple Rib

....

FLAT

(multiple of 3 sts + 1; 2-row repeat)

Row 1 (RS): K1, *k1 but do not drop st from left-hand needle, purl the same st and the following st together, then drop them from left-hand needle together, k1; repeat from * to end.

Row 2: Purl.

Repeat Rows 1 and 2 for Supple Rib Flat.

IN THE ROUND

(multiple of 3 sts; 2-rnd repeat)

Rnd 1: *K1 but do not drop st from left-hand needle, purl the same st and the following st together, then drop them from left-hand needle together, k1; repeat from * to end.

Rnd 2: Knit.

Repeat Rnds 1 and 2 for Supple Rib in the Round.

FLAT

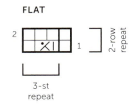

3-st
repeat

IN THE ROUND

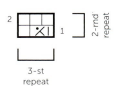

3-st
repeat

 K1 but do not drop st from left-hand needle, purl the same st and the following st together, then drop them from left-hand needle together.

Rib Checks

FLAT

(multiple of 10 sts + 5; 10-row repeat)

Row 1 (RS): P5, *k1-tbl, [p1, k1-tbl] twice, p5; repeat from * to end.

Row 2: K5, *p1-tbl, [k1, p1-tbl] twice, k5; repeat from * to end.

Rows 3 and 4: Repeat Rows 1 and 2.

Row 5: Repeat Row 1.

Row 6: P1-tbl, [k1, p1-tbl] twice, *k5, p1-tbl, [k1, p1-tbl] twice; repeat from * to end.

Row 7: K1-tbl, [p1, k1-tbl] twice, *p5, k1-tbl, [p1, k1-tbl] twice; repeat from * to end.

Rows 8 and 9: Repeat Rows 6 and 7.

Row 10: Repeat Row 6.

Repeat Rows 1–10 for Rib Checks Flat.

IN THE ROUND

(multiple of 10 sts; 10-rnd repeat)

Rnds 1–5: *K1-tbl, [p1, k1-tbl] twice, p5; repeat from * to end.

Rnds 6–10: *P5, k1-tbl, [p1, k1-tbl] twice; repeat from * to end.

Repeat Rnds 1–10 for Rib Checks in the Round.

FLAT

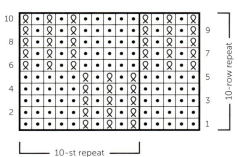

IN THE ROUND

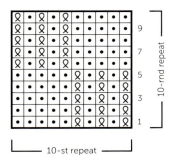

Linked Ribs

BOTTOM-UP FLAT

(multiple of 8 sts + 4; 6-row repeat)

Row 1 (RS): P4, *k1, p2, k1, p4; repeat from * to end.

Row 2 and all WS Rows: Knit the knit sts and purl the purl sts as they face you.

Row 3: Repeat Row 2.

Row 5: P4, *LC, RC, p4; repeat from * to end.

Row 6: Repeat Row 2.

Repeat Rows 1–6 for Linked Ribs Bottom-Up Flat.

BOTTOM-UP FLAT

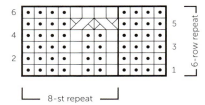

BOTTOM-UP IN THE ROUND

(multiple of 8 sts; 6-rnd repeat)

Rnds 1–4: *P4, k1, p2, k1; repeat from * to end.

Rnd 5: *P4, LC, RC; repeat from * to end.

Row 6: *P4, k4; repeat from *to end.

Repeat Rnds 1–6 for Linked Ribs Bottom-Up in the Round.

BOTTOM-UP IN THE ROUND

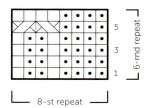

TOP-DOWN FLAT

(multiple of 8 sts + 4; 6-row repeat)

Row 1 (RS): P4, *RC, LC, p4; repeat from * to end.

Row 2: K4, *p1, k2, p1, k4; repeat from * to end.

Rows 3–5: Knit the knit sts and purl the purl sts as they face you.

Row 6: K4, *p4, k4; repeat from * to end.

Repeat Rows 1–6 for Linked Ribs Top-Down Flat.

TOP-DOWN FLAT

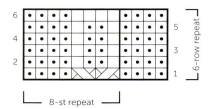

TOP-DOWN IN THE ROUND

(multiple of 8 sts; 6-rnd repeat)

Rnd 1: *P4, RC, LC; repeat from * to end.

Rnds 2–5: *P4, k1, p2, k1; repeat from * to end.

Rnd 6: *P4, k4; repeat from *to end.

Repeat Rnds 1–6 for Linked Ribs Top-Down in the Round.

TOP-DOWN IN THE ROUND

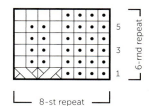

3-Stitch Twisted Rib

FLAT

(multiple of 5 sts + 2; 2-row repeat)
RC3: See key.
Note: Pattern begins with a WS row.
Row 1 (WS): K2, *p3, k2; repeat from * to end.
Row 2: P2, *RC3, p2; repeat from * to end.
Repeat Rows 1 and 2 for 3-Stitch Twisted Rib Flat.

IN THE ROUND

(multiple of 5 sts; 2-rnd repeat)
RC3: See key.
Rnd 1: *P2, k3; repeat from * to end.
Rnd 2: *P2, RC3; repeat from * to end.
Repeat Rnds 1 and 2 for 3-Stitch Twisted Rib in the Round.

FLAT

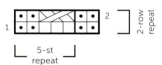

IN THE ROUND

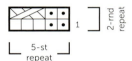

Note: Pattern begins with a WS row.

 RC3: Right Cross 3. Knit into front of third st; knit into front of first st and drop it from needle; knit into front of second st and drop second and third sts from needle together.

Granite Rib

FLAT

(multiple of 8 sts + 2; 4-row repeat)
RT3: See key.
Row 1 (RS): K2, *[RC] 3 times, k2; repeat from * to end.
Row 2: Purl.
Row 3: K2, *[RT3] twice, k2; repeat from * to end.
Row 4: Purl.
Repeat Rows 1–4 for Granite Rib Flat.

IN THE ROUND

(multiple of 8 sts; 4-rnd repeat)
RT3: See key.
Rnd 1: *K2, [RC] 3 times; repeat from * to end.
Rnd 2: Knit.
Rnd 3: *K2, [RT3] twice; repeat from * to end.
Rnd 4: Knit.
Repeat Rnds 1–4 for Granite Rib in the Round.

FLAT

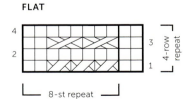

IN THE ROUND

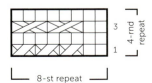

 RT3: Right Twist 3. Knit into front of third st, then second st, then first st, then drop all 3 sts from needle together.

Chain Stitch Rib

FLAT

(multiple of 3 sts + 2; 4-row repeat)

Note: *Pattern begins with a WS row.*

Row 1 (WS): K2, *p1, k2; repeat from * to end.

Row 2: P2, *k1, p2; repeat from * to end.

Row 3: Repeat Row 1.

Row 4: P2, p1b, p2; repeat from * to end.

Repeat Rows 1–4 for Chain Stitch Rib Flat.

IN THE ROUND

(multiple of 3 sts; 4-rnd repeat)

Rnds 1-3: *P2, k1; repeat from * to end.

Rnd 4: *P2, k1b; repeat from * to end.

Repeat Rnds 1–4 for Chain Stitch Rib in the Round.

FLAT

IN THE ROUND

3-st repeat

3-st repeat

Note: *Flat pattern begins with a WS row.*

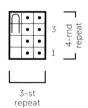 P1b on WS, k1b on RS.
K1 on RS, p1 on WS.

Square Rib

....

FLAT

(odd number of sts; 4-row repeat)

Tuck 1: Knit into st 2 rows below st on left-hand needle, dropping and unraveling sts above it.

Row 1 (RS): K1, *p1, k1; repeat from * to end.

Row 2: P1, *k1, p1; repeat from * to end.

Row 3: Repeat Row 1.

Row 4: P1, *tuck 1, p1; repeat from * to end.

Repeat Rows 1–4 for Square Rib Flat.

IN THE ROUND

(even number of sts; 4-rnd repeat)

Tuck 1: Purl into st 2 rows below st on left-hand needle, dropping and unraveling sts above it.

Rnds 1–3: *K1, p1; repeat from * to end.

Rnd 4: *K1, tuck 1; repeat from * to end.

Repeat Rnds 1–4 for Square Rib in the Round.

FLAT

4
2

3

1

4-row repeat

2-st repeat

IN THE ROUND

3

1

4-rnd repeat

2-st repeat

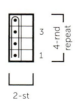

Tuck 1: Written pattern.

On first 3 rows/rnds, p1 on RS, k1 on WS.

Single Lace Rib

FLAT

(multiple of 4 sts + 1; 2-row repeat)
Row 1 (RS): K1, *yo, k2tog, p1, k1; repeat from * to end.
Row 2: P1, *yo, p2tog, k1, p1; repeat from * to end.
Repeat Rows 1 and 2 for Single Lace Rib Flat.

IN THE ROUND

(multiple of 4 sts; 2-rnd repeat)
Rnd 1: *K1, yo, k2tog, p1; repeat from * to end.
Rnd 2: *K1, p1, k2tog, yo; repeat from * to end.
Repeat Rnds 1 and 2 for Single Lace Rib in the Round.

FLAT

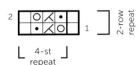

IN THE ROUND

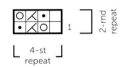

Little Chevron Rib

FLAT

(multiple of 10 sts + 1; 4-row repeat)
Row 1 (RS): P1, *k1, p1, [k2, p1] twice, k1, p1; repeat from * to end.
Row 2: K1, *p2, k1, [p1, k1] twice, p2, k1; repeat from * to end.
Row 3: P1, *k3, p3, k3, p1; repeat from * to end.
Row 4: K2, p3, k1, p3, *k3, p3, k1, p3; repeat from * to last 2 sts, k2.
Repeat Rows 1–4 for Little Chevron Rib Flat.

IN THE ROUND

(multiple of 10 sts; 4-rnd repeat)
Rnd 1: *P1, k1, p1, [k2, p1] twice, k1; repeat from * to end.
Rnd 2: *P1, k2, p1, [k1, p1] twice, k2; repeat from * to end.
Rnd 3: *P1, k3, p3, k3; repeat from * to end.
Rnd 4: P2, k3, p1, k3, *p3, k3, p1, k3; repeat from * to last st, p1.
Repeat Rnds 1–4 for Little Chevron Rib in the Round.

FLAT

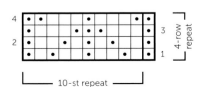

IN THE ROUND

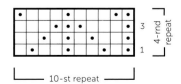

Broad Spiral Rib

FLAT

(multiple of 6 sts + 2; 4-row repeat)
Note: Pattern begins with a WS row.
Row 1 (WS): K2, *p4, k2; repeat from * to end.
Row 2: P2, *[RC] twice, p2; repeat from * to end.
Row 3: Repeat Row 1.
Row 4: P2, *k1, RC, k1, p2; repeat from * to end.
Repeat Rows 1–4 for Broad Spiral Rib Flat.

IN THE ROUND

(multiple of 6 sts; 4-rnd repeat)
Rnd 1: *P2, k4; repeat from * to end.
Rnd 2: *P2, [RC] twice; repeat from * to end.
Rnd 3: Repeat Rnd 1.
Rnd 4: *P2, k1, RC, k1; repeat from * to end.
Repeat Rnds 1–4 for Broad Spiral Rib in the Round.

FLAT

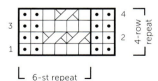

Note: *Flat pattern begins with a WS row.*

IN THE ROUND

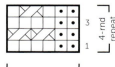

Grand Chevron Rib

FLAT

(multiple of 18 sts + 1; 4-row repeat)

Row 1 (RS): P1, *k1, p2, k2, p2, k1, p1, k1, p2, k2, p2, k1, p1; repeat from * to end.

Row 2: K3, p2, k2, p2, k1, p2, k2, p2, *k5, p2, k2, p2, k1, p2, k2, p2; repeat from * to last 3 sts, k3.

Row 3: [P2, k2] twice, *p3, k2, p2, k2; repeat from * to last 2 sts, p2.

Row 4: K1, *p2, k2, p2, k5, p2, k2, p2, k1; repeat from * to end.

Repeat Rows 1–4 for Grand Chevron Rib Flat.

IN THE ROUND

(multiple of 18 sts; 4-rnd repeat)

Rnd 1: *P1, k1, p2, k2, p2, k1, p1, k1, p2, k2, p2, k1; repeat from * to end.

Rnd 2: P3, k2, p2, k2, p1, k2, p2, k2, *p5, k2, p2, k2, p1, k2, p2, k2; repeat from * to last 2 sts, p2.

Rnd 3: [P2, k2] twice; *p3, k2, p2, k2; repeat from * to last st, p1.

Rnd 4: *P1, k2, p2, k2, p5, k2, p2, k2; repeat from * to end.

Repeat Rnds 1–4 for Grand Chevron Rib in the Round.

FLAT

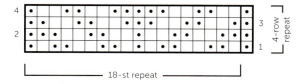

IN THE ROUND

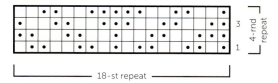

SIZE

To fit average adult (large adult)

FINISHED MEASUREMENTS

Approximately 20 (22½)" [51
(57) cm] circumference ×
9½ (10)" [24 (25.5) cm] tall

YARN

Blue Sky Fibers Royal [100%
royal alpaca; 288 yards
(263 meters) / 3½ ounces
(100 grams)]: 1 hank #709
Primrose

NEEDLES

One set of five double-pointed
needles size US 3 (3.25 mm)
Change needle size if necessary
to obtain correct gauge.

NOTIONS

Stitch markers

GAUGE

33 sts and 36 rows = 4" (10 cm)
in 3-Stitch Twisted Rib, washed
and blocked, unstretched

3-Stitch Twisted Rib Slouch Cap

This super-slouchy cap is a great vehicle for showing off the 3-Stitch Twisted Rib pattern. Customizing the length of the cap is easy. Just begin your crown shaping 3 inches (7.5 cm) before your desired length.

STITCH PATTERNS

3X2 RIB

(multiple of 5 sts; 1-rnd repeat)
All Rnds: *P2, k3; repeat from * to end.

3-STITCH TWISTED RIB

(multiple of 5 sts; 2-rnd repeat)
RC3: See key.
Rnd 1: *P2, k3; repeat from * to end.
Rnd 2: *P2, RC3; repeat from * to end.
Repeat Rnds 1 and 2 for 3-Stitch Twisted Rib.

3-STITCH TWISTED RIB

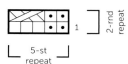

RC3: Right Cross 3. Knit into front of third st; knit into front of first st and drop it from needle; knit into front of second st and drop second and third sts from needle together.

Slouch

CO 165 (185) sts. Join for working in the rnd, being careful not to twist sts; pm for beginning of rnd. Begin 3x2 Rib; work even for 2 rnds.

Change to 3-Stitch Twisted Rib; work even until piece measures 6½ (7)" [16.5 (18) cm] from the beginning, ending with Rnd 2.

Shape Crown

Rnd 1: P2, k3, *p2tog, k3, [p2, k3] 3 times; repeat from * to end—157 (176) sts remain.
Rnd 2: P2, RC3, *p1, RC3, [p2, RC3] 3 times; repeat from * to end.
Rnd 3: Knit the knit sts and purl the purl sts as they face you.

Rnd 4: Repeat Rnd 2.
Rnd 5: P2tog, k3, *p1, k3, p2tog, k3, p2, k3, p2tog, k3; repeat from * to end—140 (157) sts remain.
Rnd 6: P1, RC3, *[p1, RC3] twice, p2, RC3, p1, RC3; repeat from * to end.
Rnd 7: Repeat Rnd 3.
Rnd 8: Repeat Rnd 6.
Rnd 9: P1, k3, *[p1, k3] twice, p2tog, k3, p1, k3; repeat from * to end—132 (148) sts remain.
Rnd 10: *P1, RC3; repeat from * to end.
Rnd 11: Repeat Rnd 3.
Rnd 12: Repeat Rnd 10.
Rnd 13: P1, k3, *p1, k2tog, k1, [p1, k3] 3 times; repeat from * to end—124 (139) sts remain.
Rnd 14: P1, RC3, *p1, RC, [p1, RC3] 3 times; repeat from * to end.
Rnd 15: Repeat Rnd 3.
Rnd 16: Repeat Rnd 14.
Rnd 17: P1, k2tog, k1, *p1, k2, p1, k2tog, k1, p1, k3, p1, k2tog, k1; repeat from * to end—107 (120) sts remain.
Rnd 18: P1, RC, *[p1, RC] twice, p1, RC3, p1, RC; repeat from * to end.
Rnd 19: Repeat Rnd 3.
Rnd 20: Repeat Rnd 18.
Rnd 21: P1, k2, *[p1, k2] twice, p1, k2tog, k1, p1, k2; repeat from * to end—99 (111) sts remain.
Rnd 22 *P1, RC; repeat from * to end.
Rnd 23: Repeat Rnd 3.
Rnd 24: P1, RC, *p1, k2tog, p1, RC; repeat from * to end—83 (93) sts remain.
Rnd 25: Repeat Rnd 3.
Rnd 26: P1, k2tog, *p1, k1, p1, k2tog; repeat from * to end—66 (74) sts remain.
Rnd 27: *K2tog; repeat from * to end—33 (37) sts remain.

Finishing

Cut yarn, leaving an 8" (20.5 cm) long tail. Thread tail through remaining sts, pull tight, and fasten off.

3 Fancy & Twisted

Here, you'll find an array of patterns that don't fit neatly into any other category. These stitch patterns contain a mixture of elements that are unusual and combine together in inventive ways. Even though the results sometimes look difficult to produce, these are actually quite fun to knit. The key with these patterns is to swatch and practice new-to-you maneuvers before diving in. One example is Mini Cables and Tassels on page 99. When I began converting this pattern from its source, I thought it'd be a tough haul. But once I got rolling with the swatch, I realized that although the stitch pattern looked daunting, it wasn't at all! The patterns in this chapter do have a lot going on, but because they are so graphic, they are easy to memorize and re-create.

Blooming Ginger

FLAT

(multiple of 10 sts + 1; 16-row repeat)

Row 1 (RS): P1, *k4, k2tog, k3, yo, p1; repeat from * to end.
Row 2: K1, *p5, k5; repeat from * to end.
Row 3: P1, *k4, k2tog, k2, yo, k1, p1; repeat from * to end.
Row 4: Repeat Row 2.
Row 5: P1, *k4, k2tog, k1, yo, k2, p1; repeat from * to end.
Row 6: Repeat Row 2.
Row 7: P1, *k4, k2tog, yo, k3, p1; repeat from * to end.
Row 8: Repeat Row 2.
Row 9: P1, *yo, k3, ssk, k4, p1; repeat from * to end.
Row 10: *K5, p5; repeat from * to last st, k1.
Row 11: P1, *k1, yo, k2, ssk, k4, p1; repeat from * to end.
Row 12: Repeat Row 10.
Row 13: P1, *k2, yo, k1, ssk, k4, p1; repeat from * to end.
Row 14: Repeat Row 10.
Row 15: P1, *k3, yo, ssk, k4, p1; repeat from * to end.
Row 16: Repeat Row 10.

Repeat Rows 1–16 for Blooming Ginger Flat.

IN THE ROUND

(multiple of 10 sts; 16-rnd repeat)

Rnd 1: *P1, k4, k2tog, k3, yo; repeat from * to end.
Rnd 2: *P5, k5; repeat from * to end.
Rnd 3: *P1, k4, k2tog, k2, yo, k1; repeat from * to end.
Rnd 4: Repeat Rnd 2.
Rnd 5: *P1, k4, k2tog, k1, yo, k2; repeat from * to end.
Rnd 6: Repeat Rnd 2.
Rnd 7: *P1, k4, k2tog, yo, k3; repeat from * to end.
Rnd 8: Repeat Rnd 2.
Rnd 9: *P1, yo, k3, ssk, k4; repeat from * to end.
Rnd 10: P1, k5, *p5, k5; repeat from * to last 4 sts, p4.
Rnd 11: *P1, k1, yo, k2, ssk, k4; repeat from * to end.
Rnd 12: Repeat Rnd 10.
Rnd 13: *P1, k2, yo, k1, ssk, k4; repeat from * to end.
Rnd 14: Repeat Rnd 10.
Rnd 15: *P1, k3, yo, ssk, k4; repeat from * to end.
Rnd 16: Repeat Rnd 10.

Repeat Rnds 1–16 for Blooming Ginger in the Round.

FLAT

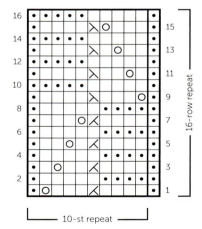

IN THE ROUND

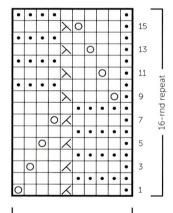

IN THE ROUND

(multiple of 13 sts; 8-rnd repeat)

Rnd 1: K5, yo, k2, s2kp2, k2, yo, *k6, yo, k2, s2kp2, k2, yo; repeat from * to last st, k1.

Rnd 2 and all Even-Numbered Rnds: Knit the knit sts and purl the purl sts as they face you; knit all yos.

Rnd 3: *C4B, k2, yo, k1, s2kp2, k1, yo, k2; repeat from * to end.

Rnd 5: K7, yo, s2kp2, yo, *k10, yo, s2kp2, yo; repeat from * to last 3 sts, k3.

Rnd 7: *C4B, p9; repeat from * to end.

Rnd 8: Repeat Rnd 2.

Repeat Rnds 1–8 for Katsura Twists in the Round.

IN THE ROUND

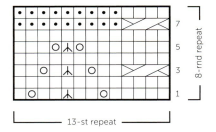

Katsura Twists

FLAT

(multiple of 13 sts + 4; 8-row repeat)

Row 1 (RS): K5, yo, k2, s2kp2, k2, yo, *k6, yo, k2, s2kp2, k2, yo; repeat from * to last 5 sts, k5.

Row 2 and all WS Rows: Knit the knit sts and purl the purl sts as they face you; purl all yos.

Row 3: C4B, *k2, yo, k1, s2kp2, k1, yo, k2, C4B; repeat from * to end.

Row 5: K7, yo, s2kp2, yo, *k10, yo, s2kp2, yo; repeat from * to last 7 sts, k7.

Row 7: C4B, *p9, C4B; repeat from * to end.

Row 8: Repeat Row 2.

Repeat Rows 1–8 for Katsura Twists Flat.

FLAT

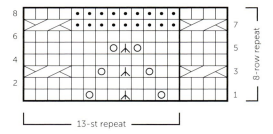

Herringbone Twist

FLAT

(multiple of 13 sts + 4; 2-row repeat)

Row 1 (RS): P1, RC, p1, *yo, k3, s2kp2, k3, yo, p1, RC, p1; repeat from * to end.

Row 2: K1, p2, k1, *p1-tbl, p7, p1-tbl, k1, p2, k1; repeat from * to end.

Repeat Rows 1 and 2 for Herringbone Twist Flat.

IN THE ROUND

(multiple of 13 sts; 2-rnd repeat)

Rnd 1: *P1, RC, p1, yo, k3, s2kp2, k3, yo; repeat from * to end.

Rnd 2: *P1, k2, p1, k1-tbl, k7, k1-tbl; repeat from * to end.

Repeat Rnds 1 and 2 for Herringbone Twist in the Round.

FLAT

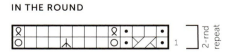

IN THE ROUND

Row 22: Repeat Row 2.
Row 23: P1, *yo, k2, ssk, p3; repeat from * to last 2 sts, p2.
Row 24: Repeat Row 8.
Row 25: P2, *yo, k2, ssk, p3; repeat from * to last st, p1.
Row 26: Repeat Row 8.
Row 27: P3, *yo, k2, ssk, p3; repeat from * to end.
Row 28: Repeat Row 8.
Row 29: P4, yo, k2, ssk, *p3, yo, k2, ssk; repeat from * to last 2 sts, p2.
Row 30: Repeat Row 8.
Row 31: P5, yo, k2, ssk, *p3, yo, k2, ssk; repeat from * to last st, p1.
Row 32: Repeat Row 8.
Repeat Rows 1–32 for Wrapped Waves Flat.

Wrapped Waves

··

FLAT

(multiple of 7 sts + 3; 32-row repeat)
Pkok: See key.
Row 1 (RS): P6, pkok, *p4, pkok; repeat from * to last st, p1.
Row 2: Knit the knit sts and purl the purl sts as they face you; purl all yos.
Row 3: P6, k3, *p4, k3; repeat from * to last st, p1.
Row 4: Repeat Row 2.
Row 5: Repeat Row 1.
Row 6: Repeat Row 2.
Row 7: P5, k2tog, k2, yo, *p3, k2tog, k2, yo; repeat from * to last st, p1.
Row 8: Knit the knit sts and purl the purl sts as they face you; knit all yos.
Row 9: P4, k2tog, k2, yo, *p3, k2tog, k2, yo; repeat from * to last 2 sts, p2.
Row 10: Repeat Row 8.
Row 11: P3, *k2tog, k2, yo, p3; repeat from * to end.
Row 12: Repeat Row 8.
Row 13: P2, *k2tog, k2, yo, p3; repeat from * to last st, p1.
Row 14: Repeat Row 8.
Row 15: P1, *k2tog, k2, yo, p3; repeat from * to last 2 sts, p2.
Row 16: Repeat Row 8.
Row 17: P1, *pkok, p4; repeat from * to last 2 sts, p2.
Row 18: Repeat Row 2.
Row 19: P1, *k3, p4; repeat from * to last 2 sts, p2.
Row 20: Repeat Row 2.
Row 21: Repeat Row 17.

FLAT

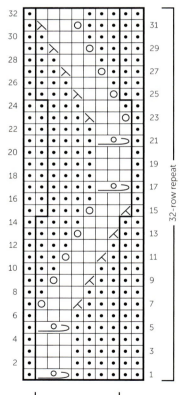

32-row repeat

7-st repeat

 Pkok: Slip third st on left-hand needle over first 2 sts and off needle; k1, yo, k1.

IN THE ROUND

(multiple of 7 sts; 32-rnd repeat)

Pkok: See key on previous page.

Rnd 1: *P4, pkok; repeat from * to end.

Rnds 2–4: Knit the knit sts and purl the purl sts as they face you; knit all yos.

Rnd 5: Repeat Rnd 1.

Rnd 6: Repeat Rnd 2.

Rnd 7: *P3, k2tog, k2, yo; repeat from * to end.

Rnd 8: Knit the knit sts and purl the purl sts as they face you; purl all yos.

Rnd 9: P2, k2tog, k2, yo, *p3, k2tog, k2, yo; repeat from * to last st, p1.

Rnd 10: Repeat Rnd 8.

Rnd 11: P1, k2tog, k2, yo, *p3, k2tog, k2, yo; repeat from * to last 2 sts, p2.

Rnd 12: Repeat Rnd 8.

Rnd 13: *K2tog, k2, yo, p3; repeat from * to end.

Rnd 14: Repeat Rnd 8 to last st; reposition beginning-of-rnd marker to before last st.

Rnd 15: Repeat Rnd 13.

Rnd 16: Repeat Rnd 8.

Rnd 17: *Pkok, p4; repeat from * to end.

Rnds 18–20: Repeat Rnd 2.

Rnd 21: Repeat Rnd 17.

Rnd 22: Repeat Rnd 2.

Rnd 23: *Yo, k2, ssk, p3; repeat from * to end, remove beginning-of-rnd marker, p1; pm for new beginning of rnd.

Rnd 24: Repeat Rnd 8.

Rnd 25: *Yo, k2, ssk, p3; repeat from * to end.

Rnd 26: Repeat Rnd 8.

Rnd 27: P1, yo, k2, ssk, *p3, yo, k2, ssk; repeat from * to last 2 sts, p2.

Rnd 28: Repeat Rnd 8.

Rnd 29: P2, yo, k2, ssk, *p3, yo, k2, ssk; repeat from * to last st, p1.

Rnd 30: Repeat Rnd 8.

Rnd 31: *P3, yo, k2, ssk; repeat from * to end.

Rnd 32: Repeat Rnd 8.

Repeat Rnds 1–32 for Wrapped Waves in the Round.

IN THE ROUND

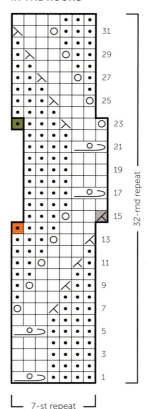

7-st repeat

32-rnd repeat

On final repeat only of Rnd 14, end rnd 1 st before beginning-of-rnd marker; reposition beginning-of-rnd marker to before last st. On all preceding repeats, purl this st.

On first repeat only of Rnd 15, work k2tog on what was last st of Rnd 14 and first sts of Rnd 15; beginning-of-rnd marker should be before this k2tog. On all following repeats, work as k2tog.

On Rnd 23 only, work this st on final repeat only; work to end of rnd, remove beginning-of-rnd marker, p1, pm for new beginning of rnd. On all preceding repeats, omit this st.

Spiders

BOTTOM-UP FLAT

(multiple of 10 sts + 5; 24-row repeat)

Tuck 1: Insert right-hand needle from back to front into st 2 rows below st on left-hand needle, purl this st, dropping and unraveling sts above it.

Row 1 (RS): Yo, ssk, k1, k2tog, yo, *k5, yo, ssk, k1, k2tog, yo; repeat from * to end.

Row 2: K2, p1, k2, *p5, k2, p1, k2; repeat from * to end.

Rows 3 and 4: Repeat Rows 1 and 2.

Row 5: Repeat Row 1.

Row 6: K2, tuck 1, k2, *p5, k2, tuck 1, k2; repeat from * to end.

Row 7: Knit.

Row 8: Purl.

Row 9: K2, MB, *k9, MB; repeat from * to last 2 sts, k2.

Row 10: Purl.

Row 11: Knit.

Row 12: Purl.

Row 13: K5, *yo, ssk, k1, k2tog, yo, k5; repeat from * to end.

Row 14: P5, *k2, p1, k2, p5; repeat from * to end.

Rows 15 and 16: Repeat Rows 13 and 14.

Row 17: Repeat Row 13.

Row 18: P5, *k2, tuck 1, k2, p5; repeat from * to end.

Row 19: Knit.

Row 20: Purl.

Row 21: K7, MB, *k9, MB; repeat from * to last 7 sts, k7.

Row 22: Purl.

Row 23: Knit.

Row 24: Purl.

Repeat Rows 1–24 for Spiders Bottom-Up Flat.

BOTTOM-UP IN THE ROUND

(multiple of 10 sts; 24-rnd repeat)

Tuck 1: Knit into st 2 rnds below st on left-hand needle, dropping and unraveling sts above this st.

Rnd 1: *Yo, ssk, k1, k2tog, yo, k5; repeat from * to end.

Rnd 2: *P2, k1, p2, k5; repeat from * to end.

Rnds 3 and 4: Repeat Rnds 1 and 2.

Rnd 5: Repeat Rnd 1.

Rnd 6: *P2, tuck 1, p2, k5; repeat from * to end.

Rnds 7 and 8: Knit.

Rnd 9: K2, MB, *k9, MB; repeat from * to last 7 sts, k7.

Rnds 10–12: Knit.

Rnd 13: *K5, yo, ssk, k1, k2tog, yo; repeat from * to end.

Rnd 14: *K5, p2, k1, p2; repeat from * to end.

Rnds 15 and 16: Repeat Rnds 13 and 14.

Rnd 17: Repeat Rnd 13.

Rnd 18: *K5, p2, tuck 1, p2; repeat from * to end.

Rnds 19 and 20: Knit.

Rnd 21: K7, MB, *k9, MB; repeat from * to last 2 sts, k2.

Rnds 22–24: Knit.

Repeat Rnds 1–24 for Spiders Bottom-Up in the Round.

BOTTOM-UP FLAT

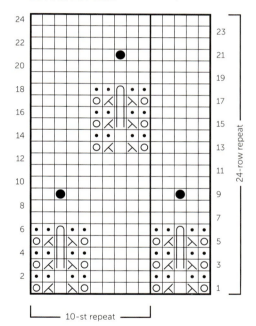

BOTTOM-UP IN THE ROUND

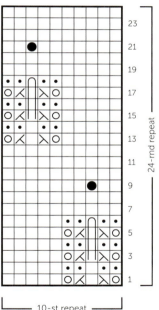

Tuck 1: See written pattern.

On first 3 rows/rnds, k1 on RS, p1 on WS.

MB: Make Bobble.

TOP-DOWN FLAT

(multiple of 10 sts + 5; 24-row repeat)

Tuck 1: Knit into st 2 rows below st on left-hand needle, dropping and unraveling sts above it.

Row 1 (RS): Knit.

Row 2: Purl.

Row 3: K7, MB, *k9, MB; repeat from * to last 7 sts, k7.

Row 4: Purl.

Row 5: Knit.

Row 6: P5, *yo, p2tog, p1, ssp, yo, p5; repeat from * to end.

Row 7: K5, *p2, k1, p2, k5; repeat from * to end.

Rows 8 and 9: Repeat Rows 6 and 7.

Row 10: Repeat Row 6.

Row 11: K5, *p2, tuck 1, p2, k5; repeat from * to end.

Row 12: Purl.

Row 13: Knit.

Row 14: Purl.

Row 15: K2, MB, *k9, MB; repeat from * to last 2 sts, k2.

Row 16: Purl.

Row 17: Knit.

Row 18: Yo, p2tog, p1, ssp, yo, *p5, yo, p2tog, p1, ssp, yo; repeat from * to end.

Row 19: P2, k1, p2, *k5, p2, k1, p2; repeat from * to end.

Rows 20 and 21: Repeat Rows 18 and 19.

Row 22: Repeat Row 18.

Row 23: P2, tuck 1, p2, *k5, p2, tuck 1, p2; repeat from * to end.

Row 24: Purl.

Repeat Rows 1–24 for Spiders Top-Down Flat.

TOP-DOWN IN THE ROUND

(multiple of 10 sts; 24-rnd repeat)

Tuck 1: Knit into st 2 rnds below st on left-hand needle, dropping and unraveling sts above it.

Rnds 1 and 2: Knit.

Rnd 3: K7, MB, *k9, MB; repeat from * to last 2 sts, k2.

Rnds 4 and 5: Knit.

Rnd 6: *K5, yo, ssk, k1, k2tog, yo; repeat from * to end.

Rnd 7: *K5, p2, k1, p2; repeat from * to end.

Rnds 8 and 9: Repeat Rnds 6 and 7.

Rnd 10: Repeat Rnd 6.

Rnd 11: *K5, p2, tuck 1, p2; repeat from * to end.

Rnds 12–14: Knit.

Rnd 15: K2, MB, *k9, MB; repeat from * to last 7 sts, k7.

Rnds 16 and 17: Knit.

Rnd 18: *Yo, ssk, k1, k2tog, yo, k5; repeat from * to end.

Rnd 19: *P2, k1, p2, k5; repeat from * to end.

Rnds 20 and 21: Repeat Rnds 18 and 19.

Rnd 22: Repeat Rnd 18.

Rnd 23: *P2, tuck 1, p2, k5; repeat from * to end.

Rnd 24: Knit.

Repeat Rnds 1–24 for Spiders Top-Down in the Round.

TOP-DOWN FLAT

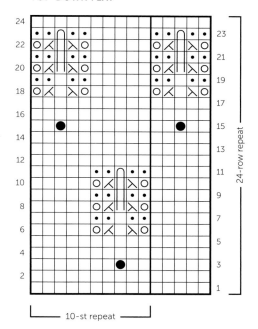

10-st repeat

24-row repeat

TOP-DOWN IN THE ROUND

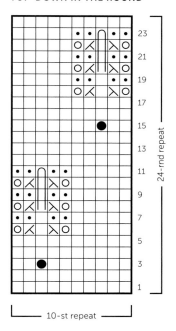

10-st repeat

24-rnd repeat

Tuck 1: See written pattern.

On first 3 rows/rnds, k1 on RS, p1 on WS.

MB: Make Bobble.

Flames

....

FLAT

(multiple of 16 sts + 9; 24-row repeat)

1/1 RTPC: See key.

1/1 LTPC: See key.

Note: You will increase 2 sts per repeat on Row 5; original st count is restored on Row 7.

Row 1 (RS): P3, k1-tbl, k1, k1-tbl, *p4, 1/1 RTPC, k1, 1/1 LTPC, p4, k1-tbl, k1, k1-tbl; repeat from * to last 3 sts, p3.

Row 2: K3, p1-tbl, k1, p1-tbl, *k4, p1-tbl, k1, p1, k1, p1-tbl, k4, p1-tbl, k1, p1-tbl; repeat from * to last 3 sts, k3.

Row 3: P3, k1-tbl, k1, k1-tbl, *p3, 1/1 RTPC, p1, k1, p1, 1/1 LTPC, p3, k1-tbl, k1, k1-tbl; repeat from * to last 3 sts, p3.

Row 4: K3, p1-tbl, k1, p1-tbl, *k3, p1-tbl, k2, p1, k2, p1-tbl, k3, p1-tbl, k1, p1-tbl; repeat from * to last 3 sts, k3.

Row 5: P3, k1-tbl, k1, k1-tbl, *p2, 1/1 RTPC, p2, knit into st 3 rows below st on left-hand needle (Row 1), yo, knit into same st to increase to 3 sts, p2, 1/1 LTPC, p2, k1-tbl, k1, k1-tbl; repeat from * to last 3 sts, p3.

Row 6: K3, p1-tbl, k1, p1-tbl, *k2, p1-tbl, k3, p3, k3, p1-tbl, k2, p1-tbl, k1, p1-tbl; repeat from * to last 3 sts, k3.

Row 7: P3, k1-tbl, k1, k1-tbl, *p2, 1/1 LTPC, p2, s2kp2, p2, 1/1 RTPC, p2, k1-tbl, k1, k1-tbl; repeat from * to last 3 sts, p3.

Row 8: K3, p1-tbl, k1, p1-tbl, *k3, p1-tbl, k5, p1-tbl, k3, p1-tbl, k1, p1-tbl; repeat from * to last 3 sts, k3.

Row 9: P3, k1-tbl, k1, k1-tbl, *p3, 1/1 LTPC, p3, 1/1 RTPC, p3, k1-tbl, k1, k1-tbl; repeat from * to last 3 sts, p3.

Row 10: K3, p1-tbl, k1, p1-tbl, *k4, p1-tbl, k3, p1-tbl, k4, p1-tbl, k1, p1-tbl; repeat from * to last 3 sts, k3.

Row 11: P3, k1-tbl, k1, k1-tbl, *p4, 1/1 LTPC, p1, 1/1 RTPC, p4, k1-tbl, k1, k1-tbl; repeat from * to last 3 sts, p3.

Row 12: K3, p1-tbl, p1, p1-tbl, *k5, p1-tbl, k1, p1-tbl, k5, p1-tbl, p1, p1-tbl; repeat from * to last 3 sts, k3.

Row 13: P2, 1/1 RTPC, k1, 1/1 LTPC, *p4, k1-tbl, k1, k1-tbl, p4, 1/1 RTPC, k1, 1/1 LTPC; repeat from * to last 2 sts, p2.

Row 14: K2, p1-tbl, p3, p1-tbl, *k4, p1-tbl, k1, p1-tbl, k4, p1-tbl, p3, p1-tbl; repeat from * to last 2 sts, k2.

Row 15: P1, 1/1 RTPC, k3, 1/1 LTPC, *p3, k1-tbl, k1, k1-tbl, p3, 1/1 RTPC, k3, 1/1 LTPC; repeat from * to last st, p1.

Row 16: K1, p1-tbl, p5, p1-tbl, *k3, p1-tbl, k1, p1-tbl, k3, p1-tbl, p5, p1-tbl; repeat from * to last st, k1.

Row 17: 1/1 RTPC, k5, 1/1 LTPC, *p2, k1-tbl, k1, k1-tbl, p2, 1/1 RTPC, k5, 1/1 LTPC; repeat from * to end.

Row 18: P1-tbl, p7, p1-tbl, *k2, p1-tbl, k1, p1-tbl, k2, p1-tbl, p7, p1-tbl; repeat from * to end.

Row 19: 1/1 LTPC, k5, 1/1 RTPC, *p2, k1-tbl, k1, k1-tbl, p2, 1/1 LTPC, k5, 1/1 RTPC; repeat from * to end.

Row 20: K1, p1-tbl, p5, p1-tbl, *k3, p1-tbl, k1, p1-tbl, k3, p1-tbl, p5, p1-tbl; repeat from * to last st, k1.

Row 21: P1, 1/1 LTPC, k3, 1/1 RTPC, *p3, k1-tbl, k1, k1-tbl, p3, 1/1 LTPC, k3, 1/1 RTPC; repeat from * to last st, p1.

Row 22: K2, p1-tbl, p3, p1-tbl, *k4, p1-tbl, k1, p1-tbl, k4, p1-tbl, p3, p1-tbl; repeat from * to last 2 sts, k2.

Row 23: P2, 1/1 LTPC, k1, 1/1 RTPC, *p4, k1-tbl, k1, k1-tbl, p4, 1/1 LTPC, k1, 1/1 RTPC; repeat from * to last 2 sts, p2.

Row 24: K3, p1-tbl, p1, p1-tbl, *k5, p1-tbl, k1, p1-tbl, k5, p1-tbl, p1, p1-tbl; repeat from * to last 3 sts, k3.

Repeat Rows 1–24 for Flames Flat.

FLAT

1/1 RTPC: Slip 1 st to cn, hold to back, k1-tbl, p1 from cn.

1/1 LTPC: Slip 1 st to cn, hold to front, p1, k1-tbl from cn.

S2kp2

K3 on RS, p3 on WS.

Knit into st 3 rows below st on left-hand needle (dropping and unraveling sts above it), yo, knit into same st to increase to 3 sts.

On first 4 rows/rnds, k1 on RS, p1 on WS.

IN THE ROUND

(multiple of 16 sts; 24-rnd repeat)

1/1 RTPC: See key.

1/1 LTPC: See key.

Note: *You will increase 2 sts per repeat on Rnd 5; original st count is restored on Rnd 7.*

Rnd 1: P2, k1-tbl, k1, k1-tbl, p4, 1/1 RTPC, k1, 1/1 LTPC, *p4, k1-tbl, k1, k1-tbl, p4, 1/1 RTPC, k1, 1/1 LTPC; repeat from * to last 2 sts, p2.

Rnd 2: P2, k1-tbl, p1, k1-tbl, p4, k1-tbl, p1, k1, p1, k1-tbl, *p4, k1-tbl, p1, k1-tbl, p4, k1-tbl, p1, k1, p1, k1-tbl; repeat from * to last 2 sts, p2.

Rnd 3: P2, k1-tbl, k1, k1-tbl, p3, 1/1 RTPC, p1, k1, p1, 1/1 LTPC, *p3, k1-tbl, k1, k1-tbl, p3, 1/1 RTPC, p1, k1, p1, 1/1 LTPC; repeat from * to last st, p1.

Rnd 4: P2, k1-tbl, p1, k1-tbl, p3, k1-tbl, p2, k1, p2, k1-tbl, *p3, k1-tbl, p1, k1-tbl, p3, k1-tbl, p2, k1, p2, k1-tbl; repeat from * to last st, p1.

Rnd 5: *P2, k1-tbl, k1, k1-tbl, p2, 1/1 RTPC, p2, knit into st 3 rnds below st on left-hand needle (Rnd 1), yo, knit into same st to increase to 3 sts, p2, 1/1 LTPC; repeat from * to end.

Rnd 6: *P2, k1-tbl, p1, k1-tbl, p2, k1-tbl, p3, k3, p3, k1-tbl; repeat from * to end.

Rnd 7: *P2, k1-tbl, k1, k1-tbl, p2, 1/1 LTPC, p2, s2kp2, p2, 1/1 RTPC; repeat from * to end.

Rnd 8: P2, k1-tbl, p1, k1-tbl, p3, k1-tbl, p5, k1-tbl, *p3, k1-tbl, p1, k1-tbl, p3, k1-tbl, p5, k1-tbl; repeat from * to last st, p1.

Rnd 9: P2, k1-tbl, k1, k1-tbl, p3, 1/1 LTPC, p3, 1/1 RTPC, *p3, k1-tbl, k1, k1-tbl, p3, 1/1 LTPC, p3, 1/1 RTPC; repeat from * to last st, p1.

Rnd 10: P2, k1-tbl, p1, k1-tbl, p4, k1-tbl, p3, k1-tbl, *p4, k1-tbl, p1, k1-tbl, p4, k1-tbl, p3, k1-tbl; repeat from * to last 2 sts, p2.

Rnd 11: P2, k1-tbl, k1, k1-tbl, p4, 1/1 LTPC, p1, 1/1 RTPC, *p4, k1-tbl, k1, k1-tbl, p4, 1/1 LTPC, p1, 1/1 RTPC; repeat from * to last 2 sts, p2.

Rnd 12: P2, k1-tbl, k1, k1-tbl, p5, k1-tbl, p1, k1-tbl, *p5, k1-tbl, k1, k1-tbl, p5, k1-tbl, p1, k1-tbl; repeat from * to last 3 sts, p2, reposition beginning-of-rnd marker to before last st.

Rnd 13: P2, 1/1 RTPC, k1, 1/1 LTPC, p4, k1-tbl, k1, k1-tbl, *p4, 1/1 RTPC, k1, 1/1 LTPC, p4, k1-tbl, k1, k1-tbl; repeat from * to last 2 sts, p2.

Rnd 14: P2, k1-tbl, k3, k1-tbl, p4, k1-tbl, p1, k1-tbl, *p4, k1-tbl, k3, k1-tbl, p4, k1-tbl, p1, k1-tbl; repeat from * to last 2 sts, p2.

Rnd 15: P1, 1/1 RTPC, k3, 1/1 LTPC, p3, k1-tbl, k1, k1-tbl, *p3, 1/1 RTPC, k3, 1/1 LTPC, p3, k1-tbl, k1, k1-tbl; repeat from * to last 2 sts, p2.

Rnd 16: P1, k1-tbl, k5, k1-tbl, p3, k1-tbl, p1, k1-tbl, *p3, k1-tbl, p5, k1-tbl, p3, k1-tbl, p1, k1-tbl; repeat from * to last 2 sts, p2.

Rnd 17: *1/1 RTPC, k5, 1/1 LTPC, p2, k1-tbl, k1, k1-tbl, p2; repeat from * to end.

Rnd 18: *K1-tbl, k7, k1-tbl, p2, k1-tbl, p1, k1-tbl, p2; repeat from * to end.

Rnd 19: *1/1 LTPC, k5, 1/1 RTPC, p2, k1-tbl, k1, k1-tbl, p2; repeat from * to end.

Rnd 20: P1, k1-tbl, k5, k1-tbl, p3, k1-tbl, p1, k1-tbl, *p3, k1-tbl, k5, k1-tbl, p3, k1-tbl, p1, k1-tbl; repeat from * to last 2 sts, p2.

Rnd 21: P1, 1/1 LTPC, k3, 1/1 RTPC, p3, k1-tbl, k1, k1-tbl, *p3, 1/1 LTPC, k3, 1/1 RTPC, p3, k1-tbl, k1, k1-tbl; repeat from * to last 2 sts, p2.

Rnd 22: P2, k1-tbl, k3, k1-tbl, p4, k1-tbl, p1, k1-tbl, *p4, k1-tbl, k3, k1-tbl, p4, k1-tbl, p1, k1-tbl; repeat from * to last 2 sts, p2.

Rnd 23: P2, 1/1 LTPC, k1, 1/1 RTPC, p4, k1-tbl, k1, k1-tbl, *p4, 1/1 LTPC, k1, 1/1 RTPC, p4, k1-tbl, k1, k1-tbl; repeat from * to last 2 sts, p2.

Rnd 24: P3, k1-tbl, k1, k1-tbl, p5, k1-tbl, p1, k1-tbl, *p5, k1-tbl, k1, k1-tbl, p5, k1-tbl, p1, k1-tbl; repeat from * to last 2 sts, p2, remove beginning-of-rnd marker, p1, pm for new beginning of rnd.

Repeat Rnds 1–24 for Flames in the Round.

IN THE ROUND

16-st repeat

24-rnd repeat

⊠ **1/1 RTPC:** Slip 1 st to cn, hold to back, k1-tbl, p1 from cn.

⊠ **1/1 LTPC:** Slip 1 st to cn, hold to front, p1, k1-tbl from cn.

S2kp2

K3 on RS, p3 on WS.

Knit into st 3 rows below st on left-hand needle (dropping and unraveling sts above it), yo, knit into same st to increase to 3 sts.
On first 4 rows/rnds, k1 on RS, p1 on WS.

On final repeat only of Rnd 12, end rnd 1 st before beginning-of-rnd marker; reposition beginning-of-rnd marker to before final st of rnd. On all preceding repeats, purl this st.

On Rnd 24 only, work this st on final repeat only; work to end of rnd, remove beginning-of-rnd marker, p1, pm for new beginning of rnd. On all preceding repeats, omit this st.

Dots and Dashes

FLAT

(multiple of 6 sts + 3; 8-row repeat)

Row 1 (RS): Knit.

Row 2: Purl.

Row 3: K3, *p3, k3; repeat from * to end.

Row 4: Purl.

Row 5: Knit.

Row 6: Purl.

Row 7: P3, *k1, MB, k1, p3; repeat from * to end.

Row 8: Purl.

Repeat Rows 1–8 for Dots and Dashes Flat.

IN THE ROUND

(multiple of 6 sts; 8-rnd repeat)

Rnds 1 and 2: Knit.

Rnd 3: *K3, p3; repeat from * to end.

Rnds 4–6: Knit.

Rnd 7: *P3, k1, MB, k1; repeat from * to end.

Rnd 8: Knit.

Repeat Rnds 1–8 for Dots and Dashes in the Round.

FLAT

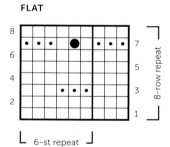

6-st repeat

8-row repeat

● **MB:** Make Bobble.

IN THE ROUND

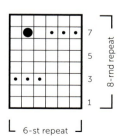

6-st repeat

8-rnd repeat

Mock Left Cable and Twist

....

FLAT

(multiple of 11 sts + 5; 8-row repeat)

Row 1 (RS): P2, k1-tbl, p2, *k1, LLI, k1, ssk, k2, p2, k1-tbl, p2; repeat from * to end.

Row 2 and all WS Rows: K2, p1-tbl, k2, *p6, k2, p1-tbl, k2; repeat from * to end.

Row 3: P2, k1-tbl, p2, *k1, LLI, k2, ssk, k1, p2, k1-tbl, p2; repeat from * to end.

Row 5: P2, k1-tbl, p2, *k2, LLI, k2, ssk, p2, k1-tbl, p2; repeat from * to end.

Row 7: P2, k1-tbl, p2, *k6, p2, k1-tbl, p2; repeat from * to end.

Row 8: Repeat Row 2.

Repeat Rows 1–8 for Mock Left Cable and Twist Flat.

IN THE ROUND

(multiple of 11 sts; 8-rnd repeat)

Rnd 1: *P2, k1-tbl, p2, k1, LLI, k1, ssk, k2; repeat from * to end.

Rnd 2 and all Even-Numbered Rnds: *P2, k1-tbl, p2, k6; repeat from * to end.

Rnd 3: *P2, k1-tbl, p2, k1, LLI, k2, ssk, k1; repeat from * to end.

Rnd 5: *P2, k1-tbl, p2, k2, LLI, k2, ssk; repeat from * to end.

Rnds 7 and 8: Repeat Rnd 2.

Repeat Rnds 1–8 for Mock Left Cable and Twist in the Round.

FLAT

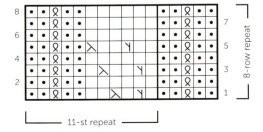

IN THE ROUND

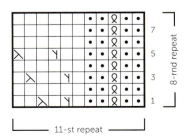

Mock Right Cable and Twist

FLAT

(multiple of 11 sts + 5; 8-row repeat)

Row 1 (RS): P2, k1-tbl, p2, *k2, k2tog, k1, RLI, k1, p2, k1-tbl, p2; repeat from * to end.

Row 2 and all WS Rows: K2, p1-tbl, k2, *p6, k2, p1-tbl, k2; repeat from * to end.

Row 3: P2, k1-tbl, p2, *k1, k2tog, k2, RLI, k1, p2, k1-tbl, p2; repeat from * to end.

Row 5: P2, k1-tbl, p2, *k2tog, k2, RLI, k2, p2, k1-tbl, p2; repeat from * to end.

Row 7: P2, k1-tbl, p2, *k6, p2, k1-tbl, p2; repeat from * to end.

Row 8: Repeat Row 2.

Repeat Rows 1–8 for Mock Right Cable and Twist Flat.

IN THE ROUND

(multiple of 11 sts; 8-rnd repeat)

Rnd 1: *P2, k1-tbl, p2, k2, k2tog, k1, RLI, k1; repeat from * to end.

Rnd 2 and all Even-Numbered Rnds: *P2, k1-tbl, p2, k6; repeat from * to end.

Rnd 3: *P2, k1-tbl, p2, k1, k2tog, k2, RLI, k1; repeat from * to end.

Rnd 5: *P2, k1-tbl, p2, k2tog, k2, RLI, k2; repeat from * to end.

Rnds 7 and 8: Repeat Rnd 2.

Repeat Rnds 1–8 for Mock Right Cable and Twist in the Round.

FLAT

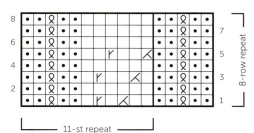

IN THE ROUND

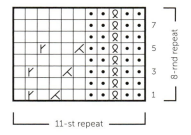

Mini Cables and Tassels

FLAT

(multiple of 14 sts + 5; 40-row repeat)

1/1 RTPC: See key.

1/1 LTPC: See key.

Pkok: See key.

Row 1 (RS): P1, k3, *p4, pkok, p4, k3; repeat from * to last st, p1.

Row 2: K1, p3, *k4, p3; repeat from * to last st, k1.

Row 3: P1, pkok, *p4, k3, p4, pkok; repeat from * to last st, p1.

Row 4: K1, p1, p1-tbl, p1, *k4, p3, k4, p1, p1-tbl, p1; repeat from * to last st, k1.

Row 5: 1/1 RTPC, k1-tbl, 1/1 LTPC, *p3, pkok, p3, 1/1 RTPC, k1-tbl, 1/1 LTPC; repeat from * to end.

Row 6: P1-tbl, [k1, p1-tbl] twice, *k3, p3, k3, p1-tbl, [k1, p1-tbl] twice; repeat from * to end.

Row 7: K1-tbl, [p1, k1-tbl] twice, *p3, k3, p3, k1-tbl, [p1, k1-tbl] twice; repeat from * to end.

Row 8: Repeat Row 6.

Row 9: K1-tbl, [p1, k1-tbl] twice, *p3, pkok, p3, k1-tbl, [p1, k1-tbl] twice; repeat from * to end.

Rows 10–13: Repeat Rows 6–9.

Rows 14–16: Repeat Rows 6–8.

Row 17: 1/1 LTPC, k1-tbl, 1/1 RTPC, *p3, pkok, p3, 1/1 LTPC, k1-tbl, 1/1 RTPC; repeat from * to end.

Row 18: K1, [p1-tbl] 3 times, *k4, p3, k4, [p1-tbl] 3 times; repeat from to last st, k1.

Row 19: Repeat Row 3.

Row 20: Repeat Row 2.

Row 21: Repeat Row 1.

Row 22: K1, p3, *k4, p1, p1-tbl, p1, k4, p3; repeat from * to last st, k1.

Row 23: P1, pkok, *p3, 1/1 RTPC, k1-tbl, 1/1 LTPC, p3, pkok; repeat from * to last st, p1.

Row 24: K1, p3, *k3, p1-tbl, [k1, p1-tbl] twice, k3, p3; repeat from * to last st, k1.

Row 25: P1, k3, *p3, k1-tbl, [p1, k1-tbl] twice, p3, k3; repeat from * to last st, p1.

Row 26: Repeat Row 24.

Row 27: P1, pkok, *p3, k1-tbl, [p1, k1-tbl] twice, p3, pkok; repeat from * to last st, p1.

Rows 28–31: Repeat Rows 24–27.

Rows 32–34: Repeat Rows 24–26.

Row 35: P1, pkok, *p3, 1/1 LTPC, k1-tbl, 1/1 RTPC, p3, pkok; repeat from * to last st, p1.

Row 36: K1, p3, *k4, [p1-tbl] 3 times, k4, p3; repeat from * to last st, k1.

Rows 37–39: Repeat Rows 1–3.

Row 40: Repeat Row 2.

Repeat Rows 1–40 for Mini Cables and Tassels Flat.

FLAT

[chart: 14-st repeat, 40-row repeat]

 1/1 RTPC: Slip 1 st to cn, hold to back, k1-tbl, p1 from cn.

 1/1 LTPC: Slip 1 st to cn, hold to front, p1, k1-tbl from cn.

Pkok: Slip third st on left-hand needle over first 2 sts and off needle; k1, yo, k1.

IN THE ROUND

(multiple of 14 sts; 40-rnd repeat)

1/1 RTPC: See key.

1/1 LTPC: See key.

Pkok: See key.

Rnd 1: P1, k3, p4, pkok, *p4, k3, p4, pkok; repeat from * to last 3 sts, p3.

Rnd 2: P1, k3, *p4, k3; repeat from * to last 3 sts, p3.

Rnd 3: P1, pkok, p4, k3, *p4, pkok, p4, k3; repeat from * to last 3 sts, p3.

Rnd 4: P1, k1, k1-tbl, k1, p4, k3, *p4, k1, k1-tbl, k1, p4, k3; repeat from * to last 3 sts, p3.

Rnd 5: *1/1 RTPC, k1-tbl, 1/1 LTPC, p3, pkok, p3; repeat from * to end.

Rnds 6–8: *K1-tbl, [p1, k1-tbl] twice, p3, k3, p3; repeat from * to end.

Rnd 9: *K1-tbl, [p1, k1-tbl] twice, p3, pkok, p3; repeat from * to end.

Rnds 10–13: Repeat Rnds 6–9.

Rnds 14–16: Repeat Rnds 6–8.

Rnd 17: *1/1 LTPC, k1-tbl, 1/1 RTPC, p3, pkok, p3; repeat from * to end.

Rnd 18: P1, [k1-tbl] 3 times, p4, k3, *p4, [k1-tbl] 3 times, p4, k3; repeat from to last 3 sts, p3.

Rnd 19: Repeat Rnd 3.

Rnd 20: Repeat Rnd 2.

Rnd 21: Repeat Rnd 1.

Rnd 22: P1, k3, p4, k1, k1-tbl, k1, *p4, k3, p4, k1, k1-tbl, k1; repeat from * to last 3 sts, p3.

Rnd 23: P1, pkok, p3, 1/1 RTPC, k1-tbl, 1/1 LTPC, *p3, pkok, p3, 1/1 RTPC, k1-tbl, 1/1 LTPC; repeat from * to last 2 sts, p2.

Rnds 24–26: P1, k3, p3, k1-tbl, [p1, k1-tbl] twice, *p3, k3, p3, k1-tbl, [p1, k1-tbl] twice; repeat from * to last 2 sts, p2.

Rnd 27: P1, pkok, p3, k1-tbl, [p1, k1-tbl] twice, *p3, pkok, p3, k1-tbl, [p1, k1-tbl] twice; repeat from * to last 2 sts, p2.

Rnds 28–31: Repeat Rnds 24–27.

Rnds 32–34: Repeat Rnds 24–26.

Rnd 35: P1, pkok, p3, 1/1 LTPC, k1-tbl, 1/1 RTPC, *p3, pkok, p3, 1/1 LTPC, k1-tbl, 1/1 RTPC; repeat from * to last 2 sts, p2.

Rnd 36: P1, k3, p4, [k1-tbl] 3 times, *p4, k3, p4, [k1-tbl] 3 times; repeat from * to last 3 sts, p3.

Rnds 37–39: Repeat Rnds 1–3.

Rnd 40: Repeat Rnd 1.

Repeat Rnds 1–40 for Mini Cables and Tassels in the Round.

IN THE ROUND

1/1 RTPC: Slip 1 st to cn, hold to back, k1-tbl, p1 from cn.

1/1 LTPC: Slip 1 st to cn, hold to front, p1, k1-tbl from cn.

Pkok: Slip third st on left-hand needle over first 2 sts and off needle; k1, yo, k1.

Banded Wraps

....

FLAT

(multiple of 4 sts + 1; 6-row repeat)

Wrap 3: See key.
Row 1 (RS): Knit.
Rows 2 and 3: Knit.
Row 4: Purl.
Row 5: K1, *wrap 3, k1; repeat from * to end.
Row 6: Purl.
Repeat Rows 1–6 for Banded Wraps Flat.

IN THE ROUND

(multiple of 4 sts; 6-rnd repeat)

Wrap 3: See key.
Rnd 1: Knit.
Rnd 2: Purl.
Rnds 3 and 4: Knit.
Rnd 5: *K1, wrap 3; repeat from * to end.
Rnd 6: Knit.
Repeat Rnds 1–6 for Banded Wraps in the Round.

FLAT

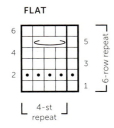

IN THE ROUND

 Wrap 3: K3, slip these 3 sts to cn; bring yarn to front and wrap yarn around these sts 3 times counterclockwise; slip sts back to right-hand needle.

Bobble Checkerboard

FLAT

(multiple of 10 sts + 7; 8-row repeat)

Row 1 (RS): K7, *p3, k7; repeat from * to end.

Row 2 and all WS Rows: Knit the knit sts and purl the purl sts as they face you; purl all bobbles.

Row 3: K3, MB, k3, *p3, k3, MB, k3; repeat from * to end.

Row 5: K2, p3, *k7, p3; repeat from * to last 2 sts, k2.

Row 7: K2, p3, *k3, MB, k3, p3; repeat from * to last 2 sts, k2.

Row 8: Repeat Row 2.

Repeat Rows 1–8 for Bobble Checkerboard Flat.

IN THE ROUND

(multiple of 10 sts; 8-rnd repeat)

Rnds 1 and 2: *K7, p3; repeat from * to end.

Rnd 3: *K3, MB, k3, p3; repeat from * to end.

Rnd 4: Repeat Rnd 1.

Rnds 5 and 6: K2, p3, *k7, p3; repeat from * to last 5 sts, k5.

Rnd 7: K2, p3, *k3, MB, k3, p3; repeat from * to last 5 sts, k3, MB, k1.

Rnd 8: Repeat Rnd 5.

Repeat Rnds 1–8 for Bobble Checkerboard in the Round.

FLAT

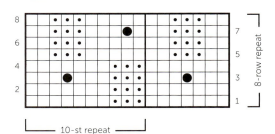

IN THE ROUND

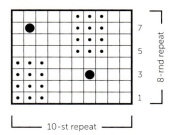

● **MB:** Make Bobble.

Bubble Clusters

FLAT

(multiple of 8 sts + 1; 10-row repeat)

Wrap 3: See key.

Row 1 (RS): P1, *k2, wrap 3, k2, p1; repeat from * to end.

Row 2 and all WS Rows: K1, *p7, k1; repeat from * to end.

Row 3: P1, *wrap 3, k1, wrap 3, p1; repeat from * to end.

Row 5: Repeat Row 1.

Rows 7 and 9: P1, *k7, p1; repeat from * to end.

Row 10: Repeat Row 2.

Repeat Rows 1–10 for Bubble Clusters Flat.

IN THE ROUND

(multiple of 8 sts; 10-rnd repeat)

Wrap 3: See key.

Rnd 1: *P1, k2, wrap 3, k2; repeat from * to end.

Rnd 2: *P1, k7; repeat from * to end.

Rnd 3: *P1, wrap 3, k1, wrap 3; repeat from * to end.

Rnd 4: Repeat Rnd 2.

Rnd 5: Repeat Rnd 1.

Rnds 6–10: Repeat Rnd 2.

Repeat Rnds 1–10 for Bubble Clusters in the Round.

FLAT

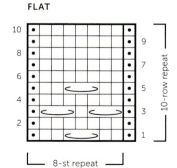

IN THE ROUND

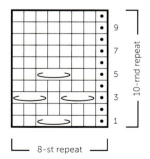

 Wrap 3: K3, slip these 3 sts to cn; bring yarn to front and wrap yarn around these sts 3 times counterclockwise; slip sts back to right-hand needle.

Crowns

FLAT

(multiple of 10 sts + 7; 8-row repeat)

WC (Work Cluster): Slip 5 sts to right-hand needle purlwise (dropping extra wraps), return same 5 sts back to left-hand needle purlwise, then (k1, p1, k1, p1, k1) into same 5 sts together.

Row 1 (RS): K6, *[k1, wrapping yarn 3 times around needle] 5 times, k5; repeat from * to last st, k1.

Row 2: P6, *WC, p5; repeat from * to last st, p1.

Row 3: Knit.

Row 4: K6, *p5, k5; repeat from * to last st, k1.

Row 5: K1, [k1, wrapping yarn 3 times around needle] 5 times, *k5, [k1, wrapping yarn 3 times around needle] 5 times; repeat from * to last st, k1.

Row 6: P1, WC, *p5, WC; repeat from * to last st, p1.

Row 7: Knit.

Row 8: P6, *k5, p5; repeat from * to last st, p1.

Repeat Rows 1–8 for Crowns Flat.

IN THE ROUND

(multiple of 10 sts; 8-rnd repeat)

WC (Work Cluster): Slip 5 sts to right-hand needle purlwise (dropping extra wraps), return same 5 sts back to left-hand needle purlwise, then (p1, k1, p1, k1, p1) into same 5 sts together.

Rnd 1: *[K1, wrapping yarn 3 times around needle] 5 times, k5; repeat from * to end.

Rnd 2: *WC, k5; repeat from * to end.

Rnd 3: Knit.

Rnd 4: *K5, p5; repeat from * to end.

Rnd 5: *K5, [k1, wrapping yarn 3 times around needle] 5 times; repeat from * to end.

Rnd 6: *K5, WC; repeat from * to end.

Rnd 7: Knit.

Rnd 8: *P5, k5; repeat from * to end.

Repeat Rnds 1–8 for Crowns In the Round.

FLAT

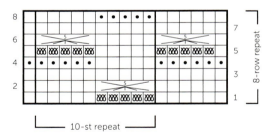

IN THE ROUND

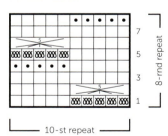

 K1, wrapping yarn 3 times around needle.

WC (Work Cluster): See written pattern.

IN THE ROUND

(multiple of 14 sts; 12-rnd repeat)

Tuck 1: Knit into st 3 rows below st on left-hand needle, dropping and unraveling sts above this st.

Rnd 1: Knit.

Rnds 2–6: *P3, k1, p3, k7; repeat from * to end.

Rnd 7: *P3, tuck 1, p3, k7; repeat from * to end.

Rnds 8–12: *K7, p3, k1, p3; repeat from * to end.

Rnd 13: *K7, p3, tuck 1, p3; repeat from * to end.

Repeat Rnds 2–13 for Butterfly Checkerboard in the Round.

FLAT

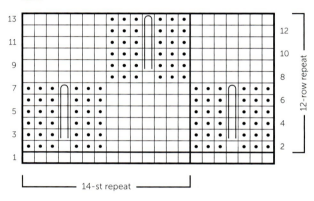

14-st repeat

Note: *Flat pattern begins with a WS row.*

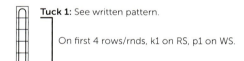

Tuck 1: See written pattern.

On first 4 rows/rnds, k1 on RS, p1 on WS.

Butterfly Checkerboard

FLAT

(multiple of 14 sts + 7; 12-row repeat)

Tuck 1: Insert right-hand needle from RS to WS into st 3 rows below st on left-hand needle, purl this st, dropping and unraveling sts above it.

Note: *Pattern begins with a WS row.*

Row 1 (WS): Purl.

Row 2: P3, k1, p3, *k7, p3, k1, p3; repeat from * to end.

Row 3: K3, p1, k3, *p7, k3, p1, k3; repeat from * to end.

Rows 4 and 5: Repeat Rows 2 and 3.

Row 6: Repeat Row 2.

Row 7: K3, tuck 1, k3, *p7, k3, tuck 1, k3; repeat from * to end.

Row 8: K7, *p3, k1, p3, k7; repeat from * to end.

Row 9: P7, *k3, p1, k3, p7; repeat from * to end.

Rows 10 and 11: Repeat Rows 8 and 9.

Row 12: Repeat Row 8.

Row 13: P7, *k3, tuck 1, k3, p7; repeat from * to end.

Repeat Rows 2–13 for Butterfly Checkerboard Flat.

IN THE ROUND

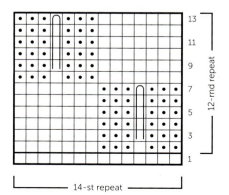

14-st repeat

Flower Bud Texture

FLAT

(multiple of 5 sts + 3; 8-row repeat)

Wrap 3: See key.

DW: Decrease Wrap. See key.

Row 1 (RS): Wrap 3, *k2, wrap 3; repeat from * to end.

Row 2: DW, *p4, DW; repeat from * to last 2 sts, p2.

Row 3: Knit.

Row 4: Purl.

Row 5: *K2, wrap 3; repeat from * to last 3 sts, k3.

Row 6: P3, *DW, p4; repeat from * to end.

Row 7: Knit.

Row 8: Purl.

Repeat Rows 1–8 for Flower Bud Texture Flat.

FLAT

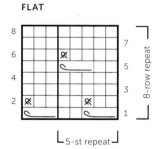

 Wrap 3: Slip 3 sts purlwise wyif, wrap yarn from front to back around left-hand needle, then to front again; keeping yarn to front and holding loop on left-hand needle in place, slip last 3 sts back to left-hand needle, yarn back, k3, slip loop to right-hand needle.

 DW: Decrease Wrap. On RS rows, k2tog (loop and preceding st). On WS rows, p2tog (loop and next st).

IN THE ROUND

(multiple of 5 sts; 8-rnd repeat)

Wrap 3: See key.

DW: Decrease Wrap. See key.

Rnd 1: *Wrap 3, k2; repeat from * to end.

Rnd 2: K2, DW, *k4, DW; repeat from * to last 2 sts, k2.

Rnds 3 and 4: Knit.

Rnd 5: *K2, wrap 3; repeat from * to end.

Rnd 6: *K4, DW; repeat from * to end.

Rnds 7 and 8: Knit.

Repeat Rnds 1–8 for Flower Bud Texture in the Round.

IN THE ROUND

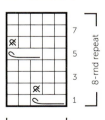

IN THE ROUND

(multiple of 5 sts; 8-rnd repeat)
LSC: Left Slipped Cross. See key.
Rnd 1: Purl.
Rnd 2: *LSC, k3; repeat from * to end.
Rnd 3: Knit.
Rnd 4: K1, LSC, *k3, LSC; repeat from * to last 2 sts, k2.
Rnd 5: Knit.
Rnd 6: K2, LSC, *k3, LSC; repeat from * to last st, k1.
Rnd 7: Knit.
Rnd 8: *K3, LSC; repeat from * to end.
Rnd 9: Purl.
Repeat Rnds 2–9 for Left Parallelograms in the Round.

FLAT

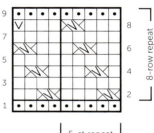

Note: Flat pattern begins with a WS row.

Left Parallelograms

....

FLAT

(multiple of 5 sts + 4; 8-row repeat)
LSC: Left Slipped Cross. See key.
Note: Pattern begins with a WS row.
Row 1 (WS): Knit.
Row 2: LSC, *k3, LSC; repeat from * to last 2 sts, k2.
Row 3: Purl.
Row 4: K1, LSC, *k3, LSC; repeat from * to last st, k1.
Row 5: Purl.
Row 6: K2, LSC, *k3, LSC; repeat from * to end.
Row 7: Purl.
Row 8: K3, *LSC, k3; repeat from * to last st, slip
1 purlwise wyib.
Row 9: Knit.
Repeat Rows 2–9 for Left Parallelograms Flat.

LSC: Left Slipped Cross. Insert
needle from back to front between
first and second sts on left-hand
needle and knit the second st
through the front loop; slip first st
purlwise to right-hand needle,
letting second st drop from
left-hand needle.

IN THE ROUND

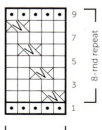

Right Parallelograms

FLAT

(multiple of 5 sts + 4; 8-row repeat)

RSC: Right Slipped Cross. See key.

Note: Pattern begins with a WS row.

Row 1 (WS): Knit.

Row 2: K2, RSC, *k3, RSC; repeat from * to end.

Row 3: Purl.

Row 4: K1, RSC, *k3, RSC; repeat from * to last st, k1.

Row 5: Purl.

Row 6: RSC, *k3, RSC; repeat from * to last 2 sts, k2.

Row 7: Purl.

Row 8: Slip 1 purlwise wyib, k3, *RSC, k3; repeat from * to end.

Row 9: Knit.

Repeat Rows 2–9 for Right Parallelograms Flat.

FLAT

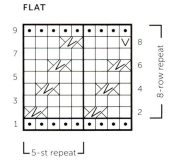

5-st repeat

8-row repeat

Note: Flat pattern begins with a WS row.

 RSC: Right Slipped Cross. Wyib, skip first st on left-hand needle and insert needle purlwise into front of second st, knit the first st through the front loop, slipping both sts from left-hand needle together.

IN THE ROUND

(multiple of 5 sts; 8-rnd repeat)

RSC: Right Slipped Cross. See key.

Rnd 1: Purl.

Rnd 2: *K3, RSC; repeat from * to end.

Rnd 3: Knit.

Rnd 4: K2, RSC, *k3, RSC; repeat from * to last st, k1.

Rnd 5: Knit.

Rnd 6: K1, RSC, *k3, RSC; repeat from * to last 2 sts, k2.

Rnd 7: Knit.

Rnd 8: *RSC, k3; repeat from * to end.

Rnd 9: Purl.

Repeat Rnds 2–9 for Right Parallelograms in the Round.

IN THE ROUND

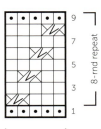

5-st repeat

8-rnd repeat

Peanuts

....

FLAT

(multiple of 6 sts + 5; 8-row repeat)

Yfskp: See key.

Row 1 (RS): Knit.

Row 2: Purl.

Row 3: K1, yfskp, *k3, yfskp; repeat from * to last st, k1.

Row 4: Purl.

Row 5: Knit.

Row 6: Purl.

Row 7: K4, *yfskp, k3; repeat from * to last st, k1.

Row 8: Purl.

Repeat Rows 1–8 for Peanuts Flat.

IN THE ROUND

(multiple of 6 sts; 8-rnd repeat)

Yfskp: See key.

Rnds 1 and 2: Knit.

Rnd 3: *Yfskp, k3; repeat from * to end.

Rnds 4–6: Knit.

Rnd 7: *K3, yfskp; repeat from * to end.

Rnd 8: Knit.

Repeat Rnds 1–8 for Peanuts in the Round.

FLAT

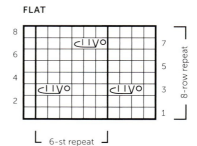

6-st repeat

8-row repeat

Yfskp: Yarn forward, slip 1 knitwise, k2, pass slipped st over last 2 sts.

IN THE ROUND

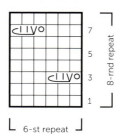

6-st repeat

8-rnd repeat

Crossed Blanket Stitch

....

FLAT

(multiple of 3 sts + 2; 2-row repeat)

Row 1 (RS): K2, *LC, k1; repeat from * to end.

Row 2: P2, *RC, p1; repeat from * to end.

Repeat Rows 1 and 2 for Crossed Blanket Stitch Flat.

IN THE ROUND

(multiple of 3 sts; 2-rnd repeat)

Rnd 1: *K1, LC; repeat from * to end.

Rnd 2: *RC, k1; repeat from * to end.

Repeat Rnds 1 and 2 for Crossed Blanket Stitch in the Round.

FLAT

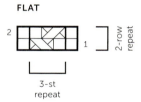

IN THE ROUND

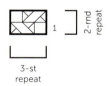

4-Point Star Texture

....

BOTTOM-UP FLAT

(multiple of 10 sts + 5; 16-row repeat)

1/1/1 LPC: See key.

Row 1 (RS): P5, *k5, p5; repeat from * to end.

Row 2 and all WS Rows: Purl.

Row 3: K1, p3, *k7, p3; repeat from * to last st, k1.

Rows 5 and 7: K1, 1/1/1 LPC, *k7, 1/1/1 LPC; repeat from * to last st, k1.

Row 9: K5, *p5, k5; repeat from * to end.

Row 11: K6, p3, *k7, p3; repeat from * to last 6 sts, k6.

Rows 13 and 15: K6, 1/1/1 LPC, *k7, 1/1/1 LPC; repeat from * to last 6 sts, k6.

Row 16: Purl.

Repeat Rows 1–16 for 4-Point Star Texture Bottom-Up Flat.

BOTTOM-UP IN THE ROUND

(multiple of 10 sts; 16-rnd repeat)

1/1/1 LPC: See key.

Rnd 1: *P5, k5; repeat from * to end.

Rnd 2 and all Even-Numbered Rnds: Knit.

Rnd 3: K1, p3, *k7, p3; repeat from * to last 6 sts, k6.

Rnds 5 and 7: K1, 1/1/1 LPC, *k7, 1/1/1 LPC; repeat from * to last 6 sts, k6.

Rnd 9: *K5, p5; repeat from * to end.

Rnd 11: K6, p3, *k7, p3; repeat from * to last st, k1.

Rnds 13 and 15: K6, 1/1/1 LPC, *k7, 1/1/1 LPC; repeat from * to last st, k1.

Rnd 16: Knit.

Repeat Rnds 1–16 for 4-Point Star Texture Bottom-Up in the Round.

TOP-DOWN FLAT

(multiple of 10 sts + 5; 16-row repeat)

1/1/1 LPC: See key.

Row 1 (RS): K6, 1/1/1 LPC, *k7, 1/1/1 LPC; repeat from * to last 6 sts, k6.

Row 2 and all WS Rows: Purl.

Row 3: Repeat Row 1.

Row 5: K6, p3, *k7, p3; repeat from * to last 6 sts, k6.

Row 7: K5, *p5, k5; repeat from * to end.

Rows 9 and 11: K1, 1/1/1 LPC, *k7, 1/1/1 LPC; repeat from * to last st, k1.

Row 13: K1, p3, *k7, p3; repeat from * to last st, k1.

Row 15: P5, *k5, p5; repeat from * to end.

Row 16: Purl.

Repeat Rows 1–16 for 4-Point Star Texture Top-Down Flat.

TOP-DOWN IN THE ROUND

(multiple of 10 sts; 16-rnd repeat)

1/1/1 LPC: See key.

Rnd 1: K1, 1/1/1 LPC, *k7, 1/1/1 LPC; repeat from * to last 6 sts, k6.

Rnd 2 and all Even-Numbered Rnds: Knit.

Rnd 3: Repeat Rnd 1.

Rnd 5: K1, p3, *k7, p3; repeat from * to last 6 sts, k6.

Rnd 7: *P5, k5; repeat from * to end.

Rnds 9 and 11: K6, 1/1/1 LPC, *k7, 1/1/1 LPC; repeat from * to last st, k1.

Rnd 13: K6, p3, *k7, p3; repeat from * to last st, k1.

Rnd 15: *K5, p5; repeat from * to end.

Rnd 16: Knit.

Repeat Rnds 1–16 for 4-Point Star Texture Top-Down in the Round.

BOTTOM-UP FLAT

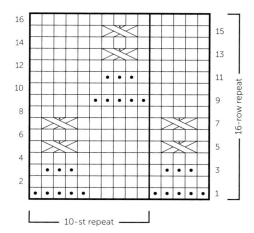

BOTTOM-UP IN THE ROUND

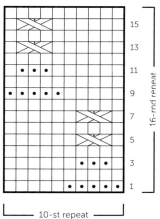

 1/1/1 LPC: Slip 1 st to cn, hold to front; slip 1 st to second cn, hold to back; k1 from left-hand needle, p1 from back cn, k1 from front cn.

TOP-DOWN FLAT

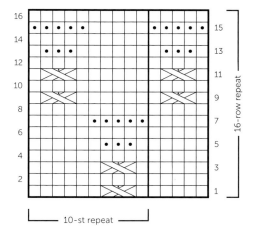

TOP-DOWN IN THE ROUND

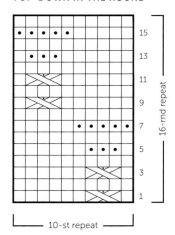

IN THE ROUND

(multiple of 4 sts; 16-rnd repeat)

Note: Slip all sts wyif.

Rnd 1: *K1, slip 3; repeat from * to end.

Rnd 2: Knit.

Rnds 3–6: Repeat Rnds 1 and 2 twice.

Rnd 7: Repeat Rnd 1.

Rnd 8: Knit to last st; reposition beginning-of-rnd marker to before last st.

Rnd 9: *Slip 3, k1; repeat from * to end.

Rnd 10: Knit.

Rnds 11–14: Repeat Rnds 9 and 10 twice.

Rnd 15: Repeat Rnd 9.

Rnd 16: Knit to end; remove beginning-of-rnd marker, k1, pm for new beginning of rnd.

Repeat Rnds 1–16 for Tatami Weave Floats in the Round.

Tatami Weave Floats

....

FLAT

(multiple of 4 sts + 1; 16-row repeat)

Note: Slip all sts wyif.

Row 1 (RS): K1, *slip 3, k1; repeat from * to end.

Row 2 and all WS Rows: Purl.

Rows 3, 5, and 7: Repeat Row 1.

Rows 9, 11, 13, and 15: Slip 2, k1, *slip 3, k1; repeat from * to last 2 sts, slip 2.

Row 16: Purl.

Repeat Rows 1–16 for Tatami Weave Floats Flat.

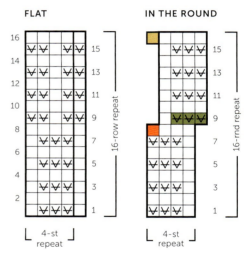

On final repeat only of Rnd 8, end rnd 1 st before beginning-of-rnd marker; reposition beginning-of-rnd marker to before last st. On all preceding repeats, knit this st.

On first repeat only of Rnd 9, first slipped st will be worked on what was last st of Rnd 8; beginning-of-rnd marker should be before this slipped st. On all following repeats, slip these 3 sts purlwise wyif.

On Rnd 16 only, work this st on final repeat only; work to end of rnd, remove beginning-of-rnd marker, k1, pm for new beginning-of-rnd. On all preceding repeats, omit this st.

Raised Parallelograms

FLAT

(multiple of 6 sts + 4; 8-row repeat)

Row 1 (RS): P4, *RC, p4; repeat from * to end.

Row 2 and all WS Rows: Purl.

Row 3: Knit.

Row 5: P1, RC, *p4, RC; repeat from * to last st, p1.

Row 7: Knit.

Row 8: Purl.

Repeat Rows 1–8 for Raised Parallelograms Flat.

IN THE ROUND

(multiple of 6 sts; 8-rnd repeat)

Rnd 1: *P4, RC; repeat from * to end.

Rnds 2–4: Knit.

Rnd 5: P1, RC, *p4, RC; repeat from * to last 3 sts, p3.

Rnds 6–8: Knit.

Repeat Rnds 1–8 for Raised Parallelograms in the Round.

FLAT

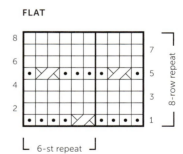

6-st repeat

8-row repeat

IN THE ROUND

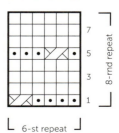

6-st repeat

8-rnd repeat

Flight of the Gulls

BOTTOM-UP FLAT

(multiple of 10 sts + 10; 12-row repeat)

Row 1 (RS): K2, 1/2 RC, 1/2 LC, *k1, k2tog, yo, k1, 1/2 RC, 1/2 LC; repeat from * to last 2 sts, k2.

Row 2 and all WS Rows: Purl.

Row 3: Knit.

Row 5: K1, 1/2 RC, k2, 1/2 LC, *k2, 1/2 RC, k2, 1/2 LC; repeat from * to last st, k1.

Row 7: Knit.

Row 9: *1/2 RC, k4, 1/2 LC; repeat from * to end.

Row 11: Knit.

Row 12: Purl.

Repeat Rows 1–12 for Flight of the Gulls Bottom-Up Flat.

BOTTOM-UP IN THE ROUND

(multiple of 10 sts; 12-rnd repeat)

Rnd 1: *1/2 LC, k1, k2tog, yo, k1, 1/2 RC; repeat from * to end.

Rnds 2–4: Knit.

Rnd 5: K1, 1/2 LC, k2, 1/2 RC, *k2, 1/2 LC, k2, 1/2 RC; repeat from * to last st, k1.

Rnds 6–8: Knit.

Rnd 9: K2, 1/2 LC, 1/2 RC, *k4, 1/2 LC, 1/2 RC; repeat from * to last 2 sts, k2.

Rnds 10–12: Knit.

Repeat Rnds 1–12 for Flight of the Gulls Bottom-Up in the Round.

BOTTOM-UP FLAT

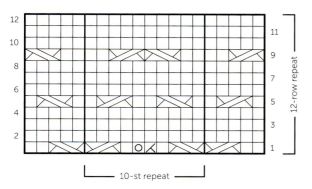

BOTTOM-UP IN THE ROUND

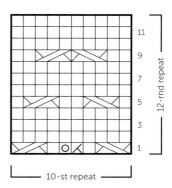

TOP-DOWN FLAT

(multiple of 10 sts + 10; 12-row repeat)

Row 1 (RS): *1/2 LC, k4, 1/2 RC; repeat from * to end.

Row 2 and all WS Rows: Purl.

Row 3: Knit.

Row 5: K1, 1/2 LC, k2, 1/2 RC, *k2, 1/2 LC, k2, 1/2 RC; repeat from * to last st, k1.

Row 7: Knit.

Row 9: K2, 1/2 LC, 1/2 RC, *k1, k2tog, yo, k1, 1/2 LC, 1/2 RC; repeat from * to last 2 sts, k2.

Row 11: Knit.

Row 12: Purl.

Repeat Rows 1–12 for Flight of the Gulls Top-Down Flat.

TOP-DOWN IN THE ROUND

(multiple of 10 sts; 12-rnd repeat)

Rnd 1: K2, 1/2 RC, 1/2 LC, *k4, 1/2 RC, 1/2 LC; repeat from * to last 2 sts, k2.

Rnd 2 and all Even-Numbered Rnds: Knit.

Rnd 3: Knit.

Rnd 5: K1, 1/2 RC, k2, 1/2 LC, *k2, 1/2 RC, k2, 1/2 LC; repeat from * to last st, k1.

Rnd 7: Knit.

Rnd 9: *1/2 RC, k1, k2tog, yo, k1, 1/2 LC; repeat from * to end.

Rnds 11 and 12: Knit.

Repeat Rnds 1–12 for Flight of the Gulls Top-Down in the Round.

TOP-DOWN FLAT

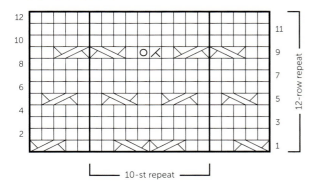

TOP-DOWN IN THE ROUND

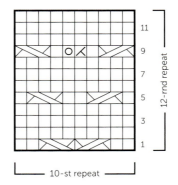

IN THE ROUND

(multiple of 4 sts; 8-rnd repeat)

Rnd 1: *Ssk, k2tog, [yo] twice; repeat from * to end.

Rnd 2: *K2, p2 into double yo (purling into front of both sts); repeat from * to end.

Rnd 3: *RC, p2; repeat from * to end.

Rnd 4: *K2, p2; repeat from * to end.

Rnd 5: *[Yo] twice, ssk, k2tog; repeat from * to end.

Rnd 6: *P2 into double yo (purling into front of both sts), k2; repeat from * to end.

Rnd 7: *P2, RC; repeat from * to end.

Rnd 8: *P2, k2; repeat from * to end.

Repeat Rnds 1–8 for Trellis Pattern in the Round.

Trellis Pattern

·····

FLAT

(multiple of 4 sts + 6; 8-row repeat)

Row 1 (RS): K1, yo, ssk, k2tog, *[yo] twice, ssk, k2tog; repeat from * to last st, yo, k1.

Row 2: P1, k1, p2, *k1 into front of first st of double yo, then k1 into back of second st, p2; repeat from * to last 2 sts, k1, p1.

Row 3: K1, p1, RC, *p2, RC; repeat from * to last 2 sts, p1, k1.

Row 4: P1, k1, p2, *k2, p2; repeat from * to last 2 sts, k1, p1.

Row 5: K1, *k2tog, [yo] twice, ssk; repeat from * to last st, k1.

Row 6: P2, *k1 into front of first st of double yo, then k1 into back of second st, p2; repeat from * to end.

Row 7: K2, p2, *RC, p2; repeat from * to last 2 sts, k2.

Row 8: P2, *k2, p2; repeat from * to end.

Repeat Rows 1–8 for Trellis Pattern Flat.

FLAT

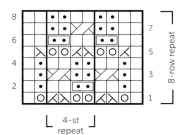

On WS, k1 into front of first st of double yo, then k1 into back of second st; on RS, p2 into double yo, purling into front of both sts.

IN THE ROUND

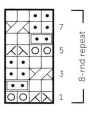

Little Tents

FLAT

(multiple of 8 sts + 9; 4-row repeat)

Catch Float: See key.

Note: Pattern begins with a WS row.

Row 1 (WS): K2, p5, *k3, p5; repeat from * to last 2 sts, k2.

Row 2: K2, slip 5 purlwise wyif, *k3, slip 5 purlwise wyif; repeat from * to last 2 sts, k2.

Row 3: Repeat Row 1.

Row 4: K4, catch float, *k7, catch float; repeat from * to last 4 sts, k4.

Repeat Rows 1–4 for Little Tents Flat.

IN THE ROUND

(multiple of 8 sts; 4-rnd repeat)

Catch Float: See key.

Rnd 1: *P3, k5; repeat from * to end.

Rnd 2: *K3, slip 5 purlwise wyif; repeat from * to end.

Rnd 3: Repeat Rnd 1.

Rnd 4: K5, catch float, *k7, catch float; repeat from * to last 2 sts, k2.

Repeat Rnds 1–4 for Little Tents in the Round.

FLAT

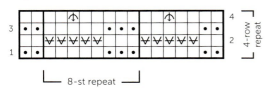

8-st repeat

4-row repeat

IN THE ROUND

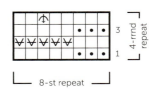

8-st repeat

4-rrnd repeat

Note: Flat pattern begins with a WS row.

⬆ **Catch Float:** Insert right-hand needle upward under float in front of slipped sts and knit next st, then lift float off over tip of right-hand needle.

Row 15: [K1-tbl] twice, *1/1 LTPC, p4, [k1-tbl] twice; repeat from * to end.

Row 17: [K1-tbl] twice, *p1, 1/2 LTPC, p2, [k1-tbl] twice; repeat from * to end.

Row 19: [K1-tbl] twice, *p3, 1/2 LTPC, [k1-tbl] twice; repeat from * to end.

Row 20: Repeat Row 2.

Repeat Rows 1–20 for Syncopated Waves Flat.

Syncopated Waves

FLAT

(multiple of 8 sts + 10; 20-row repeat)

1/1 RTPC: See key.

1/1 LTPC: See key.

1/1 RTC: See key.

1/2 RTPC: See key.

1/2 LTPC: See key.

1/2 RTC: See key.

1/2 LTC: See key.

Row 1 (RS): [K1-tbl] twice, *p5, 1/2 LTC; repeat from * to end.

Row 2 and all WS Rows: Knit the knit sts and purl the purl sts tbl as they face you.

Row 3: Repeat Row 1.

Row 5: [K1-tbl] twice, *p3, 1/2 RTPC, [k1-tbl] twice; repeat from * to end.

Row 7: [K1-tbl] twice, *p1, 1/2 RTPC, p2, [k1-tbl] twice; repeat from * to end.

Row 9: [K1-tbl] twice, *1/1 RTPC, p4, [k1-tbl] twice; repeat from * to end.

Rows 11 and 13: *1/2 RTC, p5; repeat from * to last 2 sts, 1/1 RTC.

FLAT

[chart: 20-row repeat, 8-st repeat]

1/1 RTPC: Slip 1 st to cn, hold to back, k1-tbl, p1 from cn.

1/1 LTPC: Slip 1 st to cn, hold to front, p1, k1-tbl from cn.

1/1 RTC: Slip 1 st to cn, hold to back, k1-tbl, k1-tbl from cn.

1/2 RTPC: Slip 2 sts to cn, hold to back, k1-tbl, p2 from cn.

1/2 LTPC: Slip 1 st to cn, hold to front, p2, k1-tbl from cn.

1/2 RTC: Slip 2 sts to cn, hold to back, k1-tbl, [k1-tbl] twice from cn.

1/2 LTC: Slip 1 st to cn, hold to front, [k1-tbl] twice, k1-tbl from cn.

IN THE ROUND

(multiple of 8 sts; 20-rnd repeat)

1/1 RTPC: See key.
1/1 LTPC: See key.
1/1 RTC: See key.
1/2 RTPC: See key.
1/2 LTPC: See key.
1/2 RTC: See key.
1/2 LTC: See key.
Rnd 1: *P5, 1/2 LTC; repeat from * to end.
Rnd 2: Purl the purl sts and knit the knit sts tbl as they
face you.
Rnd 3: Repeat Rnd 1.
Rnd 4: Repeat Rnd 2.
Rnd 5: *P3, 1/2 RTPC, [k1-tbl] twice; repeat from * to end.
Rnd 6: Repeat Rnd 2.
Rnd 7: *P1, 1/2 RTPC, p2, [k1-tbl] twice; repeat from * to end.
Rnd 8: Repeat Rnd 2.
Rnd 9: *1/1 RTPC, p4, [k1-tbl] twice; repeat from * to end.
Rnd 10: Repeat Rnd 2 to last 2 sts, reposition beginning-of-
rnd marker to before last 2 sts.
Rnd 11: *1/2 RTC, p5; repeat from * to end.
Rnd 12: Repeat Rnd 2.
Rnd 13: Repeat Rnd 11, remove beginning-of-rnd marker,
[k1-tbl] twice, pm for new beginning of rnd.
Rnd 14: Repeat Rnd 2.
Rnd 15: *1/1 LTPC, p4, [k1-tbl] twice; repeat from * to end.
Rnd 16: Repeat Rnd 2.
Rnd 17: *P1, 1/2 LTPC, p2, [k1-tbl] twice; repeat from * to end.
Rnd 18: Repeat Rnd 2.
Rnd 19: *P3, 1/2 LTPC, [k1-tbl] twice; repeat from * to end.
Rnd 20: Repeat Rnd 2.
Repeat Rnds 1–20 for Syncopated Waves in the Round.

IN THE ROUND

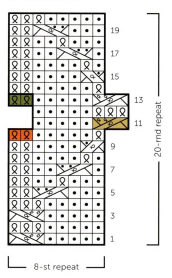

8-st repeat

 On final repeat only of Rnd 10, end rnd 2 sts
before beginning-of-rnd marker; reposition
beginning-of-rnd marker to before last 2 sts.
On all preceding repeats, work these 2 sts as
[k1-tbl] twice.

On first repeat only of Rnd 11, work 1/2 RTC
on what was last 2 sts of Rnd 10 and first st
of Rnd 11; beginning-of rnd marker should
be before this 1/2 RTC. On all following
repeats, work these sts as 1/2 RTC.

On Rnd 13 only, work to end of rnd, remove
beginning-of-rnd marker, [k1-tbl] twice, pm
for new beginning of rnd. On all preceding
repeats, omit these 2 sts.

(multiple of 8 sts; 14-rnd repeat)

Rnd 1: *P1, k1; repeat from * to end.

Rnds 2–8: Knit the purl sts and purl the knit sts as they face you.

Rnd 9: *K1, yo, ssk, k3, k2tog, yo; repeat from * to end.

Rnd 10: Knit.

Rnd 11: K2, yo, ssk, k1, k2tog, yo, *k3, yo, ssk, k1, k2tog, yo; repeat from * to last st, k1.

Rnd 12: Knit.

Rnd 13: K3, yo, sk2p, yo, *k5, yo, sk2p, yo; repeat from * to last 2 sts, k2.

Rnd 14: Knit.

Repeat Rnds 1–14 for Lace and Seed Stitch in the Round.

Lace and Seed Stitch

FLAT

(multiple of 8 sts + 1; 14-row repeat)

Row 1 (RS): P1, *k1, p1; repeat from * to end.

Rows 2–8: Knit the purl sts and purl the knit sts as they face you.

Row 9: K1, *yo, ssk, k3, k2tog, yo, k1; repeat from * to end.

Row 10: Purl.

Row 11: K2, yo, ssk, k1, k2tog, yo, *k3, yo, ssk, k1, k2tog, yo; repeat from * to last 2 sts, k2.

Row 12: Purl.

Row 13: K3, yo, sk2p, yo, *k5, yo, sk2p, yo; repeat from * to last 3 sts, k3.

Row 14: Purl.

Repeat Rows 1–14 for Lace and Seed Stitch Flat.

FLAT

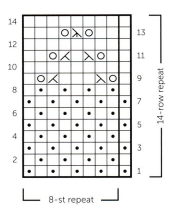

IN THE ROUND

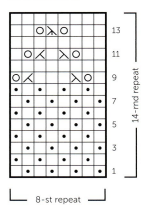

Elongated Openwork (FULLY REVERSIBLE)

FLAT

(multiple of 6 sts + 2; 4-row repeat)
Row 1 (RS): Knit.
Row 2: K1, *k1, wrapping yarn 3 times around needle; repeat from * to last st, k1.
Row 3: K1, *slip 3 sts to cable needle (dropping extra wraps), hold to back, k3 (dropping extra wraps), k3 from cable needle; repeat from * to last st, k1.
Row 4: Knit.
Repeat Rows 1–4 for Elongated Openwork Flat.

IN THE ROUND

(multiple of 6 sts; 4-rnd repeat)
Rnd 1: Knit.
Rnd 2: *P1, wrapping yarn 3 times around needle; repeat from * to end.
Rnd 3: *Slip 3 sts to cable needle (dropping extra wraps), hold to back, k3 (dropping extra wraps), k3 from cable needle; repeat from * to end.
Rnd 4: Purl.
Repeat Rnds 1–4 for Elongated Openwork in the Round.

FLAT

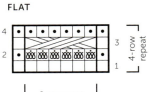

IN THE ROUND

 P1, wrapping yarn 3 times around needle on RS; k1, wrapping yarn 3 times around needle on WS.

 Slip 3 sts to cable needle (dropping extra wraps), hold to back, k3 (dropping extra wraps), k3 from cable needle.

IN THE ROUND

(multiple of 6 sts; 12-rnd repeat)

Note: You will increase 2 sts per repeat on Rnds 3 and 9; original st count is restored on Rnds 5 and 11.

Tuck 1-inc: (K1, yo, k1) into st 1 rnd below next st on left-hand needle needle (dropping and unraveling st above it) to increase to 3 sts.

Rnds 1 and 2: *P2, k1; repeat from * to end.

Rnd 3: *P2, tuck 1-inc, p2, k1; repeat from * to end.

Rnd 4: *P2, k3, p2, k1; repeat from * to end.

Rnd 5: *P2, s2kp2, p2, k1; repeat from * to end.

Rnds 6–8: Repeat Rnd 1.

Rnd 9: *P2, k1, p2, tuck 1-inc; repeat from * to end.

Rnd 10: *P2, k1, p2, k3; repeat from * to end.

Rnd 11: *P2, k1, p2, s2kp2; repeat from * to end.

Rnd 12: Repeat Rnd 1.

Repeat Rnds 1–12 for Pussy Willows in the Round.

Pussy Willows

FLAT

(multiple of 6 sts + 5; 12-row repeat)

Note: You will increase 2 sts per repeat on Rows 3 and 9, and 2 sts outside repeat on Row 3; original st count is restored on Rows 5 and 11.

Tuck 1-inc: (K1, yo, k1) into st 1 row below next st on left-hand needle (dropping and unraveling st above it) to increase to 3 sts.

Row 1 (RS): P2, *k1, p2; repeat from * to end.

Row 2: K2, *p1, k2; repeat from * to end.

Row 3: P2, tuck 1-inc, p2, *k1, p2, tuck 1-inc, p2; repeat from * to end.

Row 4: K2, p3, k2, *p1, k2, p3, k2; repeat from * to end.

Row 5: P2, s2kp2, p2, *k1, p2, s2kp2, p2; repeat from * to end.

Row 6: Repeat Row 2.

Rows 7 and 8: Repeat Rows 1 and 2.

Row 9: P2, k1, p2, *tuck 1-inc, p2, k1, p2; repeat from * to end.

Row 10: K2, p1, k2, *p3, k2, p1, k2; repeat from * to end.

Row 11: P2, k1, p2, *s2kp2, p2, k1, p2; repeat from * to end.

Row 12: Repeat Row 2.

Repeat Rows 1–12 for Pussy Willows Flat.

FLAT

(chart)

6-st repeat — 12-row repeat

⋏ S2kp2
||| K3 on RS, p3 on WS.
\3/ **Tuck 1-inc:** See written pattern.
     On first 2 rows/rnds, k1 on RS, p1 on WS.

IN THE ROUND

(chart)

6-st repeat — 12-rnd repeat

Hammocks

FLAT

(multiple of 12 sts + 7; 20-row repeat)

Note: Slip all sts purlwise with yarn to RS.

Catch Floats: See key.

Row 1 (RS): Knit.

Row 2: K1, slip 5, *k7, slip 5; repeat from * to last st, k1.

Rows 3–8: Repeat Rows 1 and 2.

Row 9: K3, catch floats, *k11, catch floats; repeat from * to last 3 sts, k3.

Row 10: Purl.

Row 11: Knit.

Row 12: K7, *slip 5, k7; repeat from * to end.

Rows 13–18: Repeat Rows 11 and 12 three times.

Row 19: K9, catch floats, *k11, catch floats; repeat from * to last 9 sts, k9.

Row 20: Purl.

Repeat Rows 1–20 for Hammocks Flat.

IN THE ROUND

(multiple of 12 sts; 20-rnd repeat)

Note: Slip all sts purlwise with yarn to front.

Catch Floats: See key.

Rnd 1: Knit.

Rnd 2: P1, slip 5, *p7, slip 5; repeat from * to last 6 sts, p6.

Rnds 3–8: Repeat Rnds 1 and 2.

Rnd 9: K3, catch floats, *k11, catch floats; repeat from * to last 8 sts, k8.

Rnds 10 and 11: Knit.

Rnd 12: *P7, slip 5; repeat from * to end.

Rnds 13–18: Repeat Rnds 11 and 12 three times.

Rnd 19: K9, catch floats, *k11, catch floats; repeat from * to last 2 sts, k2.

Rnd 20: Knit.

Repeat Rnds 1–20 for Hammocks in the Round.

FLAT

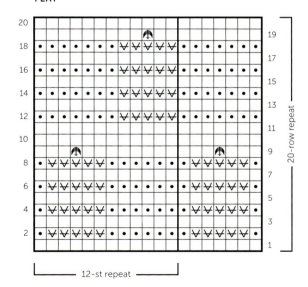

12-st repeat

 Catch Floats: Insert right-hand needle upward under the 4 floats in front of the slipped sts from the rows/rnds below and knit the next st, then draw right-hand needle with new st back under floats and slip st off left-hand needle.

IN THE ROUND

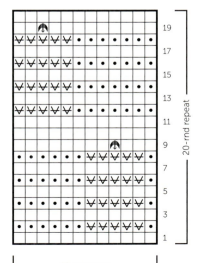

12-st repeat

Waves and Garter Ridges

FLAT

(multiple of 11 sts + 3; 16-row repeat)

Row 1 (RS): K6, k2tog, k2, RLI, *k7, k2tog, k2, RLI; repeat from * to last 4 sts, k4.

Row 2 and all WS Rows: K3, *p8, k3; repeat from * to end.

Row 3: K5, k2tog, k2, RLI, *k7, k2tog, k2, RLI; repeat from * to last 5 sts, k5.

Row 5: K4, k2tog, k2, RLI, *k7, k2tog, k2, RLI; repeat from * to last 6 sts, k6.

Row 7: K3, *k2tog, k2, RLI, k7; repeat from * to end.

Row 9: K4, LLI, k2, ssk, *k7, LLI, k2, ssk; repeat from * to last 6 sts, k6.

Row 11: K5, LLI, k2, ssk, *k7, LLI, k2, ssk; repeat from * to last 5 sts, k5.

Row 13: K6, LLI, k2, ssk, *k7, LLI, k2, ssk; repeat from * to last 4 sts, k4.

Row 15: *K7, LLI, k2, ssk; repeat from * to last 3 sts, k3.

Row 16: Repeat Row 2.

Repeat Rows 1–16 for Waves and Garter Ridges Flat.

IN THE ROUND

(multiple of 11 sts; 16-rnd repeat)

Rnd 1: K6, k2tog, k2, RLI, *k7, k2tog, k2, RLI; repeat from * to last st, k1.

Rnd 2 and all Even-Numbered Rnds: *P3, k8; repeat from * to end.

Rnd 3: K5, k2tog, k2, RLI, *k7, k2tog, k2, RLI; repeat from * to last 2 sts, k2.

Rnd 5: K4, k2tog, k2, RLI, *k7, k2tog, k2, RLI; repeat from * to last 3 sts, k3.

Rnd 7: K3, k2tog, k2, RLI, *k7, k2tog, k2, RLI; repeat from * to last 4 sts, k4.

Rnd 9: K4, LLI, k2, ssk, *k7, LLI, k2, ssk; repeat from * to last 3 sts, k3.

Rnd 11: K5, LLI, k2, ssk, *k7, LLI, k2, ssk; repeat from * to last 2 sts, k2.

Rnd 13: K6, LLI, k2, ssk, *k7, LLI, k2, ssk; repeat from * to last st, k1.

Rnd 15: *K7, LLI, k2, ssk; repeat from * to end.

Rnd 16: Repeat Rnd 2.

Repeat Rnds 1–16 for Waves and Garter Ridges in the Round.

FLAT

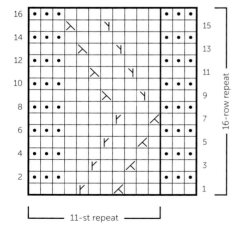

IN THE ROUND

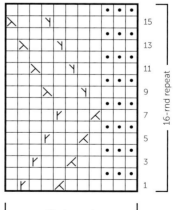

Shingle Stitch

FLAT

(multiple of 10 sts + 5; 12-row repeat)

Row 1 (RS): K5, *k1-tbl, [p1, k1-tbl] twice, k5; repeat from * to end.

Row 2: P5, *p1-tbl, [k1, p1-tbl] twice, p5; repeat from * to end.

Rows 3–6: Repeat Rows 1 and 2 twice.

Row 7: K1-tbl, [p1, k1-tbl] twice, *k5, k1-tbl, [p1, k1-tbl] twice; repeat from * to end.

Row 8: P1-tbl, [k1, p1-tbl] twice, *p5, p1-tbl, [k1, p1-tbl] twice; repeat from * to end.

Rows 9–12: Repeat Rows 7 and 8 twice.

Repeat Rows 1–12 for Shingle Stitch Flat.

IN THE ROUND

(multiple of 10 sts; 12-rnd repeat)

Rnds 1–6: *K5, k1-tbl, [p1, k1-tbl] twice; repeat from * to end.

Rnds 7–12: *K1-tbl, [p1, k1-tbl] twice, k5; repeat from * to end.

Repeat Rnds 1–12 for Shingle Stitch in the Round.

FLAT

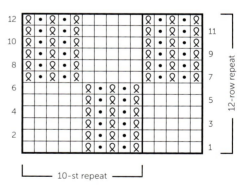

IN THE ROUND

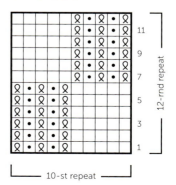

Ancient Blocks

FLAT

(multiple of 14 sts + 4; 16-row repeat)

Row 1 (RS): Knit.

Row 2: Knit.

Row 3: P1, RC, p1, *[k1-tbl] 10 times, p1, RC, p1; repeat from * to end.

Row 4: K1, p2, k1, *[p1-tbl] 10 times, k1, p2, k1; repeat from * to end.

Rows 5–8: Repeat Rows 3 and 4 twice.

Rows 9 and 10: Knit.

Row 11: [K1-tbl] 7 times, p1, RC, p1, *[k1-tbl] 10 times, p1, RC, p1; repeat from * to last 7 sts, [k1-tbl] 7 times.

Row 12: [P1-tbl] 7 times, k1, p2, k1, *[p1-tbl] 10 times, k1, p2, k1; repeat from * to last 7 sts, [p1-tbl] 7 times.

Rows 13–16: Repeat Rows 11 and 12 twice.

Repeat Rows 1–16 for Ancient Blocks Flat.

FLAT

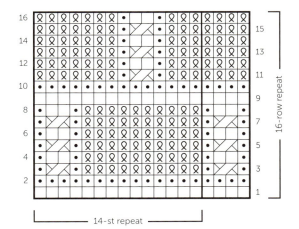

14-st repeat

16-row repeat

IN THE ROUND

(multiple of 14 sts; 16-rnd repeat)

Rnd 1: Knit.

Rnd 2: Purl.

Rnd 3: *P1, RC, p1, [k1-tbl] 10 times; repeat from * to end.

Rnd 4: *P1, k2, p1, [k1-tbl] 10 times; repeat from * to end.

Rnds 5–8: Repeat Rnds 3 and 4 twice.

Rnd 9: Knit.

Rnd 10: Purl.

Rnd 11: [K1-tbl] 7 times, p1, RC, p1, *[k1-tbl] 10 times, p1, RC, p1; repeat from * to last 3 sts, [k1-tbl] 3 times.

Rnd 12: [K1-tbl] 7 times, p1, k2, p1, *[k1-tbl] 10 times, p1, k2, p1; repeat from * to last 3 sts, [k1-tbl] 3 times.

Rnds 13–16: Repeat Rnds 11 and 12 twice.

Repeat Rnds 1–16 for Ancient Blocks in the Round.

IN THE ROUND

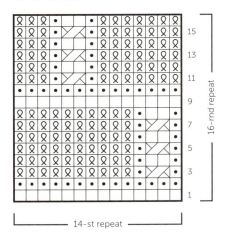

14-st repeat

16-rnd repeat

SIZES
Adult small (medium, large)

FINISHED MEASUREMENTS
Approximately 7¼ (7½, 8¼)" [18.5 (19, 21) cm] hand circumference
Approximately 13 (13½, 14¾)" [33 (34.5, 37.5) cm] long

YARN
Blue Sky Fibers Woolstok [100% fine highland wool; 123 yards (115 meters) / 2 ounces (50 grams)]: 2 hanks #1308 Golden Meadow

NEEDLES
One set of four double-pointed needles size US 6 (4 mm)
Change needle size if necessary to obtain correct gauge.

NOTIONS
Stitch markers; waste yarn; tapestry needle

GAUGE
22 sts and 30 rnds = 4" (10 cm) in Stockinette Stitch (St st), washed and blocked

Crossed Blanket Stitch Mittens

In these mittens, I incorporated a fancy stitch pattern that runs down the off-center front of the mittens. Changing the look of these mittens is super easy. For a fingerless mitt, just try on as you go, add a ribbed edge, and bind off without closing the top.

STITCH PATTERNS

2X1 RIB

(multiple of 3 sts; 1-rnd repeat)
All Rnds: *K2, p1; repeat from * to end.

CROSSED BLANKET STITCH

(multiple of 3 sts; 2-rnd repeat)
Rnd 1: *K1, LC; repeat from * to end.
Rnd 2: *RC, k1; repeat from * to end.
Repeat Rnds 1–2 for Crossed Blanket Stitch.

CROSSED BLANKET STITCH

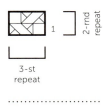

Special Techniques

Backward Loop CO: Wind yarn around thumb clockwise, insert right-hand needle into the front of the loop on thumb, remove thumb and tighten st on needle.

Kitchener Stitch: Thread a blunt tapestry needle with a length of yarn approximately 4 times the length of the section to be joined. Hold the pieces to be joined, WSs together, with the needles holding the sts parallel, both ends pointing to the right. Working from right to left, insert tapestry needle into first st on front needle as if to purl, pull yarn through, leaving st on needle; insert tapestry needle into first st on back needle as if to knit, pull yarn through, leaving st on needle; *insert tapestry needle into first st on front needle as if to knit, pull yarn through, remove st from needle; insert tapestry needle into next st on front needle as if to purl, pull yarn through, leave st on needle; insert tapestry needle into first st on back needle as if to purl, pull yarn through, remove st from needle; insert tapestry needle into next st on back needle as if to knit, pull yarn through, leave st on needle. Repeat from *, working 3 or 4 sts at a time, then go back and adjust tension to match the pieces being joined. When 1 st remains on each needle, cut yarn and pass through last 2 sts to fasten off.

Right Mitten

CO 39 (42, 45) sts. Join for working in the rnd, being careful not to twist sts; pm for beginning of rnd.

Work 2x1 Rib for 1½" (4 cm), increasing 1 (0, 1) st(s) at end of rnd—40 (42, 46) sts.

Next Rnd: K4, work 9 sts in Crossed Blanket Stitch, knit to end.

Work even until piece measures 6" (15 cm) from the beginning.

SHAPE THUMB GUSSET

Increase Rnd 1: Work 20 (21, 23) sts, pm, M1-l, k1, M1-r, pm, work to end—2 sts increased.

Work even for 2 rnds.

Increase Rnd 2: Work to marker, sm, M1-l, knit to marker, M1-r, sm, work to end—2 sts increased.

Repeat Increase Rnd 2 every 3 rnds 3 (4, 5) times—50 (54, 60) sts.

Next Rnd: Work to first marker, remove marker, transfer next 11 (13, 15) sts to waste yarn, remove marker, using Backward Loop CO, CO 1 st over gap, work to end—40 (42, 46) sts remain. Rearrange sts so that first 20 (21, 23) sts are on 1 needle and remaining 20 (21, 23) sts are on 2 needles. Work even until piece measures 4 (4¼, 4¾)" [10 (11, 12) cm] from end of thumb gusset, ending with Rnd 1 of Crossed Blanket Stitch. Pm either side of 9-st Crossed Blanket Stitch panel.

SHAPE TOP

Shift Rnd: Work to marker, M1-l, sm, work to 1 st before next marker, ssk (removing marker), pm, work to end.

Work 1 rnd even.

Decrease Rnd 1: *Needle 1:* K1, ssk, work to marker, M1-l, sm, work to 1 st before next marker, ssk (removing marker), pm, work to last 3 sts, k2tog, k1; *Needle 2:* K1, ssk, knit to end; *Needle 3:* Knit to last 3 sts, k2tog, k1—36 (38, 42) sts remain.

Work 1 rnd even.

Repeat last 2 rnds 0 (0, 1) time(s)—36 (38, 38) sts remain.

Decrease Rnd 2: *Needle 1:* K1, ssk, work to last 3 sts (removing markers on either side of Crossed Blanket Stitch panel as you come to them), k2tog, k1; *Needle 2:* K1, ssk, knit to end; *Needle 3:* Knit to last 3 sts, k2tog, k1—32 (34, 34) sts remain.

Work 1 rnd even.

Repeat last 2 rnds once (disregarding instructions to remove markers)—28 (30, 30) sts remain.

Transfer sts from Needle 2 to Needle 3. Graft sts together using Kitchener st.

THUMB

Transfer 11 (13, 15) sts from waste yarn to dpns. Rejoin yarn; pick up and knit 1 st from st CO over gap—12 (14, 16) sts. Join for working in the rnd; pm for beginning of rnd.

Work in St st until piece measures approximately 1¾ (2, 2¾)" [4.5 (5, 7) cm].

SHAPE TOP OF THUMB

Decrease Rnd: *K2tog; repeat from * to end—6 (7, 8) sts remain. Break yarn, leaving a 6" (15 cm) tail. Thread tail through remaining sts, pull tight, and fasten off.

Left Mitten

CO 39 (42, 45) sts. Join for working in the rnd, being careful not to twist sts; pm for beginning of rnd.

Work 2x1 Rib for 1½" (4 cm), increasing 1 (0, 1) st(s) at end of rnd—40 (42, 46) sts.

Next Rnd: K7 (8, 10), work 9 sts in Crossed Blanket Stitch, knit to end.

Work even until piece measures 6" (15 cm) from the beginning.

SHAPE THUMB GUSSET

Increase Rnd 1: Work to last st, pm, M1-l, k1, M1-r, sm—2 sts increased.

Work even for 2 rnds.

Increase Rnd 2: Work to marker, sm, M1-l, knit to marker, M1-r, sm—2 sts increased.

Repeat Increase Rnd 2 every 3 rnds 3 (4, 5) times—50 (54, 60) sts.

Next Rnd: Work to first marker, remove marker, transfer next 11 (13, 15) sts to waste yarn, using Backward Loop CO, CO 1 st over gap—40 (42, 46) sts remain. Rearrange sts so that first 20 (21, 23) sts are on 1 needle and remaining 20 (21, 23) sts are on 2 needles.

Work even until piece measures 4 (4¼, 4¾)" [10 (11, 12) cm] from end of thumb gusset, ending with Rnd 2 of Crossed Blanket Stitch. Pm either side of 9-st Crossed Blanket Stitch panel.

SHAPE TOP

Shift Rnd: Work to 1 st before marker, pm, k2tog (removing marker), work to next marker, sm, M1-l, work to end.

Work 1 rnd even.

Decrease Rnd 1: *Needle 1:* K1, ssk, work to 1 st before marker, pm, k2tog (removing marker), work to next marker, sm, M1-l, work to last 3 sts, k2tog, k1; *Needle 2:* K1, ssk, knit to end; *Needle 3:* Knit to last 3 sts, k2tog, k1—36 (38, 42) sts remain.

Work 1 rnd even.

Repeat last 2 rnds 0 (0, 1) time(s)—36 (38, 38) sts remain.

Decrease Rnd 2: *Needle 1:* K1, ssk, work to last 3 sts (removing markers on either side of Crossed Blanket Stitch panel as you come to them), k2tog, k1; *Needle 2:* K1, ssk, knit to end; *Needle 3:* Knit to last 3 sts, k2tog, k1—32 (34, 34) sts remain.

Work 1 rnd even.

Repeat last 2 rnds once (disregarding instructions to remove markers)—28 (30, 30) sts remain.

Transfer sts from Needle 2 to Needle 3. Graft sts together using Kitchener st.

THUMB

Work as for Right Mitten.

Finishing

Using tail at thumb gusset, close gap between gusset and hand.

Block as desired.

CHAPTER **4** Cables

When I think of cables, my mind's eye goes to Aran-knit sweaters, which are almost always knit in shades of ecru or cream. Although cabled sweaters are about as classic as you can get, cables can be used in many other items, including caps, mittens, or home accessories. Cables are versatile and feature groups of stitches that cross over another group of stitches. Cables are usually featured on a background of Reverse Stockinette stitch so they "pop," but you can use them as an all-over knitted fabric, if you like. In this chapter, you'll find both cable panels and all-over cabled stitch patterns.

IN THE ROUND

(panel of 10 sts worked on a background of Rev St st; 20-rnd repeat)

Rnd 1: C4F, k6.

Rnd 2 and all Even-Numbered Rnds: Knit.

Rnd 3: K2, C4F, C4B.

Rnd 5: [C4F] twice, k2.

Rnd 7: K6, C4F.

Rnd 9: Repeat Rnd 1.

Rnd 11: K6, C4B.

Rnd 13: C4F, C4B, k2.

Rnd 15: K2, [C4B] twice.

Rnd 17: C4B, k6.

Rnd 19: Repeat Rnd 11.

Rnd 20: Repeat Rnd 2.

Repeat Rnds 1–20 for Dragon and Cables in the Round.

Dragon and Cables

·······································

FLAT

(panel of 10 sts worked on a background of Rev St st; 20-row repeat)

Row 1 (RS): C4F, k6.

Row 2 and all WS Rows: Purl.

Row 3: K2, C4F, C4B.

Row 5: [C4F] twice, k2.

Row 7: K6, C4F.

Row 9: Repeat Row 1.

Row 11: K6, C4B.

Row 13: C4F, C4B, k2.

Row 15: K2, [C4B] twice.

Row 17: C4B, k6.

Row 19: Repeat Row 11.

Row 20: Repeat Row 2.

Repeat Rows 1–20 for Dragon and Cables Flat.

FLAT AND IN THE ROUND

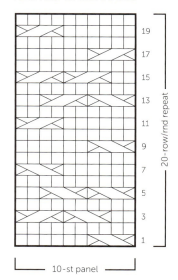

20-row/rnd repeat

10-st panel

Mock Cable and Claws

FLAT

(multiple of 14 sts + 10; 8-row repeat)

2/2/2 RC: See key.

Row 1 (RS): P2, [k2, p2] twice, *RC, LC, p2, [k2, p2] twice; repeat from * to end.

Row 2 and all WS Rows: Knit the knit sts and purl the purl sts as they face you.

Row 3: P2, 2/2/2 RC, p2, *LC, RC, p2, 2/2/2 RC, p2; repeat from * to end.

Row 5: Repeat Row 1.

Row 7: P2, [k2, p2] twice, *LC, RC, p2, [k2, p2] twice; repeat from * to end.

Row 8: Repeat Row 2.

Repeat Rows 1–8 for Mock Cable and Claws Flat.

IN THE ROUND

(multiple of 14 sts; 8-rnd repeat)

2/2/2 RC: See key.

Rnd 1: *P2, [k2, p2] twice, RC, LC; repeat from * to end.

Rnd 2 and all Even-Numbered Rnds: Knit the knit sts and purl the purl sts as they face you.

Rnd 3: *P2, 2/2/2 RC, p2, LC, RC; repeat from * to end.

Rnd 5: Repeat Rnd 1.

Rnd 7: *P2, [k2, p2] twice, LC, RC; repeat from * to end.

Rnd 8: Repeat Rnd 2.

Repeat Rnds 1–8 for Mock Cable and Claws in the Round.

FLAT

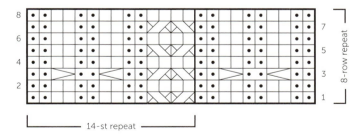

14-st repeat

8-row repeat

IN THE ROUND

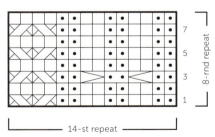

14-st repeat

8-rnd repeat

 2/2/2 RC: 2 over 2 over 2 Right Cross. Slip 2 sts to first cable needle, hold to back, slip 2 sts to second cable needle, hold to front, k2, p2 from second cable needle, k2 from first cable needle.

Twists and Eyelets

FLAT

(multiple of 8 sts + 12; 44-row repeat)

Row 1 (RS): P4, *C4F, p4; repeat from * to end.

Row 2 and all WS Rows: Knit the knit sts and purl the purl sts as they face you; purl all yos.

Row 3: Repeat Row 2.

Row 5: Repeat Row 1.

Row 7: P4, *yo, ssk, 2/1 LPC, p3; repeat from * to end.

Row 9: P4, *k2tog, yo, p1, 2/1 LPC, p2; repeat from * to end.

Row 11: P4, *yo, ssk, p2, 2/1 LPC, p1; repeat from * to end.

Row 13: P4, *k2tog, yo, p3, 2/1 LPC; repeat from * to end.

Row 15: P4, *yo, ssk, p3, 2/1 RPC; repeat from * to end.

Row 17: P4, *k2tog, yo, p2, 2/1 RPC, p1; repeat from * to end.

Row 19: P4, *yo, ssk, p1, 2/1 RPC, p2; repeat from * to end.

Row 21: P4, *k2tog, yo, 2/1 RPC, p3; repeat from * to end.

Row 23: P4, *C4B, p4; repeat from * to end.

Row 25: Repeat Row 2.

Row 27: Repeat Row 23.

Row 29: *P3, 2/1 RPC, yo, ssk; repeat from * to last 4 sts, p4.

Row 31: *P2, 2/1 RPC, p1, k2tog, yo; repeat from * to last 4 sts, p4.

Row 33: *P1, 2/1 RPC, p2, yo, ssk; repeat from * to last 4 sts, p4.

Row 35: *2/1 RPC, p3, k2tog, yo; repeat from * to last 4 sts, p4.

Row 37: *2/1 LPC, p3, yo, ssk; repeat from * to last 4 sts, p4.

Row 39: *P1, 2/1 LPC, p2, k2tog, yo; repeat from * to last 4 sts, p4.

Row 41: *P2, 2/1 LPC, p1, yo, ssk; repeat from * to last 4 sts, p4.

Row 43: *P3, 2/1 LPC, k2tog, yo; repeat from * to last 4 sts, p4.

Row 44: Repeat Row 2.

Repeat Rows 1–44 for Twists and Eyelets Flat.

FLAT

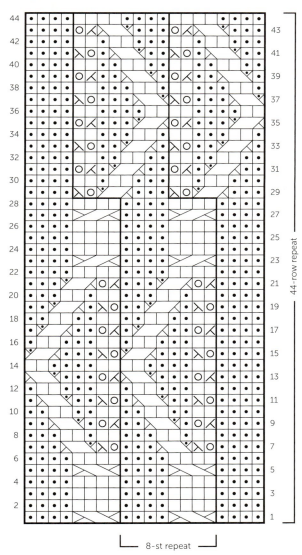

8-st repeat

44-row repeat

IN THE ROUND

(multiple of 8 sts; 44-rnd repeat)

Rnd 1: *C4F, p4; repeat from * to end. ***Note:*** *On first instance of Rnd 1, work C4F on first 4 sts of rnd as indicated. For all following instances of Rnd 1, on first repeat only, slip 2 sts to cable needle and hold to front, slip next 2 sts to right-hand needle without knitting them, then slip 2 sts from cable needle to right-hand needle without knitting them. On all following repeats, work C4F on these 4 sts.*

Rnd 2 and all Even-Numbered Rnds: Knit the knit sts and purl the purl sts as they face you; knit all yos.

Rnd 3: Repeat Rnd 2.

Rnd 5: Repeat Rnd 1.

Rnd 7: *Yo, ssk, 2/1 LPC, p3; repeat from * to end.

Rnd 9: *K2tog, yo, p1, 2/1 LPC, p2; repeat from * to end.

Rnd 11: *Yo, ssk, p2, 2/1 LPC, p1; repeat from * to end.

Rnd 13: *K2tog, yo, p3, 2/1 LPC; repeat from * to end.

Rnd 15: *Yo, ssk, p3, 2/1 RPC; repeat from * to end.

Rnd 17: *K2tog, yo, p2, 2/1 RPC, p1; repeat from * to end.

Rnd 19: *Yo, ssk, p1, 2/1 RPC, p2; repeat from * to end.

Rnd 21: *K2tog, yo, 2/1 RPC, p3; repeat from * to end.

Rnd 23: *C4B, p4; repeat from * to end.

Rnd 25: Repeat Rnd 2.

Rnd 27: Repeat Rnd 23.

Rnd 29: Remove beginning-of-rnd marker, slip 4 sts purlwise wyib, pm for new beginning of rnd, *p3, 2/1 RPC, yo, ssk; repeat from * to end.

Rnd 31: *P2, 2/1 RPC, p1, k2tog, yo; repeat from * to end.

Rnd 33: *P1, 2/1 RPC, p2, yo, ssk; repeat from * to end.

Rnd 35: *2/1 RPC, p3, k2tog, yo; repeat from * to end.

Rnd 37: *2/1 LPC, p3, yo, ssk; repeat from * to end.

Rnd 39: *P1, 2/1 LPC, p2, k2tog, yo; repeat from * to end.

Rnd 41: *P2, 2/1 LPC, p1, yo, ssk; repeat from * to end.

Rnd 43: *P3, 2/1 LPC, k2tog, yo; repeat from * to end.

Rnd 44: *P4, k4; repeat from * to end, remove beginning-of-rnd marker, slip last 4 sts worked back to left-hand needle, pm for new beginning of rnd.

Repeat Rnds 1–44 for Twists and Eyelets in the Round.

IN THE ROUND

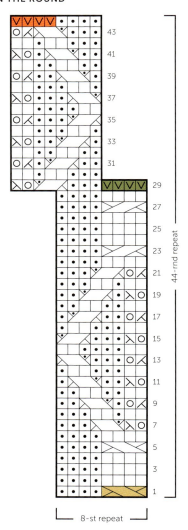

8-st repeat · 44-rnd repeat

 On first instance of Rnd 1, work C4F on first 4 sts of rnd. For all following instances of Rnd 1, on first repeat only, slip 2 sts to cable needle and hold to front, slip next 2 sts to right-hand needle without knitting them, then slip 2 sts from cable needle to right-hand needle without knitting them. On all following repeats, work C4F on these 4 sts.

V On first repeat only of Rnd 29, slip first 4 sts purlwise to right-hand needle, pm for new beginning of rnd. On all following repeats, omit these sts.

V On final repeat only of Rnd 44, remove beginning-of-rnd marker, slip last 4 sts of rnd back to left-hand needle, pm for new beginning of rnd; on all preceding repeats, knit these sts.

Water Gourd Cables

FLAT

(panel of 10 sts worked on a background of Rev St st; 20-row repeat)

Row 1 (RS): P2, C6B, p2.

Row 2 and all WS Rows: Knit the knit sts and purl the purl sts as they face you.

Row 3: Repeat Row 2.

Row 5: Repeat Row 1.

Row 7: P1, 2/1 RPC, k2, 2/1 LPC, p1.

Row 9: 2/1 RPC, p1, k2, p1, 2/1 LPC.

Rows 11–15: Repeat Row 2.

Row 17: 2/1 LPC, p1, k2, p1, 2/1 RPC.

Row 19: P1, 2/1 LPC, k2, 2/1 RPC, p1.

Row 20: Repeat Row 2.

Repeat Rows 1–20 for Water Gourd Cables Flat.

IN THE ROUND

(panel of 10 sts worked on a background of Rev St st; 20-rnd repeat)

Rnd 1: P2, C6B, p2.

Rnd 2 and all Even-Numbered Rnds: Knit the knit sts and purl the purl sts as they face you.

Rnd 3: Repeat Rnd 2.

Rnd 5: Repeat Rnd 1.

Rnd 7: P1, 2/1 RPC, k2, 2/1 LPC, p1.

Rnd 9: 2/1 RPC, p1, k2, p1, 2/1 LPC.

Rnds 11–15: Repeat Rnd 2.

Rnd 17: 2/1 LPC, p1, k2, p1, 2/1 RPC.

Rnd 19: P1, 2/1 LPC, k2, 2/1 RPC, p1.

Rnd 20: Repeat Rnd 2.

Repeat Rnds 1–20 for Water Gourd Cables in the Round.

FLAT AND IN THE ROUND

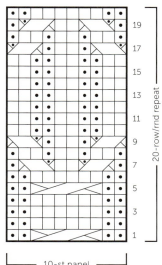

4-Column Snake Cables

FLAT

(panel of 14 sts worked on a background of Rev St st; 48-row repeat)

Row 1 (RS): K2, [p2, k2] twice, C4B.

Row 2 and all WS Rows: Knit the knit sts and purl the purl sts as they face you.

Row 3: [K2, p2] twice, C4B-p, k2.

Row 5: K2, p2, k2, C4B, p2, k2.

Row 7: K2, p2, C4B-p, k2, p2, k2.

Row 9: K2, C4B, [p2, k2] twice.

Row 11: C4B-p, k2, [p2, k2] twice.

Rows 13–23: Repeat Rows 1–11.

Row 25: C4F, k2, [p2, k2] twice.

Row 27: K2, C4F-p, [p2, k2] twice.

Row 29: K2, p2, C4F, k2, p2, k2.

Row 31: K2, p2, k2, C4F-p, p2, k2.

Row 33: [K2, p2] twice, C4F, k2.

Row 35: K2, [p2, k2] twice, C4F-p.

Rows 37–47: Repeat Rows 25–35.

Row 48: Repeat Row 2.

Repeat Rows 1–48 for 4-Column Snake Cables Flat.

IN THE ROUND

(panel of 14 sts worked on a background of Rev St st; 48-rnd repeat)

Rnd 1: K2, [p2, k2] twice, C4B.

Rnd 2 and all Even-Numbered Rnds: Knit the knit sts and purl the purl sts as they face you.

Rnd 3: [K2, p2] twice, C4B-p, k2.

Rnd 5: K2, p2, k2, C4B, p2, k2.

Rnd 7: K2, p2, C4B-p, k2, p2, k2.

Rnd 9: K2, C4B, [p2, k2] twice.

Rnd 11: C4B-p, k2, [p2, k2] twice.

Rnds 13–23: Repeat Rnds 1–11.

Rnd 25: C4F, k2, [p2, k2] twice.

Rnd 27: K2, C4F-p, [p2, k2] twice.

Rnd 29: K2, p2, C4F, k2, p2, k2.

Rnd 31: K2, p2, k2, C4F-p, p2, k2.

Rnd 33: [K2, p2] twice, C4F, k2.

Rnd 35: K2, [p2, k2] twice, C4F-p.

Rnds 37–47: Repeat Rnds 25–35.

Rnd 48: Repeat Rnd 2.

Repeat Rnds 1–48 for 4-Column Snake Cables in the Round.

FLAT AND IN THE ROUND

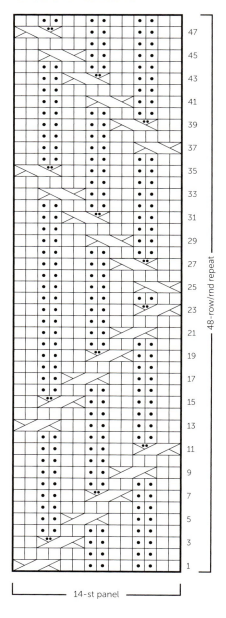

48-row/rnd repeat

14-st panel

Jeweled Cables

FLAT

(multiple of 7 sts + 5; 24-row repeat)

Row 1 (RS): K5, *p2, k5; repeat from * to end.

Row 2: Knit.

Rows 3 and 4: Repeat Rows 1 and 2.

Row 5: K1, [yo, ssk] twice, *p2, k1, [yo, ssk] twice; repeat from * to end.

Row 6: Repeat Row 2.

Rows 7 and 8: Repeat Rows 1 and 2.

Row 9: Repeat Row 1.

Rows 10–16: Knit the knit sts and purl the purl sts as they face you.

Row 17: 2/3 LC, *p2, 2/3 LC; repeat from * to end.

Rows 18–24: Repeat Row 10.

Repeat Rows 1–24 for Jeweled Cables Flat.

IN THE ROUND

(multiple of 7 sts; 24-rnd repeat)

Rnd 1: *K5, p2; repeat from * to end.

Rnd 2: Purl.

Rnds 3 and 4: Repeat Rnds 1 and 2.

Rnd 5: *K1, [yo, ssk] twice, p2; repeat from * to end.

Rnd 6: Repeat Rnd 2.

Rnds 7 and 8: Repeat Rnds 1 and 2.

Rnds 9–16: Repeat Rnd 1.

Rnd 17: *2/3 LC, p2; repeat from * to end.

Rnds 18–24: Repeat Rnd 1.

Repeat Rnds 1–24 for Jeweled Cables in the Round.

FLAT

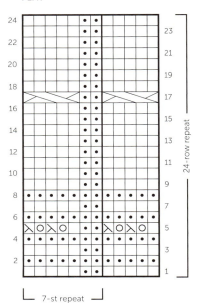

7-st repeat

24-row repeat

IN THE ROUND

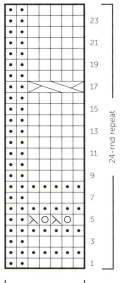

7-st repeat

24-rnd repeat

Knots and Twisted Columns

FLAT

(panel of 14 sts worked on a background of Rev St st;
20-row repeat)

Row 1 (RS): K1-tbl, p2, k2, C4B, k2, p2, k1-tbl.

Row 2: P1-tbl, k2, p8, k2, p1-tbl.

Row 3: K1-tbl, p2, [C4F] twice, p2, k1-tbl.

Row 4: Repeat Row 2.

Rows 5–8: Repeat Rows 1–4.

Rows 9 and 10: Repeat Rows 1 and 2.

Row 11: K1-tbl, p2, k8, p2, k1-tbl.

Row 12: Repeat Row 2.

Rows 13–20: Repeat Rows 11 and 12.

Repeat Rows 1–20 for Knots and Twisted Columns Flat.

IN THE ROUND

(panel of 14 sts worked on a background of Rev St st;
20-rnd repeat)

Rnd 1: K1-tbl, p2, k2, C4B, k2, p2, k1-tbl.

Rnd 2: K1-tbl, p2, k8, p2, k1-tbl.

Rnd 3: K1-tbl, p2, [C4F] twice, p2, k1-tbl.

Rnd 4: Repeat Rnd 2.

Rnds 5–8: Repeat Rnds 1–4.

Rnd 9: Repeat Rnd 1.

Rnds 10–20: Repeat Rnd 2.

Repeat Rnds 1–20 for Knots and Twisted Columns in the
Round.

FLAT AND IN THE ROUND

14-st panel

20-row/rnd repeat

Braided Diamond Cables

BOTTOM-UP FLAT

(multiple of 22 sts + 12; 32-row repeat)

Row 1 (RS): P3, C4B-p, k2, *p5, C4B, k2, p5, C4B-p, k2; repeat from * to last 3 sts, p3.

Row 2 and all WS Rows: Knit the knit sts and purl the purl sts as they face you.

Row 3: P2, 2/1 RPC, p2, 2/1 LPC, *p4, k2, C4F, p4, 2/1 RPC, p2, 2/1 LPC; repeat from * to last 2 sts, p2.

Row 5: P1, 2/1 RPC, p4, 2/1 LPC, *p3, C4B, k2, p3, 2/1 RPC, p4, 2/1 LPC; repeat from * to last st, p1.

Row 7: P1, 2/1 LPC, p4, 2/1 RPC, *p3, k2, C4F, p3, 2/1 LPC, p4, 2/1 RPC; repeat from * to last st, p1.

Row 9: P2, 2/1 LPC, p2, 2/1 RPC, *p4, C4B, k2, p4, 2/1 LPC, p2, 2/1 RPC; repeat from * to last 2 sts, p2.

Row 11: P3, k2, C4B, *p5, k2, C4F, p5, k2, C4B; repeat from * to last 3 sts, p3.

Row 13: P3, C4B, k2, *p5, C4B, k2; repeat from * to last 3 sts, p3.

Row 15: P3, k2, C4F, *p5, k2, C4F; repeat from * to last 3 sts, p3.

Row 17: P3, C4B, k2, *p5, C4B-p, k2, p5, C4B, k2; repeat from * to last 3 sts, p3.

Row 19: P3, k2, C4F, *p4, 2/1 RPC, p2, 2/1 LPC, p4, k2, C4F; repeat from * to last 3 sts, p3.

Row 21: P3, C4B, k2, *p3, 2/1 RPC, p4, 2/1 LPC, p3, C4B, k2; repeat from * to last 3 sts, p3.

Row 23: P3, k2, C4F, *p3, 2/1 LPC, p4, 2/1 RPC, p3, k2, C4F; repeat from * to last 3 sts, p3.

Row 25: P3, C4B, k2, *p4, 2/1 LPC, p2, 2/1 RPC, p4, C4B, k2; repeat from * to last 3 sts, p3.

Row 27: P3, k2, C4F, *p5, k2, C4B, p5, k2, C4F; repeat from * to last 3 sts, p3.

Row 29: Repeat Row 13.

Row 31: Repeat Row 15.

Row 32: Repeat Row 2.

Repeat Rows 1–32 for Braided Diamond Cables Bottom-Up Flat.

BOTTOM-UP IN THE ROUND

(multiple of 22 sts; 32-rnd repeat)

Rnd 1: P3, C4B-p, k2, p5, C4B, k2, *p5, C4B-p, k2, p5, C4B, k2; repeat from * to last 2 sts, p2.

Rnd 2 and all Even-Numbered Rnds: Knit the knit sts and purl the purl sts as they face you.

Rnd 3: P2, 2/1 RPC, p2, 2/1 LPC, p4, k2, C4F, *p4, 2/1 RPC, p2, 2/1 LPC, p4, k2, C4F; repeat from * to last 2 sts, p2.

Rnd 5: P1, 2/1 RPC, p4, 2/1 LPC, p3, C4B, k2, *p3, 2/1 RPC, p4, 2/1 LPC, p3, C4B, k2; repeat from * to last 2 sts, p2.

BOTTOM-UP FLAT

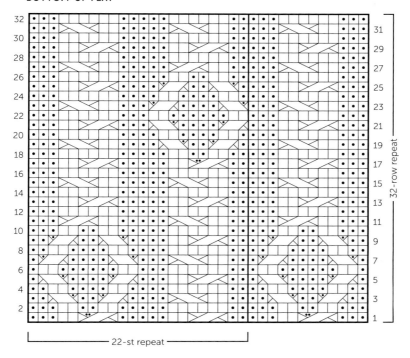

22-st repeat

32-row repeat

BOTTOM-UP IN THE ROUND

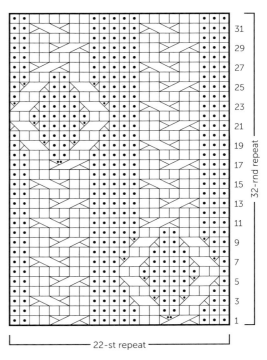

22-st repeat

32-rnd repeat

Rnd 7: P1, 2/1 LPC, p4, 2/1 RPC, p3, k2, C4F, *p3, 2/1 LPC, p4, 2/1 RPC, p3, k2, C4F; repeat from * to last 2 sts, p2.

Rnd 9: P2, 2/1 LPC, p2, 2/1 RPC, p4, C4B, k2, *p4, 2/1 LPC, p2, 2/1 RPC, p4, C4B, k2; repeat from * to last 2 sts, p2.

Rnd 11: P3, k2, C4B, p5, k2, C4F, *p5, k2, C4B, p5, k2, C4F; repeat from * to last 2 sts, p2.

Rnd 13: P3, C4B, k2, *p5, C4B, k2; repeat from * to last 2 sts, p2.

Rnd 15: P3, k2, C4F, *p5, k2, C4F; repeat from * to last 2 sts, p2.

Rnd 17: P3, C4B, k2, p5, C4B-p, k2, *p5, C4B, k2, p5, C4B-p, k2; repeat from * to last 2 sts, p2.

Rnd 19: P3, k2, C4F, p4, 2/1 RPC, p2, 2/1 LPC, *p4, k2, C4F, p4, 2/1 RPC, p2, 2/1 LPC; repeat from * to last st, p1.

Rnd 21: *P3, C4B, k2, p3, 2/1 RPC, p4, 2/1 LPC; repeat from * to end.

Rnd 23: *P3, k2, C4F, p3, 2/1 LPC, p4, 2/1 RPC; repeat from * to end.

Rnd 25: P3, C4B, k2, p4, 2/1 LPC, p2, 2/1 RPC, *p4, C4B, k2, p4, 2/1 LPC, p2, 2/1 RPC; repeat from * to last st, p1.

Rnd 27: P3, k2, C4F, p5, k2, C4B, *p5, k2, C4F, p5, k2, C4B; repeat from * to last 2 sts, p2.

Rnd 29: Repeat Rnd 13.

Rnd 31: Repeat Rnd 15.

Rnd 32: Repeat Rnd 2.

Repeat Rnds 1–32 for Braided Diamond Cables Bottom-Up in the Round.

TOP-DOWN FLAT

(multiple of 22 sts + 12; 32-row repeat)

Row 1 (RS): P3, C4F, k2, *p5, C4F, k2; repeat from * to last 3 sts, p3.

Row 2 and all WS Rows: Knit the knit sts and purl the purl sts as they face you.

Row 3: P3, k2, C4B, *p5, k2, C4B; repeat from * to last 3 sts, p3.

Row 5: P3, C4F, k2, *p5, C4B-p, k2, p5, C4F, k2; repeat from * to last 3 sts, p3.

Row 7: P3, k2, C4B, *p4, 2/1 RPC, p2, 2/1 LPC, p4, k2, C4B; repeat from * to last 3 sts, p3.

Row 9: P3, C4F, k2, *p3, 2/1 RPC, p4, 2/1 LPC, p3, C4F, k2; repeat from * to last 3 sts, p3.

Row 11: P3, k2, C4B, *p3, 2/1 LPC, p4, 2/1 RPC, p3, k2, C4B; repeat from * to last 3 sts, p3.

Row 13: P3, C4F, k2, *p4, 2/1 LPC, p2, 2/1 RPC, p4, C4F, k2; repeat from * to last 3 sts, p3.

Row 15: Repeat Row 3.

Row 17: Repeat Row 1.

Row 19: Repeat Row 3.

Row 21: P3, C4B-p, k2, *p5, C4F, k2, p5, C4B-p, k2; repeat from * to last 3 sts, p3.

Row 23: P2, 2/1 RPC, p2, 2/1 LPC, *p4, k2, C4B, p4, 2/1 RPC, p2, 2/1 LPC; repeat from * to last 2 sts, p2.

Row 25: P1, 2/1 RPC, p4, 2/1 LPC, *p3, C4F, k2, p3, 2/1 RPC, p4, 2/1 LPC; repeat from * to last st, p1.

Row 27: P1, 2/1 LPC, p4, 2/1 RPC, *p3, k2, C4B, p3, 2/1 LPC, p4, 2/1 RPC; repeat from * to last st, p1.

Row 29: P2, 2/1 LPC, p2, 2/1 RPC, *p4, C4F, k2, p4, 2/1 LPC, p2, 2/1 RPC; repeat from * to last 2 sts, p2.

Row 31: Repeat Row 3.

Row 32: Repeat Row 2.

Repeat Rows 1–32 for Braided Diamond Cables Top-Down Flat.

TOP-DOWN IN THE ROUND

(multiple of 22 sts; 32-rnd repeat)

Rnd 1: P3, C4F, k2, *p5, C4F, k2; repeat from * to last 2 sts, p2.

Rnd 2 and all Even-Numbered Rnds: Knit the knit sts and purl the purl sts as they face you.

Rnd 3: P3, k2, C4B, *p5, k2, C4B; repeat from * to last 2 sts, p2.

Rnd 5: P3, C4F, k2, p5, C4B-p, k2, *p5, C4F, k2, p5, C4B-p, k2; repeat from * to last 2 sts, p2.

Rnd 7: P3, k2, C4B, p4, 2/1 RPC, p2, 2/1 LPC, *p4, k2, C4B, p4, 2/1 RPC, p2, 2/1 LPC; repeat from * to last st, p1.

Rnd 9: *P3, C4F, k2, p3, 2/1 RPC, p4, 2/1 LPC; repeat from * to end.

Rnd 11: *P3, k2, C4B, p3, 2/1 LPC, p4, 2/1 RPC; repeat from * to end.

Rnd 13: P3, C4F, k2, p4, 2/1 LPC, p2, 2/1 RPC, *p4, C4F, k2, p4, 2/1 LPC, p2, 2/1 RPC; repeat from * to last st, p1.

Rnd 15: Repeat Rnd 3.

Rnd 17: Repeat Rnd 1.

Rnd 19: Repeat Rnd 3.

Rnd 21: P3, C4B-p, k2, p5, C4F, k2, *p5, C4B-p, k2, p5, C4F, k2; repeat from * to last 2 sts, p2.

Rnd 23: P2, 2/1 RPC, p2, 2/1 LPC, p4, k2, C4B, *p4, 2/1 RPC, p2, 2/1 LPC, p4, k2, C4B; repeat from * to last 2 sts, p2.

Rnd 25: P1, 2/1 RPC, p4, 2/1 LPC, p3, C4F, k2, *p3, 2/1 RPC, p4, 2/1 LPC, p3, C4F, k2; repeat from * to last 2 sts, p2.

Rnd 27: P1, 2/1 LPC, p4, 2/1 RPC, p3, k2, C4B, *p3, 2/1 LPC, p4, 2/1 RPC, p3, k2, C4B; repeat from * to last 2 sts, p2.

Rnd 29: P2, 2/1 LPC, p2, 2/1 RPC, p4, C4F, k2, *p4, 2/1 LPC, p2, 2/1 RPC, p4, C4F, k2; repeat from * to last 2 sts, p2.

Rnd 31: Repeat Rnd 3.

Rnd 32: Repeat Rnd 2.

Repeat Rnds 1–32 for Braided Diamond Cables Top-Down in the Round.

TOP-DOWN FLAT

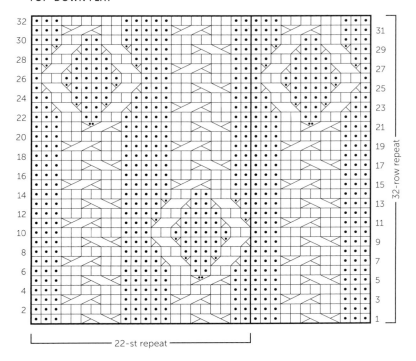

32-row repeat

22-st repeat

TOP-DOWN IN THE ROUND

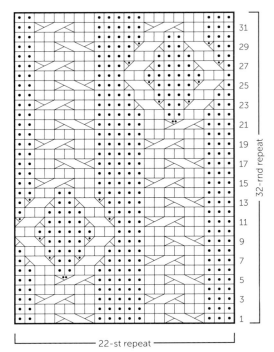

32-rnd repeat

22-st repeat

(panel of 9 sts worked on a background of Rev St st; 24-rnd repeat)

C6B-p: See key.

C6F-p: See key.

3/3 RPC: See key.

3/3 LPC: See key.

Rnd 1: P3, C6F.

Rnds 2–4: P3, k6.

Rnd 5: C6B-p, k3.

Rnds 6–8: K3, p3, k3.

Rnd 9: K3, 3/3 LPC.

Rnds 10–12: K6, p3.

Rnd 13: C6B, p3.

Rnds 14–16: K6, p3.

Rnd 17: K3, C6F-p.

Rnds 18–20: Repeat Rnd 6.

Rnd 21: 3/3 RPC, k3.

Rnds 22–24: P3, k6.

Repeat Rnds 1–24 for Nautical Twists Bottom-Up in the Round.

Nautical Twists

BOTTOM-UP FLAT

(panel of 9 sts worked on a background of Rev St st; 24-row repeat)

C6B-p: See key.

C6F-p: See key.

3/3 RPC: See key.

3/3 LPC: See key.

Row 1 (RS): P3, C6F.

Rows 2–4: Knit the knit sts and purl the purl sts as they face you.

Row 5: C6B-p, k3.

Rows 6–8: Repeat Row 2.

Row 9: K3, 3/3 LPC.

Row 10: K3, p6.

Rows 11 and 12: Repeat Row 2.

Row 13: C6B, p3.

Rows 14–16: Repeat Row 2.

Row 17: K3, C6F-p.

Rows 18–20: Repeat Row 2.

Row 21: 3/3 RPC, k3.

Row 22: P6, k3.

Rows 23 and 24: Repeat Row 2.

Repeat Rows 1–24 for Nautical Twists Bottom-Up Flat.

BOTTOM-UP FLAT AND IN THE ROUND

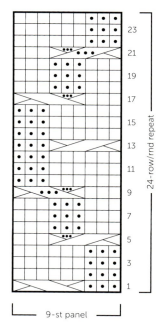

9-st panel

24-row/rnd repeat

Note: For key, see next page.

TOP-DOWN FLAT

(panel of 9 sts worked on a background of Rev St st;
24-row repeat)

C6B-p: See key.
C6F-p: See key.
3/3 RPC: See key.
3/3 LPC: See key.
Row 1 (RS): K6, p3.
Row 2: Knit the knit sts and purl the purl sts as they face you.
Row 3: K3, 3/3 RPC.
Row 4: P3, k3, p3.
Rows 5 and 6: Repeat Row 2.
Row 7: C6F-p, k3.
Rows 8–10: Repeat Row 2.
Row 11: P3, C6B.
Rows 12–14: Repeat Row 2.
Row 15: 3/3 LPC, k3.
Row 16: P3, k3, p3.
Rows 17 and 18: Repeat Row 2.
Row 19: K3, C6B-p.
Rows 20–22: Repeat Row 2.
Row 23: C6F, p3.
Row 24: Repeat Row 2.
Repeat Rows 1–24 for Nautical Twists Top-Down Flat.

TOP-DOWN IN THE ROUND

(panel of 9 sts worked on a background of Rev St st;
24-rnd repeat)

C6B-p: See key.
C6F-p: See key.
3/3 RPC: See key.
3/3 LPC: See key.
Rnds 1 and 2: K6, p3.
Rnd 3: K3, 3/3 RPC.
Rnds 4–6: K3, p3, k3.
Rnd 7: C6F-p, k3.
Rnds 8–10: P3, k6.
Rnd 11: P3, C6B.
Rnds 12–14: Repeat Rnd 8.
Rnd 15: 3/3 LPC, k3.
Rnds 16–18: Repeat Rnd 4.
Rnd 19: K3, C6B-p.
Rnds 20–22: Repeat Rnd 1.
Rnd 23: C6F, p3.
Rnd 24: Repeat Rnd 1.
Repeat Rnds 1–24 for Nautical Twists Top-Down
in the Round.

TOP-DOWN FLAT AND IN THE ROUND

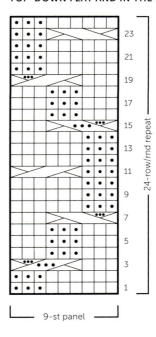

24-row/rnd repeat

9-st panel

 C6B-p: Cable 6 Back, purled. Slip 3 sts to cable needle, hold to back, k3, p3 from cable needle.

 C6F-p: Cable 6 Front, purled. Slip 3 sts to cable needle, hold to front, p3, k3 from cable needle.

 3/3 RPC: 3/3 Right Purl Cross. Slip 3 sts to cable needle, hold to back, p3, p3 from cable needle.

 3/3 LPC: 3/3 Left Purl Cross. Slip 3 sts to cable needle, hold to front, p3, p3 from cable needle.

Stacked Horned Owls

BOTTOM-UP FLAT

(panel of 8 sts worked on a background of Rev St st; 18-row repeat)

Row 1 (RS): C4B, C4F.
Row 2: Purl.
Row 3: Knit.
Row 4: Purl.
Row 5: Repeat Row 1.
Rows 6–9: Repeat Rows 2 and 3 twice.
Row 10: P2, k4, p2.
Row 11: Knit.
Rows 12–17: Repeat Rows 10 and 11 three times.
Row 18: Purl.
Repeat Rows 1–18 for Stacked Horned Owls Bottom-Up Flat.

BOTTOM-UP IN THE ROUND

(panel of 8 sts worked on a background of Rev St st; 18-rnd repeat)

Rnd 1: C4B, C4F.
Rnds 2–4: Knit.
Rnd 5: Repeat Rnd 1.
Rnds 6–9: Knit.
Rnd 10: K2, p4, k2.
Rnd 11: Knit.
Rnds 12–17: Repeat Rnds 10 and 11 three times.
Rnd 18: Knit.
Repeat Rnds 1–18 for Stacked Horned Owls Bottom-Up in the Round.

TOP-DOWN FLAT

(panel of 8 sts worked on a background of Rev St st; 18-row repeat)

Row 1 (RS): C4F, C4B.
Row 2: Purl.
Row 3: Knit.
Row 4: Purl.
Rows 5–7: Repeat Rows 1–3.
Row 8: P2, k4, p2.
Rows 9–14: Repeat Rows 7 and 8 three times.
Row 15: Knit.
Row 16: Purl.
Rows 17 and 18: Repeat Rows 15 and 16.
Repeat Rows 1–18 for Stacked Horned Owls Top-Down Flat.

TOP-DOWN IN THE ROUND

(panel of 8 sts worked on a background of Rev St st; 18-rnd repeat)

Rnd 1: C4F, C4B.
Rnds 2–4: Knit.
Rnds 5–7: Repeat Rnds 1–3.
Rnd 8: K2, p4, k2.
Rnds 9–14: Repeat Rnds 7 and 8 three times.
Rnds 15–18: Knit.
Repeat Rnds 1–18 for Stacked Horned Owls Top-Down in the Round.

BOTTOM-UP FLAT AND IN THE ROUND

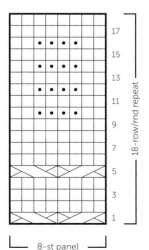

8-st panel

TOP-DOWN FLAT AND IN THE ROUND

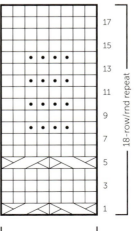

8-st panel

TOP-DOWN FLAT

(panel of 8 sts worked on a background of Rev St st; 8-row repeat)

Yo-2/2 LC-dec-yo: See key.

Row 1 (RS): Knit.

Row 2 and all WS Rows: Purl.

Row 3: K2, yo-2/2 LC-dec-yo, k2.

Row 5: Knit.

Row 7: C4F, C4B.

Row 8: Purl.

Repeat Rows 1–8 for Pitchforks Top-Down Flat.

TOP-DOWN IN THE ROUND

(panel of 8 sts worked on a background of Rev St st; 8-rnd repeat)

Yo-2/2 LC-dec-yo: See key.

Rnd 1: Knit.

Rnd 2 and all Even-Numbered Rnds: Knit.

Rnd 3: K2, yo-2/2 LC-dec-yo, k2.

Rnd 5: Knit.

Rnd 7: C4F, C4B.

Rnd 8: Knit.

Repeat Rnds 1–8 for Pitchforks Top-Down in the Round.

Pitchforks

....

BOTTOM-UP FLAT

(panel of 8 sts worked on a background of Rev St st; 8-row repeat)

Yo-2/2 LC-dec-yo: See key.

Row 1 (RS): Knit.

Row 2 and all WS Rows: Purl.

Row 3: C4B, C4F.

Row 5: Knit.

Row 7: K2, yo-2/2 LC-dec-yo, k2.

Row 8: Purl.

Repeat Rows 1–8 for Pitchforks Bottom-Up Flat.

BOTTOM-UP IN THE ROUND

(panel of 8 sts worked on a background of Rev St st; 8-rnd repeat)

Yo-2/2 LC-dec-yo: See key.

Rnds 1 and 2: Knit.

Rnd 3: C4B, C4F.

Rnds 4–6: Knit.

Rnd 7: K2, yo-2/2 LC-dec-yo, k2.

Rnd 8: Knit.

Repeat Rnds 1–8 for Pitchforks Bottom-Up in the Round.

BOTTOM-UP FLAT AND IN THE ROUND

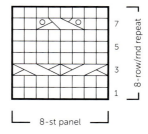

8-row/rnd repeat

8-st panel

TOP-DOWN FLAT AND IN THE ROUND

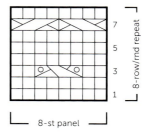

8-row/rnd repeat

8-st panel

 Yo-2/2 LC-dec-yo. Yo, slip 2 sts to cable needle, hold to front, k2tog, k2tog from cable needle, yo.

Open Crossed Columns

FLAT

(multiple of 7 sts; 10-row repeat)

1/1/1 LC: See key.

Row 1 (RS): *K2tog, yo, k1, p1, k1, yo, ssk; repeat from * to end.

Row 2: P3, k1, *p6, k1; repeat from * to last 3 sts, p3.

Rows 3–8: Repeat Rows 1 and 2 three times.

Row 9: *K2tog, yo, 1/1/1 LC, yo, ssk; repeat from * to end.

Row 10: Repeat Row 2.

Repeat Rows 1–10 for Open Crossed Columns Flat.

IN THE ROUND

(multiple of 7 sts; 10-rnd repeat)

1/1/1 LC: See key.

Rnd 1: *K2tog, yo, k1, p1, k1, yo, ssk; repeat from * to end.

Rnd 2: K3, p1, *k6, p1; repeat from * to last 3 sts, k3.

Rnds 3–8: Repeat Rnds 1 and 2 three times.

Rnd 9: *K2tog, yo, 1/1/1 LC, yo, ssk; repeat from * to end.

Rnd 10: Repeat Rnd 2.

Repeat Rnds 1–10 for Open Crossed Columns in the Round.

FLAT AND IN THE ROUND

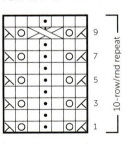

 1/1/1 LC: 1 over 1 over 1 Left Cross.
Slip 1 st to first cable needle, hold to front, slip 1 st to second cable needle, hold to back, k1, p1 from second cable needle, k1 from first cable needle.

Forked Diamonds

BOTTOM-UP FLAT

(multiple of 10 sts; 12-row repeat)

Row 1 (RS): *LPC, p2, k2, p2, RPC; repeat from * to end.
Row 2: Knit the knit sts and purl the purl sts as they face you.
Row 3: P1, LPC, p1, k2, p1, RPC, *p2, LPC, p1, k2, p1, RPC; repeat from * to last st, p1.
Row 4: Repeat Row 2.
Row 5: P2, LC, k2, RC, *p4, LC, k2, RC; repeat from * to last 2 sts, p2.
Row 6: Repeat Row 2.
Row 7: K1, p2, LC, RC, p2, *k2, p2, LC, RC, p2; repeat from * to last st, k1.
Row 8: [P1, k2] 3 times, *p2, k2, [p1, k2] twice; repeat from * to last st, p1.
Row 9: K1, p1, RPC, p2, LPC, p1, *k2, p1, RPC, p2, LPC, p1; repeat from * to last st, k1.
Row 10: P1, k1, p1, k4, p1, k1, *p2, k1, p1, k4, p1, k1; repeat from * to last st, p1.
Row 11: K1, RPC, p4, LPC, *k2, RPC, p4, LPC; repeat from * to last st, k1.
Row 12: Repeat Row 2.
Repeat Rows 1–12 for Forked Diamonds Bottom-Up Flat.

BOTTOM-UP IN THE ROUND

(multiple of 10 sts; 12-rnd repeat)

Rnd 1: *LPC, p2, k2, p2, RPC; repeat from * to end.
Rnd 2: Knit the knit sts and purl the purl sts as they face you.
Rnd 3: P1, LPC, p1, k2, p1, RPC, *p2, LPC, p1, k2, p1, RPC; repeat from * to last st, p1.
Rnd 4: Repeat Rnd 2.
Rnd 5: P2, LPC, k2, RPC, *p4, LPC, k2, RPC; repeat from * to last 2 sts, p2.
Rnd 6: Repeat Rnd 2.
Rnd 7: K1, p2, LPC, RPC, p2, *k2, p2, LPC, RPC, p2; repeat from * to last st, k1.
Rnd 8: [K1, p2] 3 times, *k2, p2, [k1, p2] twice; repeat from * to last st, k1.
Rnd 9: K1, p1, RPC, p2, LPC, p1, *k2, p1, RPC, p2, LPC, p1; repeat from * to last st, k1.
Rnd 10: K1, p1, k1, p4, k1, p1, *k2, p1, k1, p4, k1, p1; repeat from * to last st, k1.
Rnd 11: K1, RPC, p4, LPC, *k2, RPC, p4, LPC; repeat from * to last st, k1.
Rnd 12: Repeat Rnd 2.
Repeat Rnds 1–12 for Forked Diamonds Bottom-Up in the Round.

TOP-DOWN FLAT

(multiple of 10 sts; 12-row repeat)

Row 1 (RS): K1, LPC, p4, RPC, *k2, LPC, p4, RPC; repeat from * to last st, k1.

Row 2: Knit the knit sts and purl the purl sts as they face you.

Row 3: K1, p1, LPC, p2, RPC, p1, *k2, p1, LPC, p2, RPC, p1; repeat from * to last st, k1.

Row 4: Repeat Row 2.

Row 5: K1, p2, LC, RC, p2, *k2, p2, LC, RC, p2; repeat from * to last st, k1.

Row 6: K3, p4, *k6, p4; repeat from * to last 3 sts, k3.

Row 7: P2, RPC, k2, LPC, *p4, RPC, k2, LPC; repeat from * to last 2 sts, p2.

Row 8: Repeat Row 2.

Row 9: P1, RPC, p1, k2, p1, LPC, *p2, RPC, p1, k2, p1, LPC; repeat from * to last st, p1.

Row 10: Repeat Row 2.

Row 11: *RC, p2, k2, p2, LC; repeat from * to end.

Row 12: P2, k6, *p4, k6; repeat from * to last 2 sts, p2.
Repeat Rows 1–12 for Forked Diamonds Top-Down Flat.

TOP-DOWN IN THE ROUND

(multiple of 10 sts; 12-rnd repeat)

Rnd 1: K1, LPC, p4, RPC, *k2, LPC, p4, RPC; repeat from * to last st, k1.

Rnd 2: Knit the knit sts and purl the purl sts as they face you.

Rnd 3: K1, p1, LPC, p2, RPC, p1, *k2, p1, LPC, p2, RPC, p1; repeat from * to last st, k1.

Rnd 4: Repeat Rnd 2.

Rnd 5: K1, p2, LC, RC, p2, *k2, p2, LC, RC, p2; repeat from * to last st, k1.

Rnd 6: P3, k4, *p6, k4; repeat from * to last 3 sts, p3.

Rnd 7: P2, RPC, k2, LPC, *p4, RPC, k2, LPC; repeat from * to last 2 sts, p2.

Rnd 8: Repeat Rnd 2.

Rnd 9: P1, RPC, p1, k2, p1, LPC, *p2, RPC, p1, k2, p1, LPC; repeat from * to last st, p1.

Rnd 10: Repeat Rnd 2.

Rnd 11: *RC, p2, k2, p2, LC; repeat from * to end.

Rnd 12: K2, p6, *k4, p6; repeat from * to last 2 sts, k2.
Repeat Rnds 1–12 for Forked Diamonds Top-Down in the Round.

BOTTOM-UP FLAT AND IN THE ROUND

TOP-DOWN FLAT AND IN THE ROUND

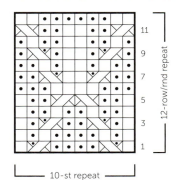

Seeded 5-Stitch Cross

FLAT

(panel of 5 sts worked on a background of Rev St st; 10-row repeat)

1/3/1 LC: See key.

Row 1 (RS): K1, [p1, k1] twice.

Row 2: P2, k1, p2.

Row 3: 1/3/1 LC.

Row 4: Repeat Row 2.

Rows 5–10: Repeat Rows 1 and 2 three times.

Repeat Rows 1–10 for Seeded 5-Stitch Cross Flat.

IN THE ROUND

(panel of 5 sts worked on a background of Rev St st; 10-rnd repeat)

1/3/1 LC: See key.

Rnd 1: K1, [p1, k1] twice.

Rnd 2: K2, p1, k2.

Rnd 3: 1/3/1 LC.

Rnd 4: Repeat Rnd 2.

Rnds 5–10: Repeat Rnds 1 and 2 three times.

Repeat Rnds 1–10 for Seeded 5-Stitch Cross in the Round.

FLAT AND IN THE ROUND

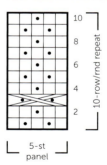

 1/3/1 LC: 1 over 3 over 1 Left Cross. Slip 1 st to first cable needle, hold to front, slip 3 sts to second cable needle, hold to back, k1, [p1, k1, p1] from second cable needle, k1 from first cable needle.

4-Stitch Cross Texture

(TWO-SIDED)

....

FLAT

(multiple of 6 sts + 2; 6-row repeat)

1/2/1 RC: See key.

Row 1 (RS): K2, *p4, k2; repeat from * to end.

Row 2: Knit.

Row 3: P2, *1/2/1 RC, p2; repeat from * to end.

Row 4: K2, *p1, k2; repeat from * to end.

Row 5: Repeat Row 1.

Row 6: P2, *k4, p2; repeat from * to end.

Repeat Rows 1–6 for 4-Stitch Cross Texture Flat.

IN THE ROUND

(multiple of 6 sts; 6-rnd repeat)

1/2/1 RC: See key.

Rnd 1: *K2, p4; repeat from * to end.

Rnd 2: Purl.

Rnd 3: *P2, 1/2/1 RC; repeat from * to end.

Rnd 4: *P2, k1; repeat from * to end.

Rnds 5 and 6: Repeat Rnd 1.

Repeat Rnds 1–6 for 4-Stitch Cross Texture in the Round.

FLAT

 1/2/1 RC: 1 over 2 over 1 Right Cross. Slip 1 st to first cable needle, hold to back, slip 2 sts to second cable needle, hold behind first cable needle, k1, p2 from second cable needle, k1 from first cable needle.

IN THE ROUND

Front (RS)

Back (WS)

BOTTOM-UP IN THE ROUND

(multiple of 13 sts; 14-rnd repeat)

Rnds 1–4: *P1, k5, p1, k6; repeat from * to end.
Rnd 5: *P1, yo, ssk, k1, k2tog, yo, p1, k6; repeat from * to end.
Rnd 6: Repeat Rnd 1.
Rnd 7: *P1, k1, yo, s2kp2, yo, k1, p1, k6; repeat from * to end.
Rnds 8–12: Repeat Rnd 1.
Rnd 13: *P1, k5, p1, C6F; repeat from * to end.
Rnd 14: Repeat Rnd 1.
Repeat Rnds 1–14 for Eyelets and Cables Bottom-Up in the Round.

TOP-DOWN FLAT

(multiple of 13 sts + 7; 14-row repeat)

Row 1 (RS): P1, k5, p1, *C6F, p1, k5, p1; repeat from * to end.
Row 2 and all WS Rows: Knit the knit sts and purl the purl sts as they face you; purl all yos.
Rows 3 and 5: Repeat Row 2.
Row 7: P1, k1, yo, s2kp2, yo, k1, p1, *k6, p1, k1, yo, s2kp2, yo, k1, p1; repeat from * to end.
Row 9: P1, yo, k2tog, k1, ssk, yo, p1, *k6, p1, yo, k2tog, k1, ssk, yo, p1; repeat from * to end.
Rows 11–14: Repeat Row 2.
Repeat Rows 1–14 for Eyelets and Cables Top-Down Flat.

TOP-DOWN IN THE ROUND

(multiple of 13 sts; 14-rnd repeat)

Rnd 1: *P1, k5, p1, C6F; repeat from * to end.
Rnd 2 and all Even-Numbered Rnds: Knit the knit sts and purl the purl sts as they face you; purl all yos.
Rnds 3 and 5: Repeat Rnd 2.
Rnd 7: *P1, k1, yo, s2kp2, yo, k1, p1, k6; repeat from * to end.
Rnd 9: *P1, yo, k2tog, k1, ssk, yo, p1, k6; repeat from * to end.
Rnds 11–14: Repeat Rnd 2.
Repeat Rnds 1–14 for Eyelets and Cables Top-Down in the Round.

Eyelets and Cables

BOTTOM-UP FLAT

(multiple of 13 sts + 7; 14-row repeat)

Row 1 (RS): P1, k5, p1, *k6, p1, k5, p1; repeat from * to end.
Row 2 and all WS Rows: Knit the knit sts and purl the purl sts as they face you; purl all yos.
Row 3: Repeat Row 1.
Row 5: P1, yo, ssk, k1, k2tog, yo, p1, *k6, p1, yo, ssk, k1, k2tog, yo, p1; repeat from * to end.
Row 7: P1, k1, yo, s2kp2, yo, k1, p1, *k6, p1, k1, yo, s2kp2, yo, k1, p1; repeat from * to end.
Rows 9 and 11: Repeat Row 2.
Row 13: P1, k5, p1, *C6F, p1, k5, p1; repeat from * to end.
Row 14: Repeat Row 2.
Repeat Rows 1–14 for Eyelets and Cables Bottom-Up Flat.

BOTTOM-UP FLAT

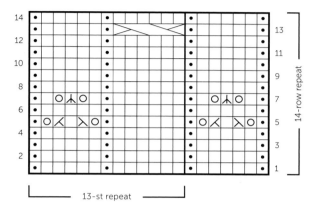

14-row repeat

13-st repeat

BOTTOM-UP IN THE ROUND

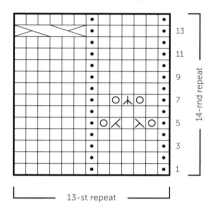

14-rnd repeat

13-st repeat

TOP-DOWN FLAT

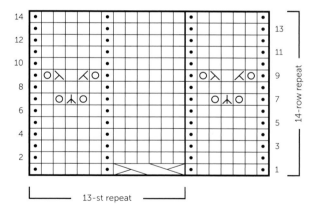

14-row repeat

13-st repeat

TOP-DOWN IN THE ROUND

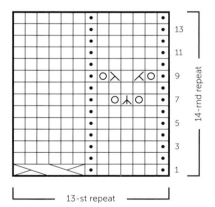

14-rnd repeat

13-st repeat

Twists and Cables

···

FLAT

(multiple of 12 sts + 8; 4-row repeat)

Row 1 (RS): P1, k1, p1, RC, p1, k1, p1, *k4, p1, k1, p1, RC, p1, k1, p1; repeat from * to end.

Row 2: K1, p1b, k1, p2, k1, p1b, k1, *p4, k1, p1b, k1, p2, k1, p1b, k1; repeat from * to end.

Row 3: P1, k1, p1, RC, p1, k1, p1, *C4B, p1, k1, p1, RC, p1, k1, p1; repeat from * to end.

Row 4: Repeat Row 2.

Repeat Rows 1–4 for Twists and Cables Flat.

IN THE ROUND

(multiple of 12 sts; 4-rnd repeat)

Rnd 1: *P1, k1, p1, RC, p1, k1, p1, k4; repeat from * to end.

Rnd 2: *P1, k1b, p1, k2, p1, k1b, p1, k4; repeat from * to end.

Rnd 3: *P1, k1, p1, RC, p1, k1, p1, C4B; repeat from * to end.

Rnd 4: Repeat Rnd 2.

Repeat Rnds 1–4 for Twists and Cables in the Round.

FLAT

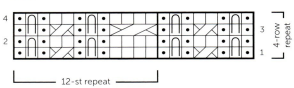

P1b on WS, k1b on RS.
K1

IN THE ROUND

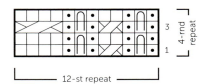

Crossed Checkerboard

FLAT

(multiple of 8 sts + 4; 16-row repeat)

Row 1 (RS): Knit.

Row 2: K4, *p4, k4; repeat from * to end.

Row 3: K4, *[RC] twice, k4; repeat from * to end.

Row 4: Repeat Row 2.

Rows 5–8: Repeat Rows 3 and 4 twice.

Row 9: Knit.

Row 10: P4, *k4, p4; repeat from * to end.

Row 11: [RC] twice, *k4, [RC] twice; repeat from * to end.

Row 12: Repeat Row 10.

Rows 13–16: Repeat Rows 11 and 12 twice.

Repeat Rows 1–16 for Crossed Checkerboard Flat.

IN THE ROUND

(multiple of 8 sts; 16-rnd repeat)

Rnd 1: Knit.

Rnd 2: *P4, k4; repeat from * to end.

Rnd 3: *K4, [RC] twice; repeat from * to end.

Rnd 4: Repeat Rnd 2.

Rnds 5–8: Repeat Rnds 3 and 4 twice.

Rnd 9: Knit.

Rnd 10: *K4, p4; repeat from * to end.

Rnd 11: *[RC] twice, k4; repeat from * to end.

Rnd 12: Repeat Rnd 10.

Rnds 13–16: Repeat Rnds 11 and 12 twice.

Repeat Rnds 1–16 for Crossed Checkerboard in the Round.

FLAT

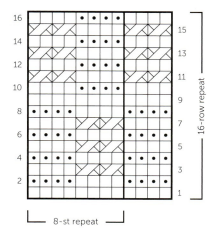

8-st repeat

16-row repeat

IN THE ROUND

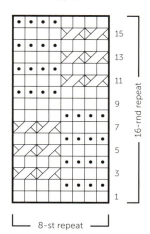

8-st repeat

16-rnd repeat

Long and Short Cables

FLAT

(multiple of 10 sts + 6; 12-row repeat)

Row 1 (RS): P1, k1-tbl, p2, k1-tbl, p1, *C4F, p1, k1-tbl, p2, k1-tbl, p1; repeat from * to end.

Row 2: K1, p1, k2, p1, k1, *p4, k1, p1, k2, p1, k1; repeat from * to end.

Rows 3–6: Repeat Rows 1 and 2 twice.

Row 7: P1, k1-tbl, p2, k1-tbl, p1, *k4, p1, k1-tbl, p2, k1-tbl, p1; repeat from * to end.

Row 8: Repeat Row 2.

Rows 9–12: Repeat Rows 7 and 8 twice.

Repeat Rows 1–12 for Long and Short Cables Flat.

IN THE ROUND

(multiple of 10 sts; 12-rnd repeat)

Rnd 1: *P1, k1-tbl, p2, k1-tbl, p1, C4F; repeat from * to end.

Rnd 2: *P1, k1, p2, k1, p1, k4; repeat from * to end.

Rnds 3–6: Repeat Rnds 1 and 2 twice.

Rnd 7: *P1, k1-tbl, p2, k1-tbl, p1, k4; repeat from * to end.

Rnd 8: Repeat Rnd 2.

Rnds 9–12: Repeat Rnds 7 and 8 twice.

Repeat Rnds 1–12 for Long and Short Cables in the Round.

FLAT

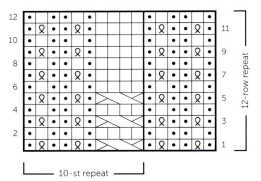

IN THE ROUND

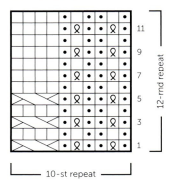

Mini Honeycomb

FLAT

(panel of 8 sts worked on a background of Rev St st; 4-row repeat)

Row 1 (RS): [RC, LC] twice.
Row 2: Purl.
Row 3: [LC, RC] twice.
Row 4: Purl.
Repeat Rows 1–4 for Mini Honeycomb Flat.

IN THE ROUND

(panel of 8 sts worked on a background of Rev St st; 4-rnd repeat)

Rnd 1: [RC, LC] twice.
Rnd 2: Knit.
Rnd 3: [LC, RC] twice.
Rnd 4: Knit.
Repeat Rnds 1–4 for Mini Honeycomb in the Round.

FLAT AND IN THE ROUND

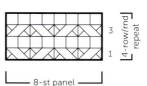

8-st panel

Open Wishbone Cables

BOTTOM-UP FLAT

(multiple of 26 sts + 16; 16-row repeat)

Row 1 (RS): P4, C4B, C4F, *p5, C4B, C4F; repeat from * to last 4 sts, p4.

Row 2: K4, p8, *k5, p8; repeat from * to last 4 sts, k4.

Row 3: P4, k8, *p4, 2/1 RPC, p4, 2/1 LPC, p4, k8; repeat from * to last 4 sts, p4.

Row 4: K4, p8, k4, *p10, k4, p8, k4; repeat from * to end.

Row 5: P4, C4B, C4F, *p4, k2, p6, k2, p4, C4B, C4F; repeat from * to last 4 sts, p4.

Row 6: Repeat Row 4.

Row 7: P4, k8, *p4, 2/1 LPC, p4, 2/1 RPC, p4, k8; repeat from * to last 4 sts, p4.

Row 8: Repeat Row 2.

Row 9: P4, C4B, C4F, *p5, C4B, C4F; repeat from * to last 4 sts, p4.

Row 10: Repeat Row 2.

Row 11: P3, 2/1 RPC, p4, 2/1 LPC, *p4, k8, p4, 2/1 RPC, p4, 2/1 LPC; repeat from * to last 3 sts, p3.

Row 12: K3, p10, *k4, p8, k4, p10; repeat from * to last 3 sts, k3.

Row 13: P3, k2, p6, k2, *p4, C4B, C4F, p4, k2, p6, k2; repeat from * to last 3 sts, p3.

Row 14: Repeat Row 12.

Row 15: P3, 2/1 LPC, p4, 2/1 RPC, *p4, k8, p4, 2/1 LPC, p4, 2/1 RPC; repeat from * to last 3 sts, p3.

Row 16: Repeat Row 2.

Repeat Rows 1–16 for Open Wishbone Cables Bottom-Up Flat.

BOTTOM-UP IN THE ROUND

(multiple of 26 sts; 16-rnd repeat)

Rnd 1: P4, C4B, C4F, *p5, C4B, C4F; repeat from * to last st, p1.

Rnd 2: P4, k8, *p5, k8; repeat from * to last st, k1.

Rnd 3: *P4, k8, p4, 2/1 RPC, p4, 2/1 LPC; repeat from * end.

Rnd 4: *P4, k8, p4, k10; repeat from * to end.

Rnd 5: *P4, C4B, C4F, p4, k2, p6, k2; repeat from * to end.

Rnd 6: Repeat Rnd 4.

Rnd 7: *P4, k8, p4, 2/1 LPC, p4, 2/1 RPC; repeat from * to end.

Rnd 8: Repeat Rnd 2.

Rnd 9: P4, C4B, C4F, *p5, C4B, C4F; repeat from * to last st, p1.

Rnd 10: Repeat Rnd 2.

Rnd 11: P3, 2/1 RPC, p4, 2/1 LPC, p4, k8, *p4, 2/1 RPC, p4, 2/1 LPC, p4, k8; repeat from * to last st, p1.

Rnd 12: P3, k10, p4, k8, *p4, k10, p4, k8; repeat from * to last st, p1.

Rnd 13: P3, k2, p6, k2, p4, C4B, C4F, *p4, k2, p6, k2, p4, C4B, C4F; repeat from * to last st, p1.

Rnd 14: Repeat Rnd 12.

Rnd 15: P3, 2/1 LPC, p4, 2/1 RPC, p4, k8, *p4, 2/1 LPC, p4, 2/1 RPC, p4, k8; repeat from * to last st, p1.

Rnd 16: Repeat Rnd 2.

Repeat Rnds 1–16 for Open Wishbone Cables Bottom-Up in the Round.

BOTTOM-UP FLAT

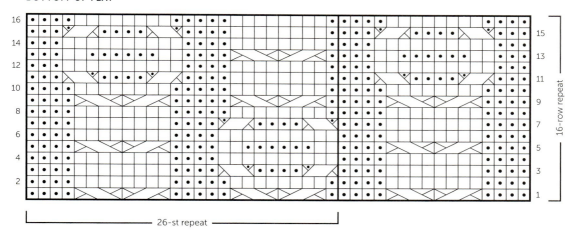

26-st repeat

16-row repeat

BOTTOM-UP IN THE ROUND

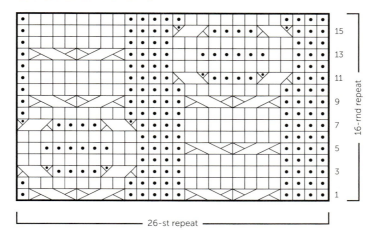

26-st repeat

16-rnd repeat

TOP-DOWN FLAT

(multiple of 26 sts + 16; 16-row repeat)

Row 1 (RS): P3, 2/1 RPC, p4, 2/1 LPC, *p4, k8, p4, 2/1 RPC, p4, 2/1 LPC; repeat from * to last 3 sts, p3.

Row 2: K3, p10, *k4, p8, k4, p10; repeat from * to last 3 sts, k3.

Row 3: P3, k2, p6, k2, *p4, C4F, C4B, p4, k2, p6, k2; repeat from * to last 3 sts, p3.

Row 4: Repeat Row 2.

Row 5: P3, 2/1 LPC, p4, 2/1 RPC, *p4, k8, p4, 2/1 LPC, p4, 2/1 RPC; repeat from * to last 3 sts, p3.

Row 6: K4, p8, *k5, p8; repeat from * to last 4 sts, k4.

Row 7: P4, C4F, C4B, *p5, C4F, C4B; repeat from * to last 4 sts, p4.

Row 8: Repeat Row 6..

Row 9: P4, k8, *p4, 2/1 RPC, p4, 2/1 LPC, p4, k8; repeat from * to last 4 sts, p4.

Row 10: K4, p8, k4, *p10, k4, p8, k4; repeat from * to end.

Row 11: P4, C4F, C4B, *p4, k2, p6, k2, p4, C4F, C4B; repeat from * to last 4 sts, p4.

Row 12: Repeat Row 10.

Row 13: P4, k8, *p4, 2/1 LPC, p4, 2/1 RPC, p4, k8; repeat from * to last 4 sts, p4.

Row 14: Repeat Row 6.

Row 15: P4, C4F, C4B, *p5, C4F, C4B; repeat from * to last 4 sts, p4.

Row 16: Repeat Row 6.

Repeat Rows 1–16 for Open Wishbone Cables Top-Down Flat.

TOP-DOWN IN THE ROUND

(multiple of 26 sts; 16-rnd repeat)

Rnd 1: P3, 2/1 RPC, p4, 2/1 LPC, p4, k8, *p4, 2/1 RPC, p4, 2/1 LPC, p4, k8; repeat from * to last st, p1.

Rnd 2: P3, k10, p4, k8, *p4, k10, p4, k8; repeat from * to last st, p1.

Rnd 3: P3, k2, p6, k2, p4, C4F, C4B, *p4, k2, p6, k2, p4, C4F, C4B; repeat from * to last st, p1.

Rnd 4: Repeat Rnd 2.

Rnd 5: P3, 2/1 LPC, p4, 2/1 RPC, p4, k8, *p4, 2/1 LPC, p4, 2/1 RPC, p4, k8; repeat from * to last st, p1.

Rnd 6: P4, k8, *p5, k8; repeat from * to last st, p1.

Rnd 7: P4, C4F, C4B, *p5, C4F, C4B; repeat from * to last st, p1.

Rnd 8: Repeat Rnd 6.

Rnd 9: *P4, k8, p4, 2/1 RPC, p4, 2/1 LPC; repeat from * to end.

Rnd 10: *P4, k8, p4, k10; repeat from * to end.

Rnd 11: *P4, C4F, C4B, p4, k2, p6, k2; repeat from * to end.

Rnd 12: Repeat Rnd 10.

Rnd 13: *P4, k8, p4, 2/1 LPC, p4, 2/1 RPC; repeat from * to end.

Rnd 14: Repeat Rnd 6.

Rnd 15: P4, C4F, C4B, *p5, C4F, C4B; repeat from * to last st, p1.

Rnd 16: Repeat Rnd 6.

Repeat Rnds 1–16 for Open Wishbone Cables Top-Down in the Round.

TOP-DOWN FLAT

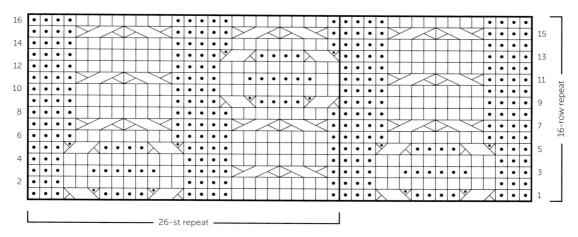

26-st repeat

16-row repeat

TOP-DOWN IN THE ROUND

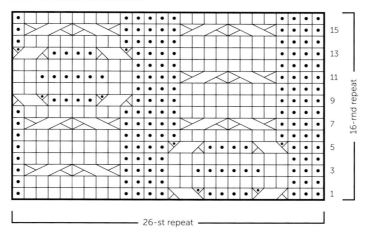

26-st repeat

16-rnd repeat

Goblets
....

BOTTOM-UP FLAT

(panel of 16 sts worked on a background of Rev St st; 12-row repeat)

Row 1 (RS): P5, C6B, p5.
Row 2: K5, p6, k5.
Row 3: P4, 3/1 RC, 3/1 LC, p4.
Row 4: K4, p3, k2, p3, k4.
Row 5: P3, 3/1 RC, k2, 3/1 LC, p3.
Row 6: K3, p3, k4, p3, k3.
Row 7: P2, 3/1 RC, k4, 3/1 LC, p2.
Row 8: K2, p3, k6, p3, k2.
Row 9: P1, 3/1 RC, k6, 3/1 LC, p1.
Row 10: K1, p3, k8, p3, k1.
Row 11: 3/1 RC, k8, 3/1 LC.
Row 12: P3, k2, p6, k2, p3.
Repeat Rows 1–12 for Goblets Bottom-Up Flat.

BOTTOM-UP IN THE ROUND

(panel of 16 sts worked on a background of Rev St st; 12-rnd repeat)

Rnd 1: P5, C6B, p5.
Rnd 2: P5, k6, p5.
Rnd 3: P4, 3/1 RC, 3/1 LC, p4.
Rnd 4: P4, k3, p2, k3, p4.
Rnd 5: P3, 3/1 RC, k2, 3/1 LC, p3.
Rnd 6: P3, k3, p4, k3, p3.
Rnd 7: P2, 3/1 RC, k4, 3/1 LC, p2.
Rnd 8: P2, k3, p6, k3, p2.
Rnd 9: P1, 3/1 RC, k6, 3/1 LC, p1.
Rnd 10: P1, k3, p8, k3, p1.
Rnd 11: 3/1 RC, k8, 3/1 LC.
Rnd 12: K3, p2, k6, p2, k3.
Repeat Rnds 1–12 for Goblets Bottom-Up in the Round.

TOP-DOWN FLAT

(panel of 16 sts worked on a background of Rev St st; 12-row repeat)

Row 1 (RS): 3/1 LC, k8, 3/1 RC.
Row 2: K1, p3, k8, p3, k1.
Row 3: P1, 3/1 LC, k6, 3/1 RC, p1.
Row 4: K2, p3, k6, p3, k2.
Row 5: P2, 3/1 LC, k4, 3/1 RC, p2.
Row 6: K3, p3, k4, p3, k3.
Row 7: P3, 3/1 LC, k2, 3/1 RC, p3.
Row 8: K4, p3, k2, p3, k4.
Row 9: P4, 3/1 LC, 3/1 RC, p4.
Row 10: K5, p6, k5.
Row 11: P5, C6B, p5.
Row 12: P3, k2, p6, k2, p3.
Repeat Rows 1–12 for Goblets Top-Down Flat.

TOP-DOWN IN THE ROUND

(panel of 16 sts worked on a background of Rev St st; 12-rnd repeat)

Rnd 1: 3/1 LC, k8, 3/1 RC.
Rnd 2: P1, k3, p8, k3, p1.
Rnd 3: P1, 3/1 LC, k6, 3/1 RC, p1.
Rnd 4: P2, k3, p6, k3, p2.
Rnd 5: P2, 3/1 LC, k4, 3/1 RC, p2.
Rnd 6: P3, k3, p4, k3, p3.
Rnd 7: P3, 3/1 LC, k2, 3/1 RC, p3.
Rnd 8: P4, k3, p2, k3, p4.
Rnd 9: P4, 3/1 LC, 3/1 RC, p4.
Rnd 10: P5, k6, p5.
Rnd 11: P5, C6B, p5.
Rnd 12: K3, p2, k6, p2, k3.
Repeat Rnds 1–12 for Goblets Top-Down in the Round.

BOTTOM-UP FLAT AND IN THE ROUND

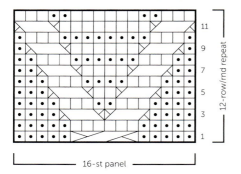

12-row/rnd repeat

16-st panel

TOP-DOWN FLAT AND IN THE ROUND

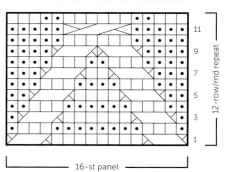

12-row/rnd repeat

16-st panel

IN THE ROUND

(panel of 10 sts worked on a background of Rev St st;
20-rnd repeat)

Rnd 1: K2, p6, k2.

Rnd 2 and all Even-Numbered Rnds: Knit the knit sts and
purl the purl sts as they face you.

Rnd 3: 2/1 LPC, p4, 2/1 RPC.

Rnd 5: P1, 2/1 LPC, p2, 2/1 RPC, p1.

Rnd 7: P2, 2/1 LPC, 2/1 RPC, p2.

Rnds 9, 11, and 13: P3, C4B, p3.

Rnd 15: P2, 2/1 RPC, 2/1 LPC, p2.

Rnd 17: P1, 2/1 RPC, p2, 2/1 LPC, p1.

Rnd 19: 2/1 RPC, p4, 2/1 LPC.

Rnd 20: Repeat Rnd 2.

Repeat Rnds 1–20 for Open and Closed Twists in the
Round.

Open and Closed Twists

....

FLAT

(panel of 10 sts worked on a background of Rev St st;
20-row repeat)

Row 1 (RS): K2, p6, k2.

Row 2 and all WS Rows: Knit the knit sts and purl the purl sts
as they face you.

Row 3: 2/1 LPC, p4, 2/1 RPC.

Row 5: P1, 2/1 LPC, p2, 2/1 RPC, p1.

Row 7: P2, 2/1 LPC, 2/1 RPC, p2.

Rows 9, 11, and 13: P3, C4B, p3.

Row 15: P2, 2/1 RPC, 2/1 LPC, p2.

Row 17: P1, 2/1 RPC, p2, 2/1 LPC, p1.

Row 19: 2/1 RPC, p4, 2/1 LPC.

Row 20: Repeat Row 2.

Repeat Rows 1–20 for Open and Closed Twists Flat.

FLAT AND IN THE ROUND

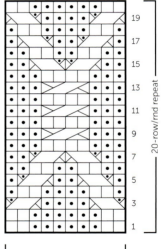

Trees

BOTTOM-UP FLAT

(panel of 9 sts worked on a background of Rev St st; 6-row repeat)

Row 1 (RS): P2, RPC, k1-tbl, LPC, p2.
Row 2: K2, p1, [k1, p1] twice, k2.
Row 3: P1, RPC, p1, k1-tbl, p1, LPC, p1.
Row 4: K1, p1, [k2, p1] twice, k1.
Row 5: RPC, p2, k1-tbl, p2, LPC.
Row 6: P1, [k3, p1] twice.
Repeat Rows 1–6 for Trees Bottom-Up Flat.

BOTTOM-UP IN THE ROUND

(panel of 9 sts worked on a background of Rev St st; 6-rnd repeat)

Rnd 1: P2, RPC, k1-tbl, LPC, p2.
Rnd 2: P2, k1, [p1, k1] twice, p2.
Rnd 3: P1, RPC, p1, k1-tbl, p1, LPC, p1.
Rnd 4: P1, k1, [p2, k1] twice, p1.
Rnd 5: RPC, p2, k1-tbl, p2, LPC.
Rnd 6: K1, [p3, k1] twice.
Repeat Rnds 1–6 for Trees Bottom-Up in the Round.

TOP-DOWN FLAT

(panel of 9 sts worked on a background of Rev St st; 6-row repeat)

Row 1 (RS): LPC, p2, k1-tbl, p2, RPC.
Row 2: K1, p1, [k2, p1] twice, k1.
Row 3: P1, LPC, p1, k1-tbl, p1, RPC, p1.
Row 4: K2, p1, [k1, p1] twice, k2.
Row 5: P2, LPC, k1-tbl, RPC, p2.
Row 6: P1, [k3, p1] twice.
Repeat Rows 1–6 for Trees Top-Down Flat.

TOP-DOWN IN THE ROUND

(panel of 9 sts worked on a background of Rev St st; 6-rnd repeat)

Rnd 1: LPC, p2, k1-tbl, p2, RPC.
Rnd 2: P1, k1, [p2, k1] twice, p1.
Rnd 3: P1, LPC, p1, k1-tbl, p1, RPC, p1.
Rnd 4: P2, k1, [p1, k1] twice, p2.
Rnd 5: P2, LPC, k1-tbl, RPC, p2.
Rnd 6: K1, [p3, k1] twice.
Repeat Rnds 1–6 for Trees Top-Down in the Round.

BOTTOM-UP FLAT AND IN THE ROUND

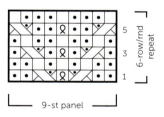

6-row/rnd repeat

9-st panel

TOP-DOWN FLAT AND IN THE ROUND

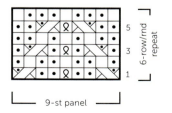

6-row/rnd repeat

9-st panel

Beetle Cable

BOTTOM-UP FLAT

(panel of 18 sts worked on a background of Rev St st;
16-row repeat)

Row 1 (RS): LPC, p3, C4B, C4F, p3, RPC.

Row 2 and all WS Rows: Knit the knit sts and purl the purl sts
as they face you.

Row 3: P1, LPC, p2, k8, p2, RPC, p1.

Row 5: P2, LPC, p1, C4B, C4F, p1, RPC, p2.

Row 7: P3, LPC, k8, RPC, p3.

Row 9: P3, RPC, k8, LPC, p3.

Row 11: P2, RPC, p1, k8, p1, LPC, p2.

Row 13: P1, RPC, p2, C4B, C4F, p2, LPC, p1.

Row 15: RPC, p3, k8, p3, LPC.

Row 16: Repeat Row 2.

Repeat Rows 1–16 for Beetle Cable Bottom-Up Flat.

BOTTOM-UP IN THE ROUND

(panel of 18 sts worked on a background of Rev St st;
16-rnd repeat)

Rnd 1: LPC, p3, C4B, C4F, p3, RPC.

Rnd 2 and all Even-Numbered Rnds: Knit the knit sts and
purl the purl sts as they face you.

Rnd 3: P1, LPC, p2, k8, p2, RPC, p1.

Rnd 5: P2, LPC, p1, C4B, C4F, p1, RPC, p2.

Rnd 7: P3, LPC, k8, RPC, p3.

Rnd 9: P3, RPC, k8, LPC, p3.

Rnd 11: P2, RPC, p1, k8, p1, LPC, p2.

Rnd 13: P1, RPC, p2, C4B, C4F, p2, LPC, p1.

Rnd 15: RPC, p3, k8, p3, LPC.

Rnd 16: Repeat Rnd 2.

Repeat Rnds 1–16 for Beetle Cable Bottom-Up in
the Round.

TOP-DOWN FLAT

(panel of 18 sts worked on a background of Rev St st;
16-row repeat)

Row 1 (RS): LPC, p3, k8, p3, RPC.

Row 2 and all WS Rows: Knit the knit sts and purl the purl sts
as they face you.

Row 3: P1, LPC, p2, C4F, C4B, p2, RPC, p1.

Row 5: P2, LPC, p1, k8, p1, RPC, p2.

Row 7: P3, LPC, k8, RPC, p3.

Row 9: P3, RPC, k8, LPC, p3.

Row 11: P2, RPC, p1, C4F, C4B, p1, LPC, p2.

Row 13: P1, RPC, p2, k8, p2, LPC, p1.

Row 15: RPC, p3, C4F, C4B, p3, LPC.

Row 16: Repeat Row 2.

Repeat Rows 1–16 for Beetle Cable Top-Down Flat.

TOP-DOWN IN THE ROUND

(panel of 18 sts worked on a background of Rev St st;
16-rnd repeat)

Rnd 1: LPC, p3, k8, p3, RPC.

Rnd 2 and all Even-Numbered Rnds: Knit the knit sts and
purl the purl sts as they face you.

Rnd 3: P1, LPC, p2, C4F, C4B, p2, RPC, p1.

Rnd 5: P2, LPC, p1, k8, p1, RPC, p2.

Rnd 7: P3, LPC, k8, RPC, p3.

Rnd 9: P3, RPC, k8, LPC, p3.

Rnd 11: P2, RPC, p1, C4F, C4B, p1, LPC, p2.

Rnd 13: P1, RPC, p2, k8, p2, LPC, p1.

Rnd 15: RPC, p3, C4F, C4B, p3, LPC.

Rnd 16: Repeat Rnd 2.

Repeat Rnds 1–16 for Beetle Cable Top-Down in the
Round.

BOTTOM-UP FLAT AND IN THE ROUND

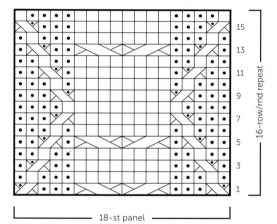

TOP-DOWN FLAT AND IN THE ROUND

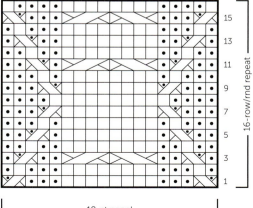

(panel of 12 sts worked on a background of Rev St st; 16-rnd repeat)

LTPC: See key.
RTPC: See key.
Rnd 1: K3, 2/1 RTPC, 2/1 LTPC, k3.
Rnd 2: K3, [k1-tbl] twice, p2, [k1-tbl] twice, k3.
Rnd 3: K2, 2/1 RTPC, k2, 2/1 LTPC, k2.
Rnd 4: K2, [k1-tbl] twice, p4, [k1-tbl] twice, k2.
Rnd 5: K1, 2/1 RTPC, k4, 2/1 LTPC, k1.
Rnd 6: K1, [k1-tbl] twice, p6, [k1-tbl] twice, k1.
Rnd 7: 2/1 RTPC, k6, 2/1 LTPC.
Rnd 8: [K1-tbl] twice, p8, [k1-tbl] twice.
Rnd 9: 2/1 LTPC, k6, 2/1 RTPC.
Rnd 10: Repeat Rnd 6.
Rnd 11: K1, 2/1 LTPC, k4, 2/1 RTPC, k1.
Rnd 12: Repeat Rnd 4.
Rnd 13: K2, 2/1 LTPC, k2, 2/1 RTPC, k2.
Rnd 14: Repeat Rnd 2.
Rnd 15: K3, 2/1 LTPC, 2/1 RTPC, k3.
Rnd 16: K4, [k1-tbl] 4 times, k4.
Repeat Rnds 1–16 for Diamond and Garter Cable in the Round.

Diamond and Garter Cable

....

FLAT

(panel of 12 sts worked on a background of Rev St st; 16-row repeat)

LTPC: See key.
RTPC: See key.
Row 1 (RS): K3, 2/1 RTPC, 2/1 LTPC, k3.
Row 2: P3, [p1-tbl] twice, k2, [p1-tbl] twice, p3.
Row 3: K2, 2/1 RTPC, k2, 2/1 LTPC, k2.
Row 4: P2, [p1-tbl] twice, k4, [p1-tbl] twice, p2.
Row 5: K1, 2/1 RTPC, k4, 2/1 LTPC, k1.
Row 6: P1, [p1-tbl] twice, k6, [p1-tbl] twice, p1.
Row 7: 2/1 RTPC, k6, 2/1 LTPC.
Row 8: [P1-tbl] twice, k8, [p1-tbl] twice.
Row 9: 2/1 LTPC, k6, 2/1 RTPC.
Row 10: Repeat Row 6.
Row 11: K1, 2/1 LTPC, k4, 2/1 RTPC, k1.
Row 12: Repeat Row 4.
Row 13: K2, 2/1 LTPC, k2, 2/1 RTPC, k2.
Row 14: Repeat Row 2.
Row 15: K3, 2/1 LTPC, 2/1 RTPC, k3.
Row 16: P4, [p1-tbl] 4 times, p4.
Repeat Rows 1–16 for Diamond and Garter Cable Flat.

FLAT AND IN THE ROUND

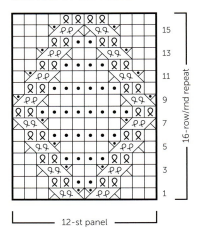

12-st panel

16-row/rnd repeat

 2/1 RTPC: 2 over 1 Right Twisted Purl Cross.
Slip 1 st to cable needle, hold to back, [k1-tbl] twice, p1 from cable needle.

2/1 LTPC: 2 over 1 Left Twisted Purl Cross.
Slip 2 sts to cable needle, hold to front, p1, [k1-tbl] twice from cable needle.

Open Medallion Cable

BOTTOM-UP FLAT

(panel of 6 sts worked on a background of Rev St st; 8-row repeat)

Row 1 (RS): K1, yo, ssk, k2tog, yo, k1.
Row 2 and all WS Rows: Purl.
Row 3: 1/2 RC, 1/2 LC.
Rows 5 and 7: Repeat Row 1.
Row 8: Purl.
Repeat Rows 1–8 for Open Medallion Cable Bottom-Up Flat.

BOTTOM-UP IN THE ROUND

(panel of 6 sts worked on a background of Rev St st; 8-rnd repeat)

Rnd 1: K1, yo, ssk, k2tog, yo, k1.
Rnd 2 and all Even-Numbered Rnds: Knit.
Rnd 3: 1/2 RC, 1/2 LC.
Rnds 5 and 7: Repeat Rnd 1.
Rnd 8: Knit.
Repeat Rnds 1–8 for Open Medallion Cable Bottom-Up in the Round.

TOP-DOWN FLAT

(panel of 6 sts worked on a background of Rev St st; 8-row repeat)

Row 1 (RS): K1, yo, ssk, k2tog, yo, k1.
Row 2 and all WS Rows: Purl.
Row 3: Repeat Row 1.
Row 5: 1/2 LC, 1/2 RC.
Row 7: Repeat Row 1.
Row 8: Purl.
Repeat Rows 1–8 for Open Medallion Cable Top-Down Flat.

TOP-DOWN IN THE ROUND

(panel of 6 sts worked on a background of Rev St st; 8-rnd repeat)

Rnd 1: K1, yo, ssk, k2tog, yo, k1.
Rnd 2 and all Even-Numbered Rnds: Knit.
Rnd 3: Repeat Rnd 1.
Rnd 5: 1/2 LC, 1/2 RC.
Rnd 7: Repeat Rnd 1.
Rnd 8: Knit.
Repeat Rnds 1–8 for Open Medallion Cable Top-Down in the Round.

BOTTOM-UP FLAT AND IN THE ROUND

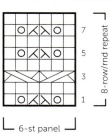

6-st panel

8-row/rnd repeat

TOP-DOWN FLAT AND IN THE ROUND

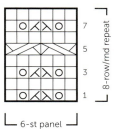

6-st panel

8-row/rnd repeat

Framed Moss and Bobble Cables

FLAT

(panel of 17 sts worked on a background of Rev St st; 20-row repeat)

Row 1 (RS): 2/1 LPC, k1, [p1, k1] 5 times, 2/1 RPC.

Row 2 and all WS Rows: Knit the knit sts and purl the purl sts as they face you; knit all bobbles.

Row 3: P1, 2/1 LPC, k1, [p1, k1] 4 times, 2/1 RPC, p1.

Row 5: P2, 2/1 LPC, k1, [p1, k1] 3 times, 2/1 RPC, p2.

Row 7: P3, 2/1 LPC, k1, [p1, k1] twice, 2/1 RPC, p3.

Row 9: P1, MB, p2, k2, p1, [k1, p1] twice, k2, p2, MB, p1.

Row 11: P3, 2/1 RPC, k1, [p1, k1] twice, 2/1 LPC, p3.

Row 13: P2, 2/1 RPC, k1, [p1, k1] 3 times, 2/1 LPC, p2.

Row 15: P1, 2/1 RPC, k1, [p1, k1] 4 times, 2/1 LPC, p1.

Row 17: 2/1 RPC, k1, [p1, k1] 5 times, 2/1 LPC.

Row 19: K3, p1, [k1, p1] 5 times, k3.

Row 20: Repeat Row 2.

Repeat Rows 1–20 for Framed Moss and Bobble Cables Flat.

IN THE ROUND

(panel of 17 sts worked on a background of Rev St st; 20-rnd repeat)

Rnd 1: 2/1 LPC, k1, [p1, k1] 5 times, 2/1 RPC.

Rnd 2 and all Even-Numbered Rnds: Knit the knit sts and purl the purl sts as they face you; purl all bobbles.

Rnd 3: P1, 2/1 LPC, k1, [p1, k1] 4 times, 2/1 RPC, p1.

Rnd 5: P2, 2/1 LPC, k1, [p1, k1] 3 times, 2/1 RPC, p2.

Rnd 7: P3, 2/1 LPC, k1, [p1, k1] twice, 2/1 RPC, p3.

Rnd 9: P1, MB, p2, k2, p1, [k1, p1] twice, k2, p2, MB, p1.

Rnd 11: P3, 2/1 RPC, k1, [p1, k1] twice, 2/1 LPC, p3.

Rnd 13: P2, 2/1 RPC, k1, [p1, k1] 3 times, 2/1 LPC, p2.

Rnd 15: P1, 2/1 RPC, k1, [p1, k1] 4 times, 2/1 LPC, p1.

Rnd 17: 2/1 RPC, k1, [p1, k1] 5 times, 2/1 LPC.

Rnd 19: K3, p1, [k1, p1] 5 times, k3.

Rnd 20: Repeat Rnd 2.

Repeat Rnds 1–20 for Framed Moss and Bobble Cables in the Round.

FLAT AND IN THE ROUND

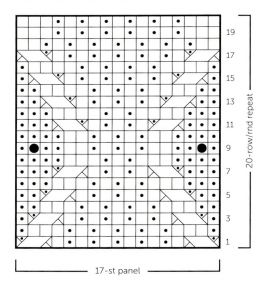

19 17 15 13 11 9 7 5 3 1

20-row/rnd repeat

17-st panel

● **MB:** Make Bobble.

Tiny Chains

FLAT

(panel of 4 sts worked on a background of Rev St st; 6-row repeat)

Row 1 (RS): P1, LC, p1.
Row 2: Knit the knit sts and purl the purl sts as they face you.
Row 3: RPC, LPC.
Row 4: Repeat Row 2.
Row 5: LPC, RPC.
Row 6: Repeat Row 2.
Repeat Rows 1–6 for Tiny Chains Flat.

IN THE ROUND

(panel of 4 sts worked on a background of Rev St st; 6-rnd repeat)

Rnd 1: P1, LC, p1.
Rnd 2: Knit the knit sts and purl the purl sts as they face you.
Rnd 3: RPC, LPC.
Rnd 4: Repeat Rnd 2.
Rnd 5: LPC, RPC.
Rnd 6: Repeat Rnd 2.
Repeat Rnds 1–6 for Tiny Chains in the Round.

FLAT AND IN THE ROUND

4-st panel

6-row/rnd repeat

Swatch shows Right Cross

Chain Mail

FLAT

(panel of 3 sts worked on a background of Rev St st; 2-row repeat)

LW: See key.

RW: See key.

Row 1 (RS): RW (for right cross) or LW (for left cross).

Row 2: Purl.

Repeat Rows 1 and 2 for Chain Mail Flat.

IN THE ROUND

(panel of 3 sts worked on a background of Rev St st; 2-rnd repeat)

LW: See key.

RW: See key.

Rnd 1: RW (for right cross) or LW (for left cross).

Rnd 2: Knit.

Repeat Rnds 1 and 2 for Chain Mail in the Round.

FLAT AND IN THE ROUND

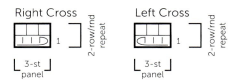

 RW: Right Wrap. Slip third st on left-hand needle over first 2 sts and onto tip of left-hand needle and knit it, k2.

 LW: Left Wrap. Slip 3 sts to right-hand needle; slip the first of these 3 sts back over the second and third sts and onto left-hand needle, slip the second and third sts back to left-hand needle; k2, k1-tbl.

Winding Rhombus

FLAT

(multiple of 10 sts + 5; 6-row repeat)

Row 1 (RS): P1, [k1-tbl, p1] twice, *RC, k1, LC, p1, [k1-tbl, p1] twice; repeat from * to end.

Row 2: K1, [p1-tbl, k1] twice, *p5, k1, [p1-tbl, k1] twice; repeat from * to end.

Row 3: P1, [k1-tbl, p1] twice, *LC, k1, RC, p1, [k1-tbl, p1] twice; repeat from * to end.

Row 4: [K1, p1-tbl] twice, *k2, p3, k2, p1-tbl, k1, p1-tbl; repeat from * to last st, k1.

Row 5: [P1, k1-tbl] twice, *p2, 1/2 RC, p2, k1-tbl, p1, k1-tbl; repeat from * to last st, p1.

Row 6: Repeat Row 4.

Repeat Rows 1–6 for Winding Rhombus Flat.

IN THE ROUND

(multiple of 10 sts; 6-rnd repeat)

Rnd 1: *P1, [k1-tbl, p1] twice, RC, k1, LC; repeat from * to end.

Rnd 2: *P1, [k1-tbl, p1] twice, k5; repeat from * to end.

Rnd 3: *P1, [k1-tbl, p1] twice, LC, k1, RC; repeat from * to end.

Rnd 4: [P1, k1-tbl] twice, p2, k3, *p2, k1-tbl, p1, k1-tbl, p2, k3; repeat from * to last st, p1.

Rnd 5: [P1, k1-tbl] twice, p2, 1/2 RC, *p2, k1-tbl, p1, k1-tbl, p2, 1/2 RC; repeat from * to last st, p1.

Rnd 6: Repeat Rnd 4.

Repeat Rnds 1–6 for Winding Rhombus in the Round.

FLAT

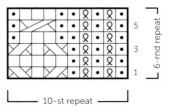

IN THE ROUND

Stacked Seed Hearts

BOTTOM-UP FLAT

(panel of 28 sts worked on a background of Rev St st; 12-row repeat)

LST: See key.

RST: See key.

3/1 LSC: See key.

3/1 RSC: See key.

3/3 LSC: See key.

3/3 RSC: See key.

Row 1 (RS): RST, p2, [3/1 LSC, p1, k1, 3/1 RSC] twice, p2, LST.

Row 2: P2, k3, [p1, k1] twice, [p2, k1] twice, [p1, k1] twice, p2, k1, p1, k3, p2.

Row 3: RST, p3, 3/1 LSC, 3/1 RSC, k1, p1, 3/1 LSC, 3/1 RSC, p3, LST.

Row 4: P2, k4, p1, k1, p2, k1, [p1, k1] twice, [p2, k1] twice, p1, k4, p2.

Row 5: RST, p4, 3/3 RSC, [p1, k1] twice, 3/3 LSC, p4, LST.

Row 6: P2, k4, p1, k1, p2, [k1, p1] 6 times, k4, p2.

Row 7: RST, p3, 3/1 RSC, [k1, p1] 5 times, 3/1 LSC, p3, LST.

Row 8: P2, k3, [p1, k1] 7 times, p2, k1, p1, k3, p2.

Row 9: RST, p2, 3/1 RSC, [p1, k1] 6 times, 3/1 LSC, p2, LST.

Row 10: P2, k2, p1, k1, p2, [k1, p1] 8 times, k2, p2.

Row 11: RST, p2, k1, p1, k2, p1, k1, p1, 3/3 RSC, [k1, p1] three times, k1, p2, LST.

Row 12: P2, k2, p1, k1, p2, [k1, p1] twice, [k1, p2] twice, [k1, p1] 3 times, k2, p2.

Repeat Rows 1–12 for Stacked Seed Hearts Bottom-Up Flat.

BOTTOM-UP IN THE ROUND

(panel of 28 sts worked on a background of Rev St st; 12-rnd repeat)

LST: See key.

RST: See key.

3/1 LSC: See key.

3/1 RSC: See key.

3/3 LSC: See key.

3/3 RSC: See key.

Rnd 1: RST, p2, [3/1 LSC, p1, k1, 3/1 RSC] twice, p2, LST.

Rnd 2: K2, p3, k1, p1, k2, p1, [k1, p1] twice, [k2, p1] twice, k1, p1, k1, p3, k2.

Rnd 3: RST, p3, 3/1 LSC, 3/1 RSC, k1, p1, 3/1 LSC, 3/1 RSC, p3, LST.

Rnd 4: K2, p4, k1, p1, [k2, p1] twice, [k1, p1] twice, k2, p1, k1, p4, k2.

Rnd 5: RST, p4, 3/3 RSC, [p1, k1] twice, 3/3 LSC, p4, LST.

Rnd 6: K2, p4, [k1, p1] 6 times, k2, p1, k1, p4, k2.

Rnd 7: RST, p3, 3/1 RSC, [k1, p1] 5 times, 3/1 LSC, p3, LST.

Rnd 8: K2, p3, k1, p1, k2, [p1, k1] 7 times, p3, k2.

Rnd 9: RST, p2, 3/1 RSC, [p1, k1] 6 times, 3/1 LSC, p2, LST.

Rnd 10: K2, p2, [k1, p1] 8 times, k2, p1, k1, p2, k2.

Rnd 11: RST, p2, k1, p1, k2, p1, k1, p1, 3/3 RSC, [k1, p1] 3 times, k1, p2, LST.

Rnd 12: K2, p2, [k1, p1] 3 times, [k2, p1] twice, [k1, p1] twice, k2, p1, k1, p2, k2.

Repeat Rnds 1–12 for Stacked Seed Hearts Bottom-Up in the Round.

BOTTOM-UP FLAT AND IN THE ROUND

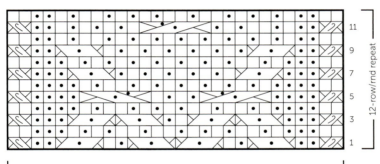

28-st panel

12-row/rnd repeat

 LST: Left Slipped Twist. Slip 2 sts one at a time knitwise to right-hand needle, slip second st on right-hand needle over first st onto tip of left-hand needle, insert left-hand needle from back to front into st on right-hand needle and knit this st tbl, then knit st on left-hand needle tbl.

 RST: Right Slipped Twist. Slip second st on left-hand needle over first st and onto tip of left-hand needle, k2 (slipped st and following st).

3/1 LSC: 3 over 1 Left Seeded Cross. Slip 3 sts to cable needle, hold to front, k1, (k1, p1, k1) from cable needle.

3/1 RSC: 3 over 1 Right Seeded Cross. Slip 1 st to cable needle, hold to back, k1, p1, k1, k1 from cable needle.

3/3 LSC: 3 over 3 Left Seeded Cross. Slip 3 sts to cable needle, hold to front, k1, p1, k1, (k1, p1, k1) from cable needle.

3/3 RSC: 3 over 3 Right Seeded Cross. Slip 3 sts to cable needle, hold to back, k1, p1, k1, (k1, p1, k1) from cable needle.

TOP-DOWN FLAT

(panel of 28 sts worked on a background of Rev St st; 12-row repeat)

LST: See key.
RST: See key.
3/1 LSC: See key.
3/1 RSC: See key.
3/3 LSC: See key.
3/3 RSC: See key.

Row 1 (RS): LST, p2, k1, [p1, k1] 3 times, 3/3 RSC, p1, k1, p1, k2, p1, k1, p2, RST.

Row 2: P2, k2, [p1, k1] 8 times, p2, k1, p1, k2, p2.

Row 3: LST, p2, 3/1 LSC, [k1, p1] 6 times, 3/1 RSC, p2, RST.

Row 4: P2, k3, p1, k1, p2, [k1, p1] 7 times, k3, p2.

Row 5: LST, p3, 3/1 LSC, [p1, k1] 5 times, 3/1 RSC, p3, RST.

Row 6: P2, k4, [p1, k1] 6 times, p2, k1, p1, k4, p2.

Row 7: LST, p4, 3/3 LSC, [k1, p1] twice, 3/3 RSC, p4, RST.

Row 8: P2, k4, p1, [k1, p2] twice, k1, [p1, k1] twice, p2, k1, p1, k4, p2.

Row 9: LST, p3, 3/1 RSC, 3/1 LSC, p1, k1, 3/1 RSC, 3/1 LSC, p3, RST.

Row 10: P2, k3, p1, k1, p2, k1, [p1, k1] twice, [p2, k1] twice, p1, k1, p1, k3, p2.

Row 11: LST, p2, [3/1 RSC, k1, p1, 3/1 LSC] twice, p2, RST.

Row 12: P2, k2, [p1, k1] 3 times, [p2, k1] twice, [p1, k1] twice, p2, k1, p1, k2, p2.

Repeat Rows 1–12 for Stacked Seed Hearts Top-Down Flat.

TOP-DOWN IN THE ROUND

(panel of 28 sts worked on a background of Rev St st; 12-rnd repeat)

LST: See key.
RST: See key.
3/1 LSC: See key.
3/1 RSC: See key.
3/3 LSC: See key.
3/3 RSC: See key.

Rnd 1: LST, p2, k1, [p1, k1] 3 times, 3/3 RSC, p1, k1, p1, k2, p1, k1, p2, RST.

Rnd 2: K2, p2, k1, p1, k2, [p1, k1] 8 times, p2, k2.

Rnd 3: LST, p2, 3/1 LSC, [k1, p1] 6 times, 3/1 RSC, p2, RST.

Rnd 4: K2, p3, [k1, p1] 7 times, k2, p1, k1, p3, k2.

Rnd 5: LST, p3, 3/1 LSC, [p1, k1] 5 times, 3/1 RSC, p3, RST.

Rnd 6: K2, p4, k1, p1, k2, [p1, k1] 6 times, p4, k2.

Rnd 7: LST, p4, 3/3 LSC, [k1, p1] twice, 3/3 RSC, p4, RST.

Rnd 8: K2, p4, k1, p1, k2, p1, [k1, p1] twice, [k2, p1] twice, k1, p4, k2.

Rnd 9: LST, p3, 3/1 RSC, 3/1 LSC, p1, k1, 3/1 RSC, 3/1 LSC, p3, RST.

Rnd 10: K2, p3, [k1, p1] twice, [k2, p1] twice, [k1, p1] twice, k2, p1, k1, p3, k2.

Rnd 11: LST, p2, [3/1 RSC, k1, p1, 3/1 LSC] twice, p2, RST.

Rnd 12: K2, p2, k1, p1, k2, p1, [k1, p1] twice, [k2, p1] twice, k1, [p1, k1] twice, p2, k2.

Repeat Rnds 1–12 for Stacked Seed Hearts Top-Down in the Round.

TOP-DOWN FLAT AND IN THE ROUND

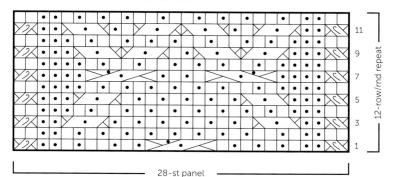

12-row/rnd repeat

11

9

7

5

3

1

28-st panel

 LST: Left Slipped Twist. Slip 2 sts one at a time knitwise to right-hand needle, slip second st on right-hand needle over first st onto tip of left-hand needle, insert left-hand needle from back to front into st on right-hand needle and knit this st tbl, then knit st on left-hand needle tbl.

 RST: Right Slipped Twist. Slip second st on left-hand needle over first st and onto tip of left-hand needle, k2 (slipped st and following st).

 3/1 LSC: 3 over 1 Left Seeded Cross. Slip 3 sts to cable needle, hold to front, k1, (k1, p1, k1) from cable needle.

 3/1 RSC: 3 over 1 Right Seeded Cross. Slip 1 st to cable needle, hold to back, k1, p1, k1, k1 from cable needle.

 3/3 LSC: 3 over 3 Left Seeded Cross. Slip 3 sts to cable needle, hold to front, k1, p1, k1, (k1, p1, k1) from cable needle.

 3/3 RSC: 3 over 3 Right Seeded Cross. Slip 3 sts to cable needle, hold to back, k1, p1, k1, (k1, p1, k1) from cable needle.

TOP-DOWN FLAT

(panel of 19 sts; 8-row repeat)

Row 1 (RS): K9, p1, k9.

Row 2 and all WS Rows: Knit the knit sts and purl the purl sts as they face you.

Row 3: C6B, k3, p1, C6B, k3.

Row 5: Repeat Row 1.

Row 7: K3, C6F, p1, k3, C6F.

Row 8: Repeat Row 2.

Repeat Rows 1–8 for 9-Stitch Braids Top-Down Flat.

TOP-DOWN IN THE ROUND

(panel of 19 sts; 8-rnd repeat)

Rnds 1 and 2: K9, p1, k9.

Rnd 3: C6B, k3, p1, C6B, k3.

Rnds 4–6: Repeat Rnd 1.

Rnd 7: K3, C6F, p1, k3, C6F.

Rnd 8: Repeat Rnd 1.

Repeat Rnds 1–8 for 9-Stitch Braids Top-Down in the Round.

9-Stitch Braids

BOTTOM-UP FLAT

(panel of 19 sts; 8-row repeat)

Row 1 (RS): K9, p1, k9.

Row 2 and all WS Rows: Knit the knit sts and purl the purl sts as they face you.

Row 3: C6F, k3, p1, C6F, k3.

Row 5: Repeat Row 1.

Row 7: K3, C6B, p1, k3, C6B.

Row 8: Repeat Row 2.

Repeat Rows 1–8 for 9-Stitch Braids Bottom-Up Flat.

BOTTOM-UP IN THE ROUND

(panel of 19 sts; 8-rnd repeat)

Rnds 1 and 2: K9, p1, k9.

Rnd 3: C6F, k3, p1, C6F, k3.

Rnds 4–6: Repeat Rnd 1.

Rnd 7: K3, C6B, p1, k3, C6B.

Rnd 8: Repeat Rnd 1.

Repeat Rnds 1–8 for 9-Stitch Braids Bottom-Up in the Round.

BOTTOM-UP FLAT AND IN THE ROUND

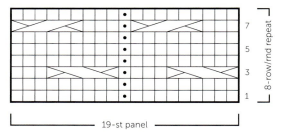

19-st panel

8-row/rnd repeat

TOP-DOWN FLAT AND IN THE ROUND

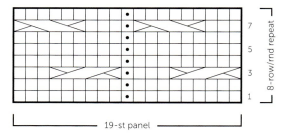

19-st panel

8-row/rnd repeat

5-Stitch Serpents

FLAT

(panel of 5 sts worked on a background of Rev St st; 12-row repeat)

Row 1 (RS): P2, 2/1 RPC.

Row 2 and all WS Rows: Knit the knit sts and purl the purl sts as they face you.

Row 3: P1, 2/1 RPC, p1.

Row 5: 2/1 RPC, p2.

Row 7: 2/1 LPC, p2.

Row 9: P1, 2/1 LPC, p1.

Row 11: P2, 2/1 LPC.

Row 12: Repeat Row 2.

Repeat Rows 1–12 for 5-Stitch Serpents Flat.

IN THE ROUND

(panel of 5 sts worked on a background of Rev St st; 12-rnd repeat)

Rnd 1: P2, 2/1 RPC.

Rnd 2 and all Even-Numbered Rnds: Knit the knit sts and purl the purl sts as they face you.

Rnd 3: P1, 2/1 RPC, p1.

Rnd 5: 2/1 RPC, p2.

Rnd 7: 2/1 LPC, p2.

Rnd 9: P1, 2/1 LPC, p1.

Rnd 11: P2, 2/1 LPC.

Rnd 12: Repeat Rnd 2.

Repeat Rnds 1–12 for 5-Stitch Serpents in the Round.

FLAT AND IN THE ROUND

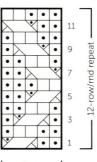

Tipsy Cables

FLAT

(panel of 16 sts worked on a background of Rev St st;
16-row repeat)

Row 1 (RS): C4B, [p2, C4B] twice.

Row 2 and all WS Rows: Knit the knit sts and purl the purl sts
as they face you; purl all yos.

Rows 3, 5, and 7: K2, yo, k2tog, [p2, k2, yo, k2tog] twice.

Row 9: Repeat Row 1.

Rows 11, 13, and 15: Ssk, yo, k2, [p2, ssk, yo, k2] twice.

Row 16: Repeat Row 2.

Repeat Rows 1–16 for Tipsy Cables Flat.

IN THE ROUND

(panel of 16 sts worked on a background of Rev St st;
16-rnd repeat)

Rnd 1: C4B, [p2, C4B] twice.

Rnd 2 and all Even-Numbered Rnds: Knit the knit sts and
purl the purl sts as they face you; knit all yos.

Rnds 3, 5, and 7: K2, yo, k2tog, [p2, k2, yo, k2tog] twice.

Rnd 9: Repeat Rnd 1.

Rnds 11, 13, and 15: Ssk, yo, k2, [p2, ssk, yo, k2] twice.

Rnd 16: Repeat Rnd 2.

Repeat Rnds 1–16 for Tipsy Cables in the Round.

FLAT AND IN THE ROUND

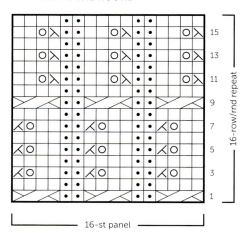

Roman Cable

BOTTOM-UP FLAT

(panel of 4 sts worked on a background of Rev St st; 2-row repeat)

Row 1 (RS): RC, LC.
Row 2: Purl.
Repeat Rows 1 and 2 for Roman Cable Bottom-Up Flat.

BOTTOM-UP IN THE ROUND

(panel of 4 sts worked on a background of Rev St st; 2-rnd repeat)

Rnd 1: RC, LC.
Rnd 2: Knit.
Repeat Rnds 1 and 2 for Roman Cable Bottom-Up in the Round.

TOP-DOWN FLAT

(panel of 4 sts worked on a background of Rev St st; 2-row repeat)

Row 1 (RS): LC, RC.
Row 2: Purl.
Repeat Rows 1 and 2 for Roman Cable Top-Down Flat.

TOP-DOWN IN THE ROUND

(panel of 4 sts worked on a background of Rev St st; 2-rnd repeat)

Rnd 1: LC, RC.
Rnd 2: Knit.
Repeat Rnds 1 and 2 for Roman Cable Top-Down in the Round.

BOTTOM-UP FLAT AND IN THE ROUND

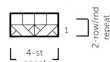

TOP-DOWN FLAT AND IN THE ROUND

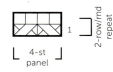

Right Cable

Left Cable

Snakes in the Sand

FLAT

(panel of 8 sts worked on a background of Rev St st; 4-row repeat)

Row 1 (RS): LC (for right cable) or RC (for left cable), k4, LC (for right cable) or RC (for left cable).

Row 2: Purl.

Row 3: LC (for right cable) or RC (for left cable), C4B (for right cable) or C4F (for left cable), LC (for right cable) or RC (for left cable).

Row 4: Purl.

Repeat Rows 1–4 for Snakes in the Sand Flat.

IN THE ROUND

(panel of 8 sts worked on a background of Rev St st; 4-rnd repeat)

Rnd 1: LC (for right cable) or RC (for left cable), k4, LC (for right cable) or RC (for left cable).

Rnd 2: Knit.

Rnd 3: LC (for right cable) or RC (for left cable), C4B (for right cable) or C4F (for left cable), LC (for right cable) or RC (for left cable).

Rnd 4: Knit.

Repeat Rnds 1–4 for Snakes in the Sand in the Round.

FLAT AND IN THE ROUND

Right Cable

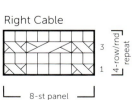

Left Cable

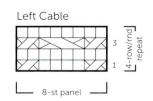

Ornamental Cable

BOTTOM-UP FLAT

(panel of 30 sts worked on a background of Rev St st; 8-row repeat)

Row 1 (RS): K9, C6B, C6F, k9.

Row 2 and all WS Rows: Purl.

Row 3: K6, C6B, k6, C6F, k6.

Row 5: K3, C6B, k12, C6F, k3.

Row 7: C6B, k18, C6F.

Row 8: Purl.

Repeat Rows 1–8 for Ornamental Cable Bottom-Up Flat.

BOTTOM-UP IN THE ROUND

(panel of 30 sts worked on a background of Rev St st; 8-rnd repeat)

Rnd 1: K9, C6B, C6F, k9.

Rnd 2 and all Even-Numbered Rnds: Knit.

Rnd 3: K6, C6B, k6, C6F, k6.

Rnd 5: K3, C6B, k12, C6F, k3.

Rnd 7: C6B, k18, C6F.

Rnd 8: Knit.

Repeat Rnds 1–8 for Ornamental Cable Bottom-Up in the Round.

TOP-DOWN FLAT

(panel of 30 sts worked on a background of Rev St st; 8-row repeat)

Row 1 (RS): C6F, k18, C6B.

Row 2 and all WS Rows: Purl.

Row 3: K3, C6F, k12, C6B, k3.

Row 5: K6, C6F, k6, C6B, k6.

Row 7: K9, C6F, C6B, k9.

Row 8: Purl.

Repeat Rows 1–8 for Ornamental Cable Top-Down Flat.

TOP-DOWN IN THE ROUND

(panel of 30 sts worked on a background of Rev St st; 8-rnd repeat)

Rnd 1: C6F, k18, C6B.

Rnd 2 and all Even-Numbered Rnds: Knit.

Rnd 3: K3, C6F, k12, C6B, k3.

Rnd 5: K6, C6F, k6, C6B, k6.

Rnd 7: K9, C6F, C6B, k9.

Rnd 8: Knit.

Repeat Rnds 1–8 for Ornamental Cable Top-Down in the Round.

BOTTOM-UP FLAT AND IN THE ROUND

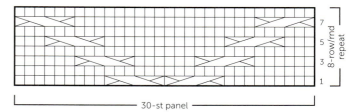

30-st panel

8-row/rnd repeat

TOP-DOWN FLAT AND IN THE ROUND

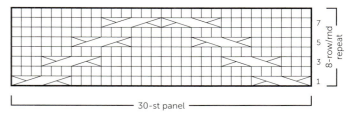

30-st panel

8-row/rnd repeat

Slipped Zigzag Cable

FLAT

(panel of 7 sts worked on a background of Rev St st; 8-row repeat)

Note: *Pattern begins with a WS row.*

1/2 LSC: See key.
1/2 RSC: See key.
Row 1 (WS): K2, p3, k2.
Row 2: P2, slip 1 purlwise wyib, k2, p2.
Row 3: K2, p2, slip 1 purlwise wyif, k2.
Row 4: P2, 1/2 LSC, p2.
Row 5: Repeat Row 1.
Row 6: P2, k2, slip 1 purlwise wyib, p2.
Row 7: K2, slip 1 purlwise wyif, p2, k2.
Row 8: P2, 1/2 RSC, p2.
Repeat Rows 1–8 for Slipped Zigzag Cable Flat.

IN THE ROUND

(panel of 7 sts worked on a background of Rev St st; 8-rnd repeat)

1/2 LSC: See key.
1/2 RSC: See key.
Rnd 1: P2, k3, p2.
Rnds 2 and 3: P2, slip 1 purlwise wyib, k2, p2.
Rnd 4: P2, 1/2 LSC, p2.
Rnd 5: Repeat Rnd 1.
Rnds 6 and 7: P2, k2, slip 1 purlwise wyib, p2.
Rnd 8: P2, 1/2 RSC, p2.
Repeat Rnds 1–8 for Slipped Zigzag Cable in the Round.

FLAT AND IN THE ROUND

Note: *Flat pattern begins with a WS row.*

 1/2 LSC: 1 over 2 Left Slipped Cross. Drop slipped st off left-hand needle and leave to front, k2, pick up dropped st and knit it.

 1/2 RSC: 1 over 2 Right Slipped Cross. Slip 2 wyib, drop slipped st from previous row off left-hand needle and leave to front, slip 2 sts from right-hand needle back to left-hand needle, pick up dropped st and knit it, k2.

Cross-Stitch Cable

FLAT

(panel of 10 sts worked on a background of Rev St st; 4-row repeat)

Row 1 (RS): K1-tbl, p2, k4, p2, k1-tbl.

Row 2: P1-tbl, k2, [p1, wrapping yarn twice around needle] 4 times, k2, p1-tbl.

Row 3: K1-tbl, p2, 2/2 RSC (for right cross) or 2/2 LSC (for left cross), p2, k1-tbl.

Row 4: P1-tbl, k2, p4, k2, p1-tbl.

Repeat Rows 1–4 for Cross-Stitch Cable Flat.

IN THE ROUND

(panel of 10 sts worked on a background of Rev St st; 4-rnd repeat)

Rnd 1: K1-tbl, p2, k4, p2, k1-tbl.

Rnd 2: K1-tbl, p2, [k1, wrapping yarn twice around needle] 4 times, p2, k1-tbl.

Rnd 3: K1-tbl, p2, 2/2 RSC (for right cross) or 2/2 LSC (for left cross), p2, k1-tbl.

Rnd 4: Repeat Rnd 1.

Repeat Rnds 1–4 for Cross-Stitch Cable in the Round.

FLAT AND IN THE ROUND

Right Cross

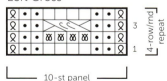

10-st panel

Left Cross

10-st panel

 K1 on RS (p1 on WS), wrapping yarn twice around needle.

 2/2 RSC: 2 over 2 Right Slipped Cross. Slip 4 sts, dropping extra wraps, slip same 4 sts back to left-hand needle, pass last 2 slipped sts over first 2 sts and onto tip of left-hand needle, k4.

2/2 LSC: 2 over 2 Left Slipped Cross. Slip 4 sts, dropping extra wraps, pass first 2 slipped sts over last 2 sts and onto left-hand needle, slip last 2 sts back to left-hand needle, k4.

Right Cross

Left Cross

Snow Tracks

BOTTOM-UP FLAT

(panel of 18 sts worked on a background of Rev St st;
10-row repeat)

Row 1 (RS): P7, k4, p7.
Row 2: K7, p4, k7.
Row 3: P6, 2/1 RC, 2/1 LC, p6.
Row 4: K6, p2, k2, p2, k6.
Row 5: P5, 2/1 RC, k2, 2/1 LC, p5.
Row 6: K5, p2, k4, p2, k5.
Row 7: P4, 2/1 RC, k4, 2/1 LC, p4.
Row 8: K4, p2, k6, p2, k4.
Row 9: P3, 2/1 RC, k6, 2/1 LC, p3.
Row 10: K3, p2, k8, p2, k3.
Repeat Rows 1–10 for Snow Tracks Bottom-Up Flat.

BOTTOM-UP IN THE ROUND

(panel of 18 sts worked on a background of Rev St st;
10-rnd repeat)

Rnds 1 and 2: P7, k4, p7.
Rnd 3: P6, 2/1 RC, 2/1 LC, p6.
Rnd 4: P6, k2, p2, k2, p6.
Rnd 5: P5, 2/1 RC, k2, 2/1 LC, p5.
Rnd 6: P5, k2, p4, k2, p5.
Rnd 7: P4, 2/1 RC, k4, 2/1 LC, p4.
Rnd 8: P4, k2, p6, k2, p4.
Rnd 9: P3, 2/1 RC, k6, 2/1 LC, p3.
Rnd 10: P3, k2, p8, k2, p3.
Repeat Rnds 1–10 for Snow Tracks Bottom-Up in the
Round.

TOP-DOWN FLAT

(panel of 18 sts worked on a background of Rev St st;
10-row repeat)

Row 1 (RS): P3, 2/1 LC, k6, 2/1 RPC, p3.
Row 2: K4, p2, k6, p2, k4.
Row 3: P4, 2/1 LPC, k4, 2/1 RPC, p4.
Row 4: K5, p2, k4, p2, k5.
Row 5: P5, 2/1 LPC, k2, 2/1 RPC, p5.
Row 6: K6, p2, k2, p2, k6.
Row 7: P6, 2/1 LPC, 2/1 RPC, p6.
Row 8: K7, p4, k7.
Row 9: P7, k4, p7.
Row 10: K3, p2, k8, p2, k3.
Repeat Rows 1–10 for Snow Tracks Top-Down Flat.

TOP-DOWN IN THE ROUND

(panel of 18 sts worked on a background of Rev St st;
10-rnd repeat)

Rnd 1: P3, 2/1 LPC, k6, 2/1 RPC, p3.
Rnd 2: P4, k2, p6, k2, p4.
Rnd 3: P4, 2/1 LPC, k4, 2/1 RPC, p4.
Rnd 4: P5, k2, p4, k2, p5.
Rnd 5: P5, 2/1 LPC, k2, 2/1 RPC, p5.
Rnd 6: P6, k2, p2, k2, p6.
Rnd 7: P6, 2/1 LPC, 2/1 RPC, p6.
Rnds 8 and 9: P7, k4, p7.
Rnd 10: P3, k2, p8, k2, p3.
Repeat Rnds 1–10 for Snow Tracks Top-Down in the Round.

BOTTOM-UP FLAT AND IN THE ROUND

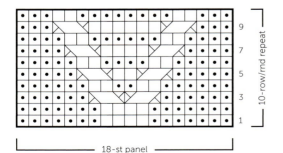

TOP-DOWN FLAT AND IN THE ROUND

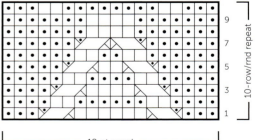

SIZES

To fit bust sizes 28–30 (34–36, 40–42, 46–48, 52–54)" [71–76 (86.5–91.5, 101.5–106.5, 117–122, 132–137) cm]

FINISHED MEASUREMENTS

57 (62, 68½, 73½, 80½)" [145 (157.5, 174, 186.5, 204.5) cm] bust

YARN

Blue Sky Fibers Techno [68% baby alpaca, 22% silk, 10% extra fine merino; 120 yards (110 meters) / 2 ounces (50 grams)]: 8 (9, 10, 11, 12) hanks #1983 Fringe

NEEDLES

One pair straight needles size US 10½ (6.5 mm)
One set of five double-pointed needles size US 10½ (6.5 mm)
Change needle size if necessary to obtain correct gauge.

NOTIONS

Stitch markers; cable needle

GAUGE

12 sts and 19 rows = 4" (10 cm) in Stockinette stitch (St st), washed and blocked
Note: Because this piece is worked from side to side, the row gauge will affect the bust measurements given and the stitch gauge will affect the length.

Sideways Cable Pulli

Cables are usually placed in the center of a pullover. This time I changed it up by working the cables sideways. Check out the section on combining stitch patterns (on page 14) to come up with your own version.

STITCH PATTERNS

CHAIN MAIL RIGHT

(panel of 3 sts; 2-row repeat)
RW: See key.
Row 1 (RS): RW.
Row 2: Purl.
Repeat Rows 1 and 2 for Chain Mail Right.

CHAIN MAIL LEFT

(panel of 3 sts; 2-row repeat)
LW: See key.
Row 1 (RS): LW.
Row 2: Purl.
Repeat Rows 1 and 2 for Chain Mail Left.

CHAIN MAIL RIGHT   **CHAIN MAIL LEFT**

|‖ ⌐| RW: **Right Wrap.** Slip third st on left-hand needle over first 2 sts and onto tip of left-hand needle and knit it, k2.

|⌐ ‖| LW: **Left Wrap.** Slip 3 sts to right-hand needle; slip the first of these 3 sts back over the second and third sts and onto left-hand needle, slip the second and third sts back to left-hand needle; k2, k1-tbl.

RIBBED CABLES

(panel of 10 sts; 20-row repeat)
Row 1 (RS): P2, C6B, p2.
Row 2: K2, p6, k2.
Row 3: P2, k6, p2.
Row 4: Repeat Row 2.
Rows 5 and 6: Repeat Rows 1 and 2.
Row 7: P1, 2/1 RPC, k2, 2/1 LPC, p1.
Row 8: K1, [p2, k1] 3 times.
Row 9: 2/1 RPC, p1, k2, p1, 2/1 LPC.
Row 10: P2, [k2, p2] twice.
Row 11: K2, [p2, k2] twice.
Rows 12–15: Repeat Rows 10 and 11 twice.
Row 16: Repeat Row 10.
Row 17: 2/1 LPC, p1, k2, p1, 2/1 RPC.
Row 18: Repeat Row 8.
Row 19: P1, 2/1 LPC, k2, 2/1 RPC, p1.
Row 20: Repeat Row 2.
Repeat Rows 1–20 for Ribbed Cables.

RIBBED CABLES

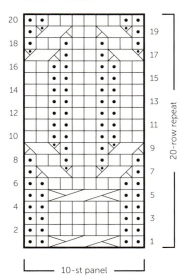

Back

CO 14 (16, 17, 19, 19) sts, pm, CO 26 sts, pm, CO 30 (30, 32, 32, 32) sts—70 (72, 75, 77, 77) sts.

Set-Up Row (WS): Slip 1 purlwise wyib, purl to marker, sm, p1-tbl, k2, p3, k2, work Ribbed Cables beginning with Row 16 (20, 12, 16, 18), k2, p3, k2, p1-tbl, sm, purl to end.

Row 1: Slip 1 purlwise wyib, knit to marker, sm, k1-tbl, p2, work Chain Mail Right, p2, work Ribbed Cables, p2, work Chain Mail Left, p2, k1-tbl, sm, knit to end.

Slipping first st of every row purlwise wyib, work even through Row 20 of Ribbed Cables, then work Rows 1–20 six (7, 7, 8, 9) times, then work through Row 10 (6, 14, 10, 8); you should have a total of 135 (147, 163, 175, 191) rows from the beginning. BO all sts in pattern.

Front

Work as for Back until piece measures 10¼ (11½, 12¾, 14, 15½)" [26 (29, 32.5, 35.5, 39.5) cm] from the beginning, ending with a WS row.

SHAPE NECK

BO 2 sts at beginning of next 4 RS rows, then 1 st at beginning of following RS row—61 (63, 66, 68, 68) sts remain.

Work even for 4 (4, 4¾, 4¾, 5¼)" [10 (10, 12, 12, 13.5) cm], ending with a WS row.

CO 1 st at beginning of next RS row, then 2 sts at beginning of following 4 RS rows—70 (72, 75, 77, 77) sts.

Complete as for Back.

Lightly block pieces, if desired. Sew shoulder seams, working from armhole edge toward neck edge. Pm 6 (6¼, 7, 7¾, 7¾)" [15 (16, 18, 19.5, 19.5) cm] down from each shoulder seam on Front and Back. Sew side seams from lower edge to markers.

Sleeves

With RS facing, using dpns and beginning at center underarm, pick up and knit 36 (38, 42, 46, 46) sts around armhole edge. Join for working in the rnd; pm for beginning of rnd.

Work in St st (knit every rnd) until piece measures 4 (5, 5½, 6, 6)" [10 (12.5, 14, 15, 15) cm] from underarm.

SHAPE SLEEVE

Decrease Rnd: K1, k2tog, knit to last 3 sts, ssk, k1—2 sts decreased.

Repeat Decrease Rnd every 5 rnds 3 (4, 4, 4, 4) times—28 (28, 32, 36, 36) sts remain.

Work even until piece measures 13 (14, 14½, 15, 15)" [33 (35.5, 37, 38, 38) cm] from underarm. BO all sts.

Finishing

Block lightly.

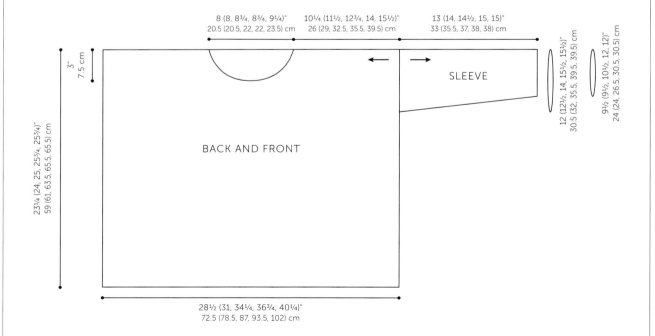

8 (8, 8¾, 8¾, 9¼)"
20.5 (20.5, 22, 22, 23.5) cm

10¼ (11½, 12¾, 14, 15½)"
26 (29, 32.5, 35.5, 39.5) cm

13 (14, 14½, 15, 15)"
33 (35.5, 37, 38, 38) cm

3"
7.5 cm

SLEEVE

12 (12½, 14, 15½, 15½)"
30.5 (32, 35.5, 39.5, 39.5) cm

9½ (9½, 10½, 12, 12)"
24 (24, 26.5, 30.5, 30.5) cm

23¼ (24, 25, 25¾, 25¾)"
59 (61, 63.5, 65.5, 65.5) cm

BACK AND FRONT

28½ (31, 34¼, 36¾, 40¼)"
72.5 (78.5, 87, 93.5, 102) cm

CHAPTER **5** Lace

Since most knitters begin with simple knit and purl projects like scarves, making lace is typically considered an intermediate or advanced skill. While this is true, lace doesn't have to be difficult. After all, in addition to the basic knit and purl stitches, lace consists of only three other actions: the increase, the decrease, and yarn over. Although there are variations of increases and decreases, they are easy to execute and explained in the back of this book. Most lace patterns such as Waving Wheat on page 203 and Field of Flowers on page 222 have "resting rows," which means the wrong-side rows are simply purled (or in the case of in-the-round versions, they are knitted). On the other hand, some have actions happening on both sides of the knitting. Regardless of whether the actual knitting is simple or complex, both have a distinctive, elegantly patterned appearance and look best when knit with solid or semi-solid yarn. Lace is usually knit with finer yarns like fingering weight, but if you want a visual punch, try knitting lace with a chunky-weight yarn like I used in the Little Berries Bulky Scarf on page 263.

Zigzag and Garter Lace

....

FLAT

(multiple of 11 sts; 12-row repeat)

Row 1 (RS): *K2, k2tog, yo, k2, p3, k2tog, yo; repeat from * to end.

Row 2 and all WS Rows: Purl.

Row 3: K1, k2tog, yo, k2, p3, k2tog, yo, *k2, k2tog, yo, k2, p3, k2tog, yo; repeat from * to last st, k1.

Row 5: *K2tog, yo, k2, p3, k2tog, yo, k2; repeat from * to end.

Row 7: P1, [k2, yo, ssk] twice, *p3, [k2, yo, ssk] twice; repeat from * to last 2 sts, p2.

Row 9: P2, [k2, yo, ssk] twice, *p3, [k2, yo, ssk] twice; repeat from * to last st, p1.

Row 11: *P3, [k2, yo, ssk] twice; repeat from * to end.

Row 12: Purl.

Repeat Rows 1–12 for Zigzag and Garter Lace Flat.

IN THE ROUND

(multiple of 11 sts; 12-rnd repeat)

Rnd 1: *K2, k2tog, yo, k2, p3, k2tog, yo; repeat from * to end.

Rnd 2 and all Even-Numbered Rnds: Knit.

Rnd 3: K1, k2tog, yo, k2, p3, k2tog, yo, *k2, k2tog, yo, k2, p3, k2tog, yo; repeat from * to last st, k1.

Rnd 5: *K2tog, yo, k2, p3, k2tog, yo, k2; repeat from * to end.

Rnd 7: P1, [k2, yo, ssk] twice, *p3, [k2, yo, ssk] twice; repeat from * to last 2 sts, p2.

Rnd 9: P2, [k2, yo, ssk] twice, *p3, [k2, yo, ssk] twice; repeat from * to last st, p1.

Rnd 11: *P3, [k2, yo, ssk] twice; repeat from * to end.

Rnd 12: Knit.

Repeat Rnds 1–12 for Zigzag and Garter Lace in the Round.

FLAT AND IN THE ROUND

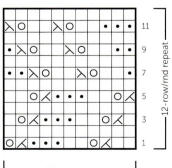

Waving Wheat

FLAT

(multiple of 16 sts; 12-row repeat)

Row 1 (RS): *K9, yo, k1, yo, k3, sk2p; repeat from * to end.

Row 2 and all WS Rows: Purl.

Row 3: *K10, yo, k1, yo, k2, sk2p; repeat from * to end.

Row 5: *K3tog, k4, yo, k1, yo, k3, [yo, k1] twice, sk2p; repeat from * to end.

Row 7: *K3tog, k3, yo, k1, yo, k9; repeat from * to end.

Row 9: *K3tog, k2, yo, k1, yo, k10; repeat from * to end.

Row 11: *K3tog, [k1, yo] twice, k3, yo, k1, yo, k4, sk2p; repeat from * to end.

Row 12: Purl.

Repeat Rows 1–12 for Waving Wheat Flat.

IN THE ROUND

(multiple of 16 sts; 12-rnd repeat)

Rnd 1: *K9, yo, k1, yo, k3, sk2p; repeat from * to end.

Rnd 2 and all Even-Numbered Rnds: Knit.

Rnd 3: *K10, yo, k1, yo, k2, sk2p; repeat from * to end.

Rnd 5: *K3tog, k4, yo, k1, yo, k3, [yo, k1] twice, sk2p; repeat from * to end.

Rnd 7: *K3tog, k3, yo, k1, yo, k9; repeat from * to end.

Rnd 9: *K3tog, k2, yo, k1, yo, k10; repeat from * to end.

Rnd 11: *K3tog, [k1, yo] twice, k3, yo, k1, yo, k4, sk2p; repeat from * to end.

Rnd 12: Knit.

Repeat Rnds 1–12 for Waving Wheat in the Round.

FLAT AND IN THE ROUND

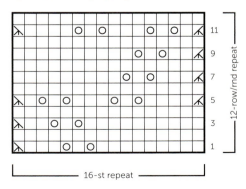

Overlapping Spearheads

FLAT

(multiple of 14 sts + 15; 20-row repeat)

Row 1 (RS): K1, *yo, sk2p, [yo, k1] twice, s2kp2, [k1, yo] twice, k3tog, yo, k1; repeat from * to end.

Row 2 and all WS Rows: Purl.

Row 3: K1, *yo, k1, sk2p, yo, k1, yo, s2kp2, yo, k1, yo, k3tog, k1, yo, k1; repeat from * to end.

Row 5: K1, *yo, k2, sk2p, yo, k3, yo, k3tog, k2, yo, k1; repeat from * to end.

Row 7: K1, *yo, k3, sk2p, yo, k1, yo, k3tog, k3, yo, k1; repeat from * to end.

Row 9: K1, *yo, k4, ssk, k1, k2tog, k4, yo, k1; repeat from * to end.

Row 11: K3, *k2tog, yo, k5, yo, ssk, k5; repeat from * to last 12 sts, k2tog, yo, k5, yo, ssk, k3.

Row 13: K2, *k2tog, yo, k1, yo, ssk, k1, k2tog, yo, k1, yo, ssk, k3; repeat from * to last 13 sts, k2tog, yo, k1, yo, ssk, k1, k2tog, yo, k1, yo, ssk, k2.

Row 15: K1, *k2tog, yo, k3, yo, s2kp2, yo, k3, yo, ssk, k1; repeat from * to end.

Row 17: K2tog, yo, k11, *yo, sk2p, yo, k11; repeat from * to last 2 sts, yo, ssk.

Row 19: K6, yo, s2kp2, yo, *k11, yo, s2kp2, yo; repeat from * to last 6 sts, k6.

Row 20: Purl.

Repeat Rows 1–20 for Overlapping Spearheads Flat.

IN THE ROUND

(multiple of 14 sts; 20-rnd repeat)

Rnd 1: *K1, yo, sk2p, [yo, k1] twice, s2kp2, [k1, yo] twice, k3tog, yo; repeat from * to end.

Rnd 2: Knit.

Rnd 3: *K1, yo, k1, sk2p, yo, k1, yo, s2kp2, yo, k1, yo, k3tog, k1, yo; repeat from * to end.

Rnd 4: Knit.

Rnd 5: *K1, yo, k2, sk2p, yo, k3, yo, k3tog, k2, yo; repeat from * to end.

Rnd 6: Knit.

Rnd 7: *K1, yo, k3, sk2p, yo, k1, yo, k3tog, k3, yo; repeat from * to end.

Rnd 8: Knit.

Rnd 9: *K1, yo, k4, ssk, k1, k2tog, k4, yo; repeat from * to end.

FLAT

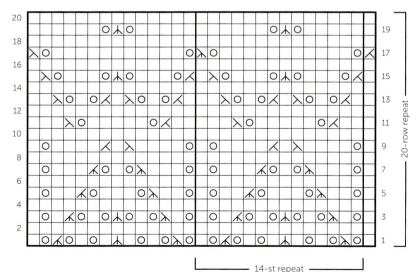

Rnd 10: Knit.

Rnd 11: K3, k2tog, yo, k5, yo, ssk, *k5, k2tog, yo, k5, yo, ssk; repeat from * to last 2 sts, k2.

Rnd 12: Knit.

Rnd 13: *K2, [k2tog, yo, k1, yo, ssk, k1] twice; repeat from * to end.

Rnd 14: Knit.

Rnd 15: *K1, k2tog, yo, k3, yo, s2kp2, yo, k3, yo, ssk; repeat from * to end.

Rnd 16: Knit to last st, reposition beginning-of-rnd marker to before last st.

Rnd 17: *Sk2p, yo, k11, yo; repeat from * to end.

Rnd 18: Knit.

Rnd 19: K6, yo, s2kp2, yo, *k11, yo, s2kp2, yo; repeat from * to last 5 sts, k5.

Rnd 20: Knit.

Repeat Rnds 1–20 for Overlapping Spearheads in the Round.

IN THE ROUND

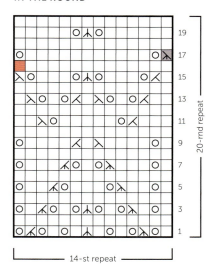

On final repeat only of Rnd 16, end rnd 1 st before beginning-of-rnd marker; reposition beginning-of-rnd marker to before last st. On all preceding repeats, knit this st.

On first repeat only of Rnd 17, work sk2p on what was last st of Rnd 16 and first 2 sts of Rnd 17; beginning-of-rnd marker should be before this sk2p. On all following repeats, work sk2p.

Candelabra

(multiple of 12 sts + 13; 16-row repeat)

Wrap 3: See key.

Wrap 5: See key.

Row 1 (RS): K4, wrap 5, *k7, wrap 5; repeat from * to last 4 sts, k4.

Row 2: K4, p5, *k7, p5; repeat from * to last 4 sts, k4.

Row 3: P3, k2tog, [k1, yo] twice, k1, ssk, *p5, k2tog, [k1, yo] twice, k1, ssk; repeat from * to last 3 sts, p3.

Row 4: Knit the knit sts and purl the purl sts as they face you; purl all yos.

Row 5: P2, k2tog, k1, yo, k3, yo, k1, ssk, *p3, k2tog, k1, yo, k3, yo, k1, ssk; repeat from * to last 2 sts, p2.

Row 6: Repeat Row 4.

Row 7: P1, *k2tog, k1, yo, k2tog, yo, k1, yo, ssk, yo, k1, ssk, p1; repeat from * to end.

Row 8: Repeat Row 4.

Row 9: Wrap 3, k7, *wrap 5, k7; repeat from * to last 3 sts, wrap 3.

Row 10: P3, k7, *p5, k7; repeat from * to last 3 sts, p3.

Row 11: K1, yo, k1, ssk, p5, *k2tog, [k1, yo] twice, k1, ssk, p5; repeat from * to last 4 sts, k2tog, k1, yo, k1.

Row 12: Repeat Row 4.

Row 13: K2, yo, k1, ssk, p3, *k2tog, k1, yo, k3, yo, k1, ssk, p3; repeat from * to last 5 sts, k2tog, k1, yo, k2.

Row 14: Repeat Row 4.

Row 15: K1, *yo, ssk, yo, k1, ssk, p1, k2tog, k1, yo, k2tog, yo, k1; repeat from * to end.

Row 16: Repeat Row 4.

Repeat Rows 1–16 for Candelabra Flat.

IN THE ROUND

(multiple of 12 sts; 16-rnd repeat)

Wrap 5: See key.

Rnd 1: K4, *wrap 5, k7; repeat from * to last 8 sts, wrap 5, k3.

Rnd 2: P4, *k5, p7; repeat from * to last 8 sts, k5, p3.

Rnd 3: P3, k2tog, [k1, yo] twice, k1, ssk, *p5, k2tog, [k1, yo] twice, k1, ssk; repeat from * to last 2 sts, p2.

Rnd 4: Knit the knit sts and purl the purl sts as they face you; knit all yos.

Rnd 5: P2, k2tog, k1, yo, k3, yo, k1, ssk, *p3, k2tog, k1, yo, k3, yo, k1, ssk; repeat from * to last st, p1.

Rnd 6: Repeat Rnd 4.

Rnd 7: *P1, k2tog, k1, yo, k2tog, yo, k1, yo, ssk, yo, k1, ssk; repeat from * to end.

Rnd 8: *P1, k11; repeat from * to last 12 sts, p1, k9.

Rnd 9: *Wrap 5, k7; repeat from * to last 2 sts, k2. **Note:** *On first repeat only, work wrap 5 on last 2 sts of Rnd 8 and first 3 sts of Rnd 9, leaving beginning-of-rnd marker in place as you work.*

Rnd 10: K3, *p7, k5; repeat from * to last 9 sts, p7, k2.

Rnd 11: *K1, yo, k1, ssk, p5, k2tog, k1, yo; repeat from * to end.

Rnd 12: Repeat Rnd 4.

Rnd 13: K2, yo, k1, ssk, p3, k2tog, k1, yo, *k3, yo, k1, ssk, p3, k2tog, k1, yo; repeat from * to last st, k1.

Rnd 14: Repeat Rnd 4.

Rnd 15: *K1, yo, ssk, yo, k1, ssk, p1, k2tog, k1, yo, k2tog, yo; repeat from * to end.

Rnd 16: Repeat Rnd 4.

Repeat Rnds 1–16 for Candelabra in the Round.

FLAT

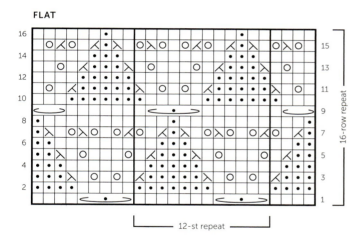

Wrap 3: K3, slip these 3 sts to cn; bring yarn to front and wrap yarn around these sts 3 times counterclockwise; slip sts back to right-hand needle.

Wrap 5: K2, p1, k2, slip these 5 sts to cn; bring yarn to front and wrap yarn around these 5 sts 3 times counterclockwise; slip sts back to right-hand needle.

IN THE ROUND

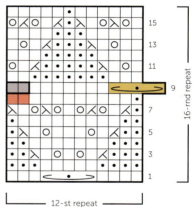

On final repeat only of Rnd 8, end 2 sts before beginning-of-rnd marker; the last 2 sts will be worked with the first wrap 5 of Rnd 9. On all preceding repeats, knit these sts.

On first repeat only of Rnd 9, work wrap 5 on last 2 sts of Rnd 8 and first 3 sts of Rnd 9, leaving beginning-of-rnd marker in place as you work. On all following repeats, work wrap 5 as before.

After final repeat of Rnd 9 is complete, knit. On all preceding repeats, omit these sts.

Row 11: K2tog, yo, k7, yo, ssk, *k1, k2tog, yo, k7, yo, ssk; repeat from * to end.
Row 12: Repeat Row 10.
Row 13: Ssk, k3, yo, k1, yo, k3, k2tog, *k1, ssk, k3, yo, k1, yo, k3, k2tog; repeat from * to end.
Rows 14–17: Repeat Rows 12 and 13 twice.
Row 18: Repeat Row 10.
Row 19: Yo, ssk, k7, k2tog, yo, *k1, yo, ssk, k7, k2tog, yo; repeat from * to end.
Row 20: Repeat Row 10.
Row 21: P1, yo, ssk, k5, k2tog, yo, *p1, k1, p1, yo, ssk, k5, k2tog, yo; repeat from * to last st, p1.
Row 22: Repeat Row 6.
Row 23: P1, k1, yo, ssk, k3, k2tog, yo, *[k1, p1] twice, k1, yo, ssk, k3, k2tog, yo; repeat from * to last 2 sts, k1, p1.
Row 24: Repeat Row 6.
Row 25: P1, k1, p1, yo, ssk, k1, k2tog, yo, *[p1, k1] 3 times, p1, yo, ssk, k1, k2tog, yo; repeat from * to last 3 sts, p1, k1, p1.
Row 26: Repeat Row 4.
Rows 27–38: Repeat Rows 1–4 three times.
Repeat Rows 1–38 for Gothic Seeded Arches Flat.

Gothic Seeded Arches

FLAT

(multiple of 12 sts + 11; 38-row repeat)
Row 1 (RS): [P1, k1] twice, *yo, s2kp2, yo, [k1, p1] 4 times, k1; repeat from * to last 7 sts, yo, s2kp2, yo, [k1, p1] twice.
Rows 2 and 3: P1, k1, p1, k5, *[k1, p1] 3 times, p1, k5; repeat from * to last 3 sts, p1, k1, p1.
Row 4: [P1, k1] twice, p3, *[k1, p1] 4 times, k1, p3; repeat from * to last 4 sts, [k1, p1] twice.
Row 5: P1, k1, p1, k2tog, yo, k1, yo, ssk, *[p1, k1] 3 times, p1, k2tog, yo, k1, yo, ssk; repeat from * to last 3 sts, p1, k1, p1.
Row 6: P1, k1, p7, *[k1, p1] twice, k1, p7; repeat from * to last 2 sts, k1, p1.
Row 7: P1, k1, k2tog, yo, k3, yo, ssk, *[k1, p1] twice, k1, k2tog, yo, k3, yo, ssk; repeat from * to last 2 sts, k1, p1.
Row 8: Repeat Row 6.
Row 9: P1, k2tog, yo, k5, yo, ssk, *p1, k1, p1, k2tog, yo, k5, yo, ssk; repeat from * to last st, p1.
Row 10: P11, *k1, p11; repeat from * to end.

IN THE ROUND

(multiple of 12 sts; 38-rnd repeat)
Rnd 1: [P1, k1] twice, yo, s2kp2, yo, *[k1, p1] 4 times, k1, yo, s2kp2, yo; repeat from * to last 5 sts, [k1, p1] twice, k1.
Rnd 2: K1, p1, k1, p5, *[k1, p1] 3 times, k1, p5; repeat from * to last 4 sts, [k1, p1] twice.
Rnd 3: P1, k1, p1, k5, *[p1, k1] 3 times, p1, k5; repeat from * to last 4 sts, [p1, k1] twice.
Rnd 4: [K1, p1] twice, k3, *[p1, k1] 4 times, p1, k3; repeat from * to last 5 sts, [p1, k1] twice, p1.
Rnd 5: P1, k1, p1, k2tog, yo, k1, yo, ssk, *[p1, k1] 3 times, p1, k2tog, yo, k1, yo, ssk; repeat from * to last 4 sts, [p1, k1] twice.
Rnd 6: K1, p1, k7, *[p1, k1] twice, p1, k7; repeat from * to last 3 sts, p1, k1, p1.
Rnd 7: P1, k1, k2tog, yo, k3, yo, ssk, *[k1, p1] twice, k1, k2tog, yo, k3, yo, ssk; repeat from * to last 3 sts, k1, p1, k1.
Rnd 8: Repeat Rnd 6.
Rnd 9: *P1, k2tog, yo, k5, yo, ssk, p1, k1; repeat from * to end.
Rnd 10: *K11, p1; repeat from * to end.
Rnd 11: *K2tog, yo, k7, yo, ssk, k1; repeat from * to end.
Rnd 12: Repeat Rnd 10.
Rnd 13: *Ssk, k3, yo, k1, yo, k3, k2tog, k1; repeat from * to end.
Rnds 14–17: Repeat Rnds 12 and 13 twice.
Rnd 18: Repeat Rnd 10.
Rnd 19: *Yo, ssk, k7, k2tog, yo, k1; repeat from * to end.
Rnd 20: Repeat Rnd 10.

Rnd 21: *P1, yo, ssk, k5, k2tog, yo, p1, k1; repeat from * to end.

Rnd 22: Repeat Rnd 6.

Rnd 23: P1, k1, yo, ssk, k3, k2tog, yo, *[k1, p1] twice, k1, yo, ssk, k3, k2tog, yo; repeat from * to last 3 sts, k1, p1, k1.

Rnd 24: Repeat Rnd 6.

Rnd 25: P1, k1, p1, yo, ssk, k1, k2tog, yo, *[p1, k1] 3 times, p1, yo, ssk, k1, k2tog, yo; repeat from * to last 4 sts, [p1, k1] twice.

Rnd 26: Repeat Rnd 4.

Rnds 27–38: Repeat Rnds 1–4 three times.

Repeat Rnds 1–38 for Gothic Seeded Arches in the Round.

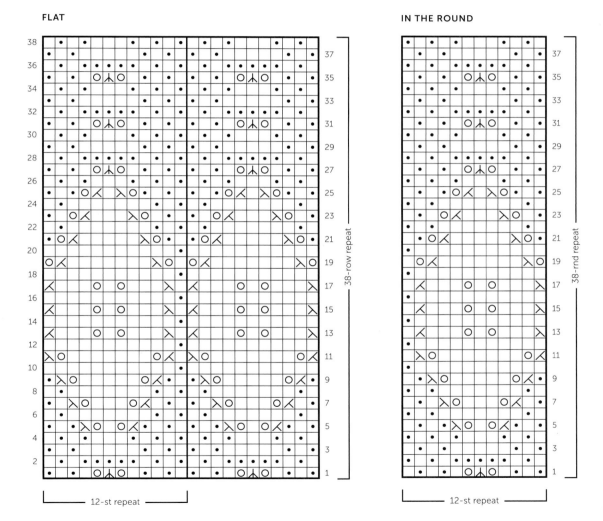

FLAT

IN THE ROUND

38-row repeat

38-rnd repeat

12-st repeat

12-st repeat

Wheat Sheaves

....

FLAT

(multiple of 8 sts + 9; 16-row repeat)

Wrap 3: See key.

Row 1 (RS): P1, k1, p1, yo, sk2p, yo, *[p1, k1] twice, p1, yo, sk2p, yo; repeat from * to last 3 sts, p1, k1, p1.

Row 2: Knit the knit sts and purl the purl sts as they face you; purl all yos.

Row 3: [P1, k1] twice, yo, ssk, *p1, wrap 3, p1, k1, yo, ssk; repeat from * to last 3 sts, p1, k1, p1.

Row 4: K1, *p1, k1; repeat from * to end.

Row 5: P1, *k1, k2tog, yo, p1, yo, ssk, k1, p1; repeat from * to end.

Row 6: K1, *p3, k1; repeat from * to end.

Row 7: P1, *k2tog, yo, k1, p1, k1, yo, ssk, p1; repeat from * to end.

Row 8: Repeat Row 4.

Row 9: K2tog, yo, [p1, k1] twice, p1, *yo, sk2p, yo, [p1, k1] twice, p1; repeat from * to last 2 sts, yo, ssk.

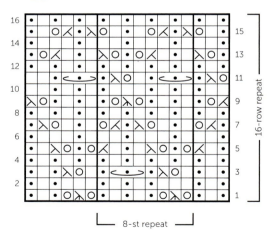

FLAT

 Wrap 3: K1, p1, k1, slip these 3 sts to cn; bring yarn to front and wrap yarn around these sts 3 times counterclockwise; slip sts back to right-hand needle.

Row 10: Repeat Row 2.

Row 11: *Yo, ssk, p1, wrap 3, p1, k1; repeat from * to last st, k1.

Row 12: Repeat Row 4.

Row 13: P1, *yo, ssk, k1, p1, k1, k2tog, yo, p1; repeat from * to end.

Row 14: Repeat Row 6.

Row 15: P1, *k1, yo, ssk, p1, k2tog, yo, k1, p1; repeat from * to end.

Row 16: Repeat Row 4.

Repeat Rows 1–16 for Wheat Sheaves Flat.

IN THE ROUND

(multiple of 8 sts; 16-rnd repeat)

Wrap 3: See key.

Rnd 1: *P1, yo, sk2p, yo, [p1, k1] twice; repeat from * to end.

Rnd 2: Knit the knit sts and purl the purl sts as they face you; knit all yos.

Rnd 3: *P1, k1, yo, ssk, p1, wrap 3; repeat from * to end.

Rnd 4: *P1, k1; repeat from * to end.

Rnd 5: *K2tog, yo, p1, yo, ssk, k1, p1, k1; repeat from * to end.

Rnd 6: K2, *p1, k3; repeat from * to last 2 sts, p1, k1, remove beginning-of-rnd marker, k1, pm for new beginning of rnd.

Rnd 7: *Yo, k1, p1, k1, yo, ssk, p1, k2tog; repeat from * to end.

Rnd 8: Repeat Rnd 4.

Rnd 9: *[P1, k1] twice, p1, yo, sk2p, yo; repeat from * to end.

Rnd 10: Repeat Rnd 2.

Rnd 11: *P1, wrap 3, p1, k1, yo, ssk; repeat from * to end.

Rnd 12: *P1, k1; repeat from * to last 2 sts, p1, reposition beginning-of-rnd marker to before last st.

Rnd 13: *Ssk, k1, p1, k1, k2tog, yo, p1, yo; repeat from * to end. **Note:** *On first repeat of Rnd 13 only, work ssk on what was last st of Rnd 12 and first st of Rnd 13; beginning-of-rnd marker should be before this ssk.*

Rnd 14: K2, *p1, k3; repeat from * to last 2 sts, p1, k1.

Rnd 15: *Yo, ssk, p1, k2tog, yo, k1, p1, k1; repeat from * to end.

Rnd 16: Repeat Rnd 4.

Repeat Rnds 1–16 for Wheat Sheaves in the Round.

IN THE ROUND

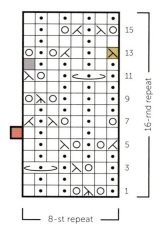

8-st repeat

At end of Rnd 6, remove beginning-of-rnd marker, k1, pm for new beginning of rnd. On all preceding repeats, omit this st.

On final repeat only of Rnd 12, end rnd 1 st before beginning-of-rnd marker; reposition beginning-of-rnd marker to before last st. On all preceding repeats, knit this st.

On first repeat only of Rnd 13, work ssk on what was last st of Rnd 12 and first st of Rnd 13; beginning-of-rnd marker should be before this ssk. On all following repeats, ssk.

Peacock Feathers

FLAT

(panel of 13 sts worked on a background of Rev St st; 18-row repeat)

Row 1 (RS): K4tog, [yo, k1] 5 times, yo, ssssk.

Row 2: Purl.

Row 3: Knit.

Row 4: Purl.

Rows 5–8: Repeat Rows 1–4.

Row 9: Repeat Row 1.

Rows 10 and 11: Knit.

Rows 12–15: K1, *p1, k1; repeat from * to end.

Rows 16–18: Purl.

Repeat Rows 1–18 for Peacock Feathers Flat.

IN THE ROUND

(panel of 13 sts worked on a background of Rev St st; 18-rnd repeat)

Rnd 1: K4tog, [yo, k1] 5 times, yo, ssssk.

Rnds 2–4: Knit.

Rnds 5–8: Repeat Rnds 1–4.

Rnd 9: Repeat Rnd 1.

Rnd 10: Purl.

Rnd 11: Knit.

Rnd 12: P1, *k1, p1; repeat from * to end.

Rnds 13–15: Knit the purl sts and purl the knit sts as they face you.

Rnd 16: Knit.

Rnd 17: Purl.

Rnd 18: Knit.

Repeat Rnds 1–18 for Peacock Feathers in the Round.

FLAT AND IN THE ROUND

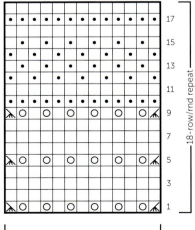

13-st panel

18-row/rnd repeat

 K4tog   Ssssk

Little Berries (TWO-SIDED)

FLAT

(multiple of 6 sts + 3; 4-row repeat)

Row 1 (RS): Yo, s2kp2, yo, *p3, yo, s2kp2, yo; repeat from * to end.

Row 2: K3, *p3, k3; repeat from * to end.

Row 3: P3, *yo, s2kp2, yo, p3; repeat from * to end.

Row 4: P3, *k3, p3; repeat from * to end.

Repeat Rows 1–4 for Little Berries Flat.

IN THE ROUND

(multiple of 6 sts; 4-rnd repeat)

Rnd 1: *Yo, s2kp2, yo, p3; repeat from * to end.

Rnd 2: *P3, k3; repeat from * to end.

Rnd 3: *P3, yo, s2kp2, yo; repeat from * to end.

Rnd 4: *K3, p3; repeat from * to end.

Repeat Rnds 1–4 for Little Berries in the Round.

FLAT

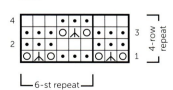

IN THE ROUND

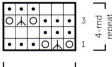

Halved Hourglasses

FLAT

(multiple of 16 sts + 17; 24-row repeat)

Row 1 (RS): K1, *yo, k3, ssk, k5, k2tog, k3, yo, k1; repeat from * to end.

Row 2: K2, p13, *k3, p13; repeat from * to last 2 sts, k2.

Row 3: K2, *yo, k3, ssk, k3, k2tog, k3, yo, k3; repeat from * to last 15 sts, yo, k3, ssk, k3, k2tog, k3, yo, k2.

Row 4: K3, p11, *k5, p11; repeat from * to last 3 sts, k3.

Row 5: K3, *yo, k3, ssk, k1, k2tog, k3, yo, k5; repeat from * to last 14 sts, yo, k3, ssk, k1, k2tog, k3, yo, k3.

Row 6: K4, p9, *k7, p9; repeat from * to last 4 sts, k4.

Row 7: K4, *yo, k3, s2kp2, k3, yo, k7; repeat from * to last 13 sts, yo, k3, s2kp2, k3, yo, k4.

Rows 8–11: Repeat Rows 6 and 7 twice.

Row 12: Purl.

Row 13: K3, *k2tog, k3, yo, k1, yo, k3, ssk, k5; repeat from * to last 14 sts, k2tog, k3, yo, k1, yo, k3, ssk, k3.

Row 14: P7, k3, *p13, k3; repeat from * to last 7 sts, p7.

Row 15: K2, *k2tog, [k3, yo] twice, k3, ssk, k3; repeat from * to last 15 sts, k2tog, [k3, yo] twice, k3, ssk, k2.

Row 16: P6, k5, *p11, k5; repeat from * to last 6 sts, p6.

Row 17: K1, *k2tog, k3, yo, k5, yo, k3, ssk, k1; repeat from * to end.

Row 18: P5, k7, *p9, k7; repeat from * to last 5 sts, p5.

Row 19: Ssk, k3, yo, k7, yo, k3, *s2kp2, k3, yo, k7, yo, k3; repeat from * to last 2 sts, k2tog.

Rows 20–23: Repeat Rows 18 and 19 twice.

Row 24: Purl.

Repeat Rows 1–24 for Halved Hourglasses Flat.

IN THE ROUND

(multiple of 16 sts; 24-rnd repeat)

Rnd 1: *K1, yo, k3, ssk, k5, k2tog, k3, yo; repeat from * to end.

Rnd 2: P2, k13, *p3, k13; repeat from * to last st, p1.

Rnd 3: K2, *yo, k3, ssk, k3, k2tog, k3, yo, k3; repeat from * to last 14 sts, yo, k3, ssk, k3, k2tog, k3, yo, k1.

Rnd 4: P3, k11, *p5, k11; repeat from * to last 2 sts, p2.

Rnd 5: K3, *yo, k3, ssk, k1, k2tog, k3, yo, k5; repeat from * to last 13 sts, yo, k3, ssk, k1, k2tog, k3, yo, k2.

Rnd 6: P4, k9, *p7, k9; repeat from * to last 3 sts, p3.

Rnd 7: K4, yo, k3, s2kp2, k3, yo, *k7, yo, k3, s2kp2, k3, yo; repeat from * to last 3 sts, k3.

Rnds 8–11: Repeat Rnds 6 and 7 twice.

Rnd 12: Knit.

Rnd 13: K3, *k2tog, k3, yo, k1, yo, k3, ssk, k5; repeat from * to last 13 sts, k2tog, k3, yo, k1, yo, k3, ssk, k2.

Rnd 14: K7, p3, *k13, p3; repeat from * to last 6 sts, k6.

Rnd 15: K2, *k2tog, [k3, yo] twice, k3, ssk, k3; repeat from * to last 14 sts, k2tog, [k3, yo] twice, k3, ssk, k1.

Rnd 16: K6, p5, *k11, p5; repeat from * to last 5 sts, k5.

Rnd 17: *K1, k2tog, k3, yo, k5, yo, k3, ssk; repeat from * to end.

Rnd 18: K5, p7, *k9, p7; repeat from * to last 3 sts, k3, reposition beginning-of-rnd marker to before last st.

Note: On first repeat only, work s2kp2 on what was last st of previous rnd and first 2 sts of current rnd; beginning-of-rnd marker should be before this s2kp2.

Rnd 19: *S2kp2, k3, yo, k7, yo, k3; repeat from * to end.

Rnds 20–23: Repeat Rnds 18 and 19 twice.

Rnd 24: Knit.

Repeat Rnds 1–24 for Halved Hourglasses in the Round.

FLAT

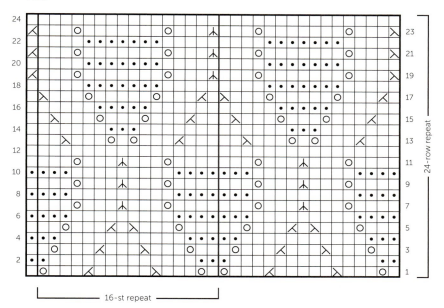

16-st repeat

24-row repeat

IN THE ROUND

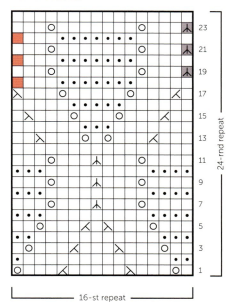

16-st repeat

24-rnd repeat

On final repeat only of Rnds 18, 20, and 22, end rnd 1 st before beginning-of-rnd marker; reposition beginning-of-rnd marker to before last st. On all preceding repeats, knit this st.

On first repeat only of Rnds 19, 21, and 23, work s2kp2 on what was last st of previous rnd and first 2 sts of current rnd; beginning-of-rnd marker should be before this s2kp2. On all following repeats, s2kp2.

Cherry Blossoms

....

FLAT

(multiple of 7 sts; 6-row repeat)
Row 1 (RS): Knit.
Row 2: Purl.
Rows 3 and 4: Repeat Rows 1 and 2.
Row 5: K1, k2tog, yo, k1, yo, ssk, *k2, k2tog, yo, k1, yo, ssk; repeat from * to last st, k1.
Row 6: *Ssp, yo, p3, yo, p2tog; repeat from * to end.
Repeat Rows 1–6 for Cherry Blossoms Flat.

IN THE ROUND

(multiple of 7 sts; 6-rnd repeat)
Rnds 1–4: Knit.
Rnd 5: K1, k2tog, yo, k1, yo, ssk, *k2, k2tog, yo, k1, yo, ssk; repeat from * to last st, k1.
Rnd 6: *K2tog, yo, k3, yo, ssk; repeat from * to end.
Repeat Rnds 1–6 for Cherry Blossoms in the Round.

FLAT AND IN THE ROUND

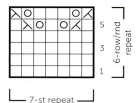

Lily of the Valley

FLAT

(multiple of 9 sts + 1; 24-row repeat)

Row 1 (RS): Knit.

Row 2: Purl.

Row 3: K1, *[ssk] 3 times, [yo, k1] 3 times; repeat from * to end.

Row 4: Purl.

Rows 5–12: Repeat Rows 1–4 twice.

Row 13: Knit.

Row 14: Purl.

Row 15: *[K1, yo] 3 times, [k2tog] 3 times; repeat from * to last st, k1.

Row 16: Purl.

Rows 17–24: Repeat Rows 13–16 twice.

Repeat Rows 1–24 for Lily of the Valley Flat.

IN THE ROUND

(multiple of 9 sts; 24-rnd repeat)

Rnds 1 and 2: Knit.

Rnd 3: K1, [ssk] 3 times, *[yo, k1] 3 times, [ssk] 3 times; repeat from * to last 2 sts, [yo, k1] twice, yo.

Rnd 4: Knit.

Rnds 5–12: Repeat Rnds 1–4 twice.

Rnds 13 and 14: Knit.

Rnd 15: *[K1, yo] 3 times, [k2tog] 3 times; repeat from * to end.

Rnd 16: Knit.

Rnds 17–24: Repeat Rnds 13–16 twice.

Repeat Rnds 1–24 for Lily of the Valley in the Round.

FLAT

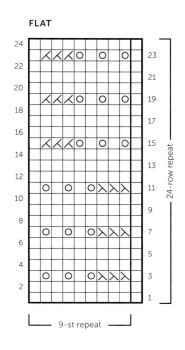

IN THE ROUND

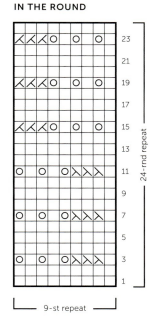

Figs

FLAT

(multiple of 8 sts + 9; 16-row repeat)

Row 1 (RS): *Yo, k1, k2tog, k5; repeat from * to last st, k1.

Row 2 and all WS Rows: Purl.

Row 3: K1, yo, k1, k2tog, k1, *ssk, [k1, yo] twice, k1, k2tog, k1; repeat from * to last 4 sts, ssk, k1, yo, k1.

Row 5: K2, *yo, k1, s2kp2, k1, yo, k3; repeat from * to last 7 sts, yo, k1, s2kp2, k1, yo, k2.

Row 7: Knit.

Row 9: K4, yo, k1, k2tog, *k5, yo, k1, k2tog; repeat from * to last 2 sts, k2.

Row 11: K1, *ssk, [k1, yo] twice, k1, k2tog, k1; repeat from * to end.

Row 13: Ssk, k1, yo, k3, *yo, k1, s2kp2, k1, yo, k3; repeat from * to last 3 sts, yo, k1, ssk.

Row 15: Knit.

Row 16: Purl.

Repeat Rows 1–16 for Figs Flat.

IN THE ROUND

(multiple of 8 sts; 16-rnd repeat)

Rnd 1: K3, yo, k1, k2tog, *k5, yo, k1, k2tog; repeat from * to last 2 sts, k2.

Rnd 2: Knit.

Rnd 3: *Ssk, k1, [yo, k1] twice, k2tog, k1; repeat from * to end.

Rnd 4: Knit to end, remove beginning-of-rnd marker, k1, pm for new beginning of rnd.

Rnd 5: *K1, yo, k3, yo, k1, s2kp2; repeat from * to end.

Rnds 6–8: Knit.

Rnd 9: *K1, k2tog, k5, yo; repeat from * to end.

Rnd 10: Knit to last st, reposition beginning-of-rnd marker to before last st.

Rnd 11: *Yo, k1, k2tog, k1, ssk, k1, yo, k1; repeat from * to end.

Rnd 12: Knit.

Rnd 13: K1, yo, k1, s2kp2, k1, yo, *k3, yo, k1, s2kp2, k1, yo; repeat from * to last 2 sts, k2.

Rnds 14–16: Knit.

Repeat Rnds 1–16 for Figs in the Round.

FLAT

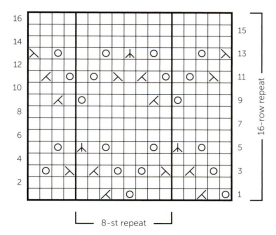

IN THE ROUND

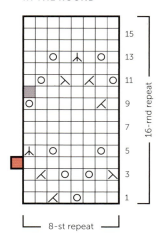

At end of Rnd 4, remove beginning-of-rnd marker, k1, pm for new beginning of rnd. On all preceding repeats, omit this st.

On final repeat only of Rnd 10, end rnd 1 st before beginning-of-rnd marker; reposition beginning-of-rnd marker to before last st. On all preceding repeats, knit this st.

Arrow Bands

....

FLAT

(multiple of 24 sts + 1; 8-row repeat)

Row 1 (RS): K1, *[yo, ssk] 5 times, yo, s2kp2, yo, [k2tog, yo] 5 times, k1; repeat from * to end.

Row 2: Purl.

Row 3: K1, *yo, k10, s2kp2, k10, yo, k1; repeat from * to end.

Rows 4–7: Repeat Rows 2 and 3 twice.

Row 8: Purl.

Repeat Rows 1–8 for Arrow Bands Flat.

IN THE ROUND

(multiple of 24 sts; 8-rnd repeat)

Rnd 1: *K1, [yo, ssk] 5 times, yo, s2kp2, yo, [k2tog, yo] 5 times; repeat from * to end.

Rnd 2: Knit.

Rnd 3: *K1, yo, k10, s2kp2, k10, yo; repeat from * to end.

Rnds 4–7: Repeat Rnds 2 and 3 twice.

Rnd 8: Knit.

Repeat Rnds 1–8 for Arrow Bands in the Round.

FLAT

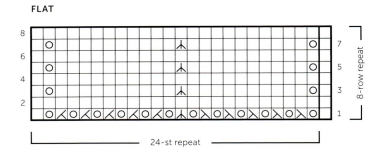

IN THE ROUND

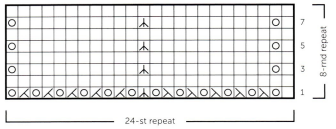

Rising Suns

....

FLAT

(multiple of 17 sts + 4; 6-row repeat)

Row 1 (RS): P1, k2, p1, *yo, k5, k3tog, k5, yo, p1, k2, p1; repeat from * to end.

Row 2: K1, p2, k1, *p1, yo, p4, p3tog, p4, yo, p1, k1, p2, k1; repeat from * to end.

Row 3: P1, k2, p1, *k2, yo, k3, k3tog, k3, yo, [k2, p1] twice; repeat from * to end.

Row 4: K1, p2, k1, *p3, yo, p2, p3tog, p2, yo, p3, k1, p2, k1; repeat from * to end.

Row 5: P1, k2, p1, *k4, yo, k1, k3tog, k1, yo, k4, p1, k2, p1; repeat from * to end.

Row 6: K1, p2, k1, *p5, yo, p3tog, yo, p5, k1, p2, k1; repeat from * to end.

Repeat Rows 1–6 for Rising Suns Flat.

IN THE ROUND

(multiple of 17 sts; 6-rnd repeat)

Rnd 1: K1, p1, yo, k5, k3tog, k5, yo, p1, *k2, p1, yo, k5, k3tog, k5, yo, p1; repeat from * to last st, k1.

Rnd 2: K1, p1, k1, yo, k4, k3tog, k4, yo, k1, p1, *k2, p1, k1, yo, k4, k3tog, k4, yo, k1, p1; repeat from * to last st, k1.

Rnd 3: K1, p1, k2, yo, k3, k3tog, k3, yo, k2, p1, *k2, p1, k2, yo, k3, k3tog, k3, yo, k2, p1; repeat from * to last st, k1.

Rnd 4: K1, p1, k3, yo, k2, k3tog, k2, yo, k3, p1, *k2, p1, k3, yo, k2, k3tog, k2, yo, k3, p1; repeat from * to last st, k1.

Rnd 5: K1, p1, k4, yo, k1, k3tog, k1, yo, k4, p1, *k2, p1, k4, yo, k1, k3tog, k1, yo, k4, p1; repeat from * to last st, k1.

Rnd 6: K1, p1, k5, yo, k3tog, yo, k5, p1, *k2, p1, k5, yo, k3tog, yo, k5, p1; repeat from * to last st, k1.

Repeat Rnds 1–6 for Rising Suns in the Round.

FLAT

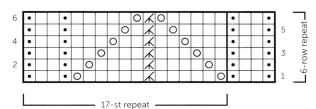

IN THE ROUND

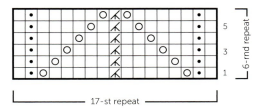

Field of Flowers

....

IN FLAT

(multiple of 12 sts + 11; 16-row repeat)

Row 1 (RS): K2tog, yo, k7, *yo, k1, sk2p, k1, yo, k7; repeat from * to last 2 sts, yo, ssk.

Row 2 and all WS Rows: Purl.

Row 3: K2tog, k1, yo, k5, *yo, k2, sk2p, k2, yo, k5; repeat from * to last 3 sts, yo, k1, ssk.

Row 5: K2tog, k2, yo, k3, *yo, k3, sk2p, k3, yo, k3; repeat from * to last 4 sts, yo, k2, ssk.

Row 7: K2tog, k3, yo, k1, *yo, k4, sk2p, k4, yo, k1; repeat from * to last 5 sts, yo, k3, ssk.

Row 9: Yo, k4, sk2p, k4, yo, *k1, yo, k4, sk2p, k4, yo; repeat from * to end.

Row 11: K1, yo, k3, sk2p, k3, yo, *k3, yo, k3, sk2p, k3, yo; repeat from * to last st, k1.

Row 13: K2, yo, k2, sk2p, k2, yo, *k5, yo, k2, sk2p, k2, yo; repeat from * to last 2 sts, k2.

Row 15: K3, yo, k1, sk2p, k1, yo, *k7, yo, k1, sk2p, k1, yo; repeat from * to last 3 sts, k3.

Row 16: Purl.

Repeat Rows 1–16 for Field of Flowers Flat.

IN THE ROUND

(multiple of 12 sts; 16-rnd repeat)

Rnd 1: K4, yo, k1, sk2p, k1, yo, *k7, yo, k1, sk2p, k1, yo; repeat from * to last 3 sts, k3.

Rnd 2: Knit.

Rnd 3: K3, yo, k2, sk2p, k2, yo, *k5, yo, k2, sk2p, k2, yo; repeat from * to last 2 sts, k2.

Rnd 4: Knit.

Rnd 5: K2, yo, k3, sk2p, k3, yo, *k3, yo, k3, sk2p, k3, yo; repeat from * to last st, k1.

Rnd 6: Knit.

Rnd 7: *K1, yo, k4, sk2p, k4, yo; repeat from * to end.

Rnd 8: Knit to last st, reposition beginning-of-rnd marker to before last st.

Rnd 9: *Sk2p, k4, yo, k1, yo, k4; repeat from * to end.

Rnd 10: Repeat Rnd 8.

Rnd 11: *Sk2p, [k3, yo] twice, k3; repeat from * to end.

Rnd 12: Repeat Rnd 8.

Rnd 13: *Sk2p, k2, yo, k5, yo, k2; repeat from * to end.

Rnd 14: Repeat Rnd 8.

Rnd 15: *Sk2p, k1, yo, k7, yo, k1; repeat from * to end.

Rnd 16: Knit.

Repeat Rnds 1–16 for Field of Flowers in the Round.

FLAT

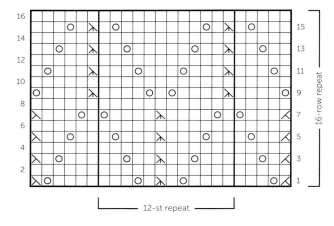

IN THE ROUND

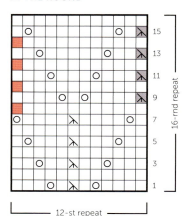

On final repeat only of Rnds 8, 10, 12, and 14, end rnd 1 st before beginning-of-rnd marker; reposition beginning-of-rnd marker to before last st. On all preceding repeats, knit this st.

On first repeat only of Rnds 9, 11, 13, and 15, work sk2p on what was last st of Rnds 8, 10, 12, and 14 and first 2 sts of Rnds 9, 11, 13, and 15; beginning-of-rnd marker should be before this sk2p. On all following repeats, sk2p.

Row 7: Ssk, yo, k5, *yo, s2kp2, yo, k5; repeat from * to last 2 sts, yo, k2tog.
Row 9: K1, *k2tog, yo, k3, yo, ssk, k1; repeat from * to end.
Row 11: K2, k2tog, yo, k1, yo, ssk, *k3, k2tog, yo, k1, yo, ssk; repeat from * to last 2 sts, k2.
Row 12: Purl.
Repeat Rows 1–12 for Sparkling Diamonds Flat.

IN THE ROUND

(multiple of 8 sts; 12-rnd repeat)
Rnd 1: K3, yo, s2kp2, yo, *k5, yo, s2kp2, yo; repeat from * to last 2 sts, k2.
Rnd 2: Knit.
Rnd 3: K2, yo, ssk, k1, k2tog, yo, *k3, yo, ssk, k1, k2tog, yo; repeat from * to last st, k1.
Rnd 4: Knit.
Rnd 5: *K1, yo, ssk, k3, k2tog, yo; repeat from * to end.
Rnd 6: Knit to last st, reposition beginning-of-rnd marker to before last st.
Rnd 7: *S2kp2, yo, k5, yo; repeat from * to end.
Rnd 8: Knit.
Rnd 9: *K1, k2tog, yo, k3, yo, ssk; repeat from * to end.
Rnd 10: Knit.
Rnd 11: K2, k2tog, yo, k1, yo, ssk, *k3, k2tog, yo, k1, yo, ssk; repeat from * to last st, k1.
Rnd 12: Knit.
Repeat Rnds 1–12 for Sparkling Diamonds in the Round.

Sparkling Diamonds

FLAT

(multiple of 8 sts + 9; 12-row repeat)
Row 1 (RS): K3, yo, s2kp2, yo, *k5, yo, s2kp2, yo; repeat from * to last 3 sts, k3.
Row 2 and all WS Rows: Purl.
Row 3: K2, yo, ssk, k1, k2tog, yo, *k3, yo, ssk, k1, k2tog, yo; repeat from * to last 2 sts, k2.
Row 5: K1, *yo, ssk, k3, k2tog, yo, k1; repeat from * to end.

FLAT

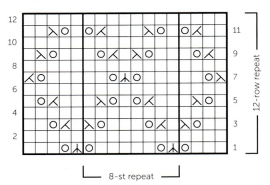

IN THE ROUND

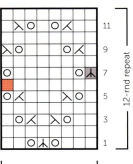

On final repeat only of Rnd 6, end rnd 1 st before beginning-of-rnd marker; reposition beginning-of-rnd marker to before last st. On all preceding repeats, knit this st.

On first repeat only of Rnd 7, work s2kp2 on what was last st of Rnd 6 and first 2 sts of Rnd 7; beginning-of-rnd marker should be before this s2kp2. On all following repeats, s2kp2.

Eyelet Grid

FLAT

(multiple of 8 sts + 2; 16-row repeat)

Row 1 (RS): *Yo, k2tog; repeat from * to end.

Row 2: Purl.

Row 3: Yo, k2tog, *k6, yo, k2tog; repeat from * to end.

Rows 4–15: Repeat Rows 2 and 3 six times.

Row 16: Purl.

Repeat Rows 1–16 for Eyelet Grid Flat.

IN THE ROUND

(multiple of 8 sts; 16-rnd repeat)

Rnd 1: *Yo, k2tog; repeat from * to end.

Rnd 2: Knit.

Rnd 3: *K6, yo, k2tog; repeat from * to end.

Rnds 4–15: Repeat Rows 2 and 3 six times.

Rnd 16: Knit.

Repeat Rnds 1–16 for Eyelet Grid in the Round.

FLAT

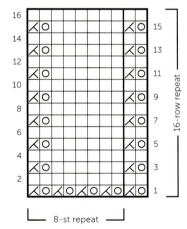

8-st repeat

IN THE ROUND

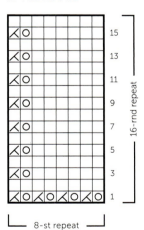

8-st repeat

Acorns and Eyelets

FLAT

(multiple of 12 sts + 13; 20-row repeat)

Row 1 (RS): K1, *yo, ssk, k7, k2tog, yo, k1; repeat from * to end.

Row 2: P3, k7, *p5, k7; repeat from * to last 3 sts, p3.

Row 3: K2, yo, ssk, k5, k2tog, yo, *k3, yo, ssk, k5, k2tog, yo; repeat from * to last 2 sts, k2.

Row 4: P4, k5, *p7, k5; repeat from * to last 4 sts, p4.

Row 5: K3, yo, ssk, k3, k2tog, yo, *k5, yo, ssk, k3, k2tog, yo; repeat from * to last 3 sts, k3.

Row 6: P5, k3, *p9, k3; repeat from * to last 5 sts, p5.

Row 7: K4, yo, ssk, k1, k2tog, yo, *k7, yo, ssk, k1, k2tog, yo; repeat from * to last 4 sts, k4.

Row 8: P6, k1, *p11, k1; repeat from * to last 6 sts, p6.

Row 9: K5, yo, sk2p, yo, *k9, yo, sk2p, yo; repeat from * to last 5 sts, k5.

Row 10: P1, k4, p3, *k9, p3; repeat from * to last 5 sts, k4, p1.

Row 11: K4, k2tog, yo, k1, yo, ssk, *k7, k2tog, yo, k1, yo, ssk; repeat from * to last 4 sts, k4.

Row 12: P1, k3, p5, *k7, p5; repeat from * to last 4 sts, k3, p1.

Row 13: K3, k2tog, yo, k3, yo, ssk, *k5, k2tog, yo, k3, yo, ssk; repeat from * to last 3 sts, k3.

Row 14: P1, k2, p7, *k5, p7; repeat from * to last 3 sts, k2, p1.

Row 15: K2, k2tog, yo, k5, yo, ssk, *k3, k2tog, yo, k5, yo, ssk; repeat from * to last 2 sts, k2.

Row 16: P1, k1, p9, *k3, p9; repeat from * to last 2 sts, k1, p1.

Row 17: K1, *k2tog, yo, k7, yo, ssk, k1; repeat from * to end.

Row 18: P12, *k1, p11; repeat from * to last st, p1.

Row 19: K2tog, yo, k9, *yo, sk2p, yo, k9; repeat from * to last 2 sts, yo, ssk.

Row 20: P2, k9, *p3, k9; repeat from * to last 2 sts, p2.

Repeat Rows 1–20 for Acorns and Eyelets Flat.

IN THE ROUND

(multiple of 12 sts; 20-rnd repeat)

Rnd 1: *K1, yo, ssk, k7, k2tog, yo; repeat from * to end.

Rnd 2: K3, p7, *k5, p7; repeat from * to last 2 sts, k2.

Rnd 3: K2, yo, ssk, k5, k2tog, yo, *k3, yo, ssk, k5, k2tog, yo; repeat from * to last st, k1.

Rnd 4: K4, p5, *k7, p5; repeat from * to last 3 sts, k3.

Rnd 5: K3, yo, ssk, k3, k2tog, yo, *k5, yo, ssk, k3, k2tog, yo; repeat from * to last 2 sts, k2.

Rnd 6: K5, p3, *k9, p3; repeat from * to last 4 sts, k4.

Rnd 7: K4, yo, ssk, k1, k2tog, yo, *k7, yo, ssk, k1, k2tog, yo; repeat from * to last 3 sts, k3.

Rnd 8: K6, p1, *k11, p1; repeat from * to last 5 sts, k5.

Rnd 9: K5, yo, sk2p, yo, *k9, yo, sk2p, yo; repeat from * to last 4 sts, k4.

Rnd 10: P5, k3, *p9, k3; repeat from * to last 4 sts, p4.

Rnd 11: K4, k2tog, yo, k1, yo, ssk, *k7, k2tog, yo, k1, yo, ssk; repeat from * to last 3 sts, k3.

Rnd 12: P4, k5, *p7, k5; repeat from * to last 3 sts, p3.

Rnd 13: K3, k2tog, yo, k3, yo, ssk, *k5, k2tog, yo, k3, yo, ssk; repeat from * to last 2 sts, k2.

Rnd 14: P3, k7, *p5, k7; repeat from * to last 2 sts, p2.

Rnd 15: K2, k2tog, yo, k5, yo, ssk, *k3, k2tog, yo, k5, yo, ssk; repeat from * to last st, k1.

Rnd 16: P2, k9, *p3, k9; repeat from * to last st, p1.

Rnd 17: *K1, k2tog, yo, k7, yo, ssk; repeat from * to end.

Rnd 18: *P1, k11; repeat from * to last 11 sts, p1, k10, reposition beginning-of-rnd marker to before last st.

Rnd 19: *Sk2p, yo, k9, yo; repeat from * to end. ***Note:*** *On first repeat of Rnd 19 only, work sk2p on what was last st of Rnd 18 and first 2 sts of Rnd 19; beginning-of-rnd marker should be before this sk2p. On all following repeats, sk2p.*

Rnd 20: K2, p9, *k3, p9; repeat from * to last st, k1.

Repeat Rnds 1–20 for Acorns and Eyelets in the Round.

FLAT

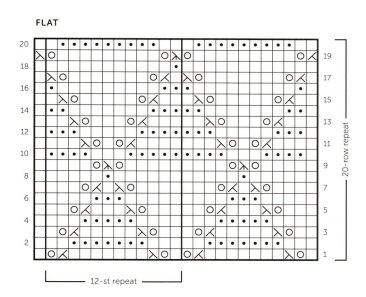

12-st repeat

20-row repeat

IN THE ROUND

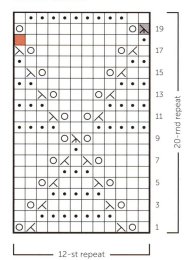

12-st repeat

20-rnd repeat

On last repeat only of Rnd 18, end rnd 1 st before beginning-of-rnd marker; reposition beginning-of-rnd marker to before last st. On all preceding repeats, knit this st.

On first repeat only of Rnd 19, work sk2p on what was last st of Rnd 18 and first 2 sts of Rnd 19; beginning-of-rnd marker should be before this sk2p. On all following repeats, sk2p.

(multiple of 14 sts; 12-rnd repeat)

Rnds 1 and 2: Knit.

Rnd 3: [K1, yo] twice, [ssk] twice, k3, [k2tog] twice, *[yo, k1] 3 times, yo, [ssk] twice, k3, [k2tog] twice; repeat from * to last st, yo, k1, yo.

Rnd 4: Knit.

Rnds 5 and 6: P5, k5, *p9, k5; repeat from * to last 4 sts, p4.

Rnds 7 and 8: Knit.

Rnd 9: K2, [k2tog] twice, [yo, k1] 3 times, yo, [ssk] twice, *k3, [k2tog] twice, [yo, k1] 3 times, yo, [ssk] twice; repeat from * to last st, k1.

Rnd 10: Knit.

Rnds 11 and 12: K3, p9, *k5, p9; repeat from * to last 2 sts, k2.

Repeat Rnds 1–12 for Wheat Bales in the Round.

Wheat Bales

FLAT

(multiple of 14 sts + 1; 12-row repeat)

Row 1 (RS): Knit.

Row 2 and all WS Rows: Knit the knit sts and purl the purl sts as they face you; purl all yos.

Row 3: [K1, yo] twice, [ssk] twice, k3, [k2tog] twice, *[yo, k1] 3 times, yo, [ssk] twice, k3, [k2tog] twice; repeat from * to last 2 sts, [yo, k1] twice.

Row 5: P5, k5, *p9, k5; repeat from * to last 5 sts, p5.

Row 7: Knit.

Row 9: K2, [k2tog] twice, [yo, k1] 3 times, yo, [ssk] twice, *k3, [k2tog] twice, [yo, k1] 3 times, yo, [ssk] twice; repeat from * to last 2 sts, k2.

Row 11: K3, p9, *k5, p9; repeat from * to last 3 sts, k3.

Row 12: Repeat Row 2.

Repeat Rows 1–12 for Wheat Bales Flat.

FLAT

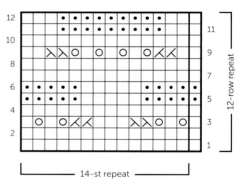

IN THE ROUND

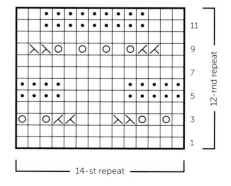

Ants on a Log

FLAT

(multiple of 8 sts + 5; 12-row repeat)

Row 1 (RS): Purl.

Row 2: Knit.

Rows 3 and 4: Purl.

Row 5: K1, yo, sk2p, yo, *k5, yo, sk2p, yo; repeat from * to last st, k1.

Rows 6 and 7: Purl.

Row 8: Knit.

Rows 9 and 10: Purl.

Row 11: K5, *yo, sk2p, yo, k5; repeat from * to end.

Row 12: Purl.

Repeat Rows 1–12 for Ants on a Log Flat.

FLAT

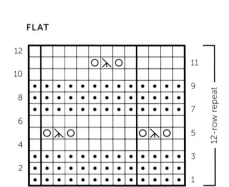

8-st repeat

IN THE ROUND

(multiple of 8 sts; 12-rnd repeat)

Rnds 1–3: Purl.

Rnd 4: Knit.

Rnd 5: *K5, yo, sk2p, yo; repeat from * to end.

Rnd 6: Knit.

Rnds 7–9: Purl.

Rnd 10: Knit.

Rnd 11: K1, yo, sk2p, yo, *k5, yo, sk2p, yo; repeat from * to last 4 sts, k4.

Rnd 12: Knit.

Repeat Rnds 1–12 for Ants on a Log in the Round.

IN THE ROUND

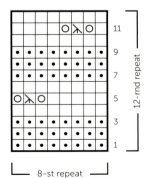

8-st repeat

Sails

....

FLAT

(multiple of 16 sts + 17; 32-row repeat)

Row 1 (RS): Knit.

Row 2: Knit.

Row 3: K1, *yo, k6, s2kp2, k6, yo, k1; repeat from * to end.

Row 4: Purl.

Row 5: K2, yo, k5, s2kp2, k5, yo, *k3, yo, k5, s2kp2, k5, yo; repeat from * to last 2 sts, k2.

Row 6: Purl.

Row 7: K3, yo, k4, s2kp2, k4, yo, *k5, yo, k4, s2kp2, k4, yo; repeat from * to last 3 sts, k3.

Row 8: Purl.

Row 9: K4, yo, k3, s2kp2, k3, yo, *k7, yo, k3, s2kp2, k3, yo; repeat from * to last 4 sts, k4.

Row 10: Purl.

Row 11: K5, yo, k2, s2kp2, k2, yo, *k9, yo, k2, s2kp2, k2, yo; repeat from * to last 5 sts, k5.

Row 12: Purl.

Row 13: K6, yo, k1, s2kp2, k1, yo, *k11, yo, k1, s2kp2, k1, yo; repeat from * to last 6 sts, k6.

FLAT

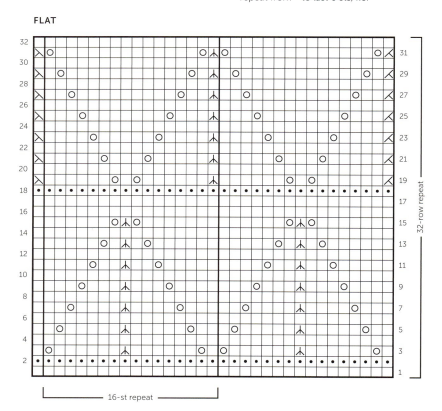

Row 14: Purl.

Row 15: K7, yo, s2kp2, yo, *k13, yo, s2kp2, yo; repeat from * to last 7 sts, k7.

Row 16: Purl.

Rows 17 and 18: Knit.

Row 19: K2tog, k6, yo, k1, yo, k6, *s2kp2, k6, yo, k1, yo, k6; repeat from * to last 2 sts, ssk.

Row 20: Purl.

Row 21: K2tog, k5, yo, k3, yo, k5, *s2kp2, k5, yo, k3, yo, k5; repeat from * to last 2 sts, ssk.

Row 22: Purl.

Row 23: K2tog, k4, yo, k5, yo, k4, *s2kp2, k4, yo, k5, yo, k4; repeat from * to last 2 sts, ssk.

Row 24: Purl.

Row 25: K2tog, k3, yo, k7, yo, k3, *s2kp2, k3, yo, k7, yo, k3; repeat from * to last 2 sts, ssk.

Row 26: Purl.

Row 27: K2tog, k2, yo, k9, yo, k2, *s2kp2, k2, yo, k9, yo, k2; repeat from * to last 2 sts, ssk.

Row 28: Purl.

Row 29: K2tog, k1, yo, k11, yo, k1, *s2kp2, k1, yo, k11, yo, k1; repeat from * to last 2 sts, ssk.

Row 30: Purl.

Row 31: K2tog, yo, k13, *yo, s2kp2, yo, k13; repeat from * to last 2 sts, yo, ssk.

Row 32: Purl.

Repeat Rows 1–32 for Sails Flat.

IN THE ROUND

(multiple of 16 sts; 32-rnd repeat)

Rnd 1: Knit.

Rnd 2: Purl.

Rnd 3: *K1, yo, k6, s2kp2, k6, yo; repeat from * to end.

Rnd 4: Knit.

Rnd 5: K2, yo, k5, s2kp2, k5, yo, *k3, yo, k5, s2kp2, k5, yo; repeat from * to last st, k1.

Rnd 6: Knit.

Rnd 7: K3, yo, k4, s2kp2, k4, yo, *k5, yo, k4, s2kp2, k4, yo; repeat from * to last 2 sts, k2.

Rnd 8: Knit.

Rnd 9: K4, yo, k3, s2kp2, k3, yo, *k7, yo, k3, s2kp2, k3, yo; repeat from * to last 3 sts, k3.

Rnd 10: Knit.

Rnd 11: K5, yo, k2, s2kp2, k2, yo, *k9, yo, k2, s2kp2, k2, yo; repeat from * to last 4 sts, k4.

Rnd 12: Knit.

Rnd 13: K6, yo, k1, s2kp2, k1, yo, *k11, yo, k1, s2kp2, k1, yo; repeat from * to last 5 sts, k5.

Rnd 14: Knit.

Rnd 15: K7, yo, s2kp2, yo, *k13, yo, s2kp2, yo; repeat from * to last 6 sts, k6.

Rnds 16 and 17: Knit.

Rnd 18: Purl to last st, reposition beginning-of-rnd marker to before last st.

Rnd 19: *S2kp2, k6, yo, k1, yo, k6; repeat from * to end.

Rnd 20: Repeat Rnd 18.

Rnd 21: *S2kp2, k5, yo, k3, yo, k5; repeat from * to end.

Rnd 22: Repeat Rnd 18.

Rnd 23: *S2kp2, k4, yo, k5, yo, k4; repeat from * to end.

Rnd 24: Repeat Rnd 18.

Rnd 25: *S2kp2, k3, yo, k7, yo, k3; repeat from * to end.

Rnd 26: Repeat Rnd 18.

Rnd 27: *S2kp2, k2, yo, k9, yo, k2; repeat from * to end.

Rnd 28: Repeat Rnd 18.

Rnd 29: *S2kp2, k1, yo, k11, yo, k1; repeat from * to end.

Rnd 30: Repeat Rnd 18.

Rnd 31: *S2kp2, yo, k13, yo; repeat from * to end.

Rnd 32: Knit.

Repeat Rnds 1–32 for Sails in the Round.

IN THE ROUND

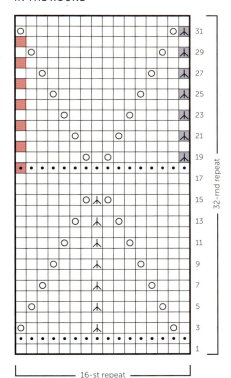

On last repeat only of Rnds 18, 20, 22, 24, 26, 28, and 30, end rnd 1 st before beginning-of-rnd marker; reposition beginning-of-rnd marker to before last st. On all preceding repeats, knit or purl this st as indicated.

On first repeat only of Rnds 19, 21, 23, 25, 27, 29, and 31, work s2kp2 on what was last st of Rnds 18, 20, 22, 24, 26, 28, and 30 and first 2 sts of Rnds 19, 21, 23, 25, 27, 29, and 31; beginning-of-rnd marker should be before this s2kp2. On all following repeats, s2kp2.

Ribbons

FLAT

(multiple of 14 sts + 3; 24-row repeat)

Row 1 (RS): P3, *yo, k1, p3, k5, k2tog, p3; repeat from * to end.

Row 2 and all WS Rows: Knit the knit sts and purl the purl sts as they face you; purl all yos.

Row 3: P3, *k1, yo, k1, p3, k4, k2tog, p3; repeat from * to end.

Row 5: P3, *k2, yo, k1, p3, k3, k2tog, p3; repeat from * to end.

Row 7: P3, *k3, yo, k1, p3, k2, k2tog, p3; repeat from * to end.

Row 9: P3, *k4, yo, k1, p3, k1, k2tog, p3; repeat from * to end.

Row 11: P3, *k5, yo, k1, p3, k2tog, p3; repeat from * to end.

Row 13: P3, *ssk, k5, p3, k1, yo, p3; repeat from * to end.

Row 15: P3, *ssk, k4, p3, k1, yo, k1, p3; repeat from * to end.

Row 17: P3, *ssk, k3, p3, k1, yo, k2, p3; repeat from * to end.

Row 19: P3, *ssk, k2, p3, k1, yo, k3, p3; repeat from * to end.

Row 21: P3, *ssk, k1, p3, k1, yo, k4, p3; repeat from * to end.

Row 23: P3, *ssk, p3, k1, yo, k5, p3; repeat from * to end.

Row 24: Repeat Row 2.

Repeat Rows 1–24 for Ribbons Flat.

IN THE ROUND

(multiple of 14 sts; 24-rnd repeat)

Rnd 1: *P3, yo, k1, p3, k5, k2tog; repeat from * to end.

Rnd 2 and all Even-Numbered Rnds: Knit the knit sts and purl the purl sts as they face you; knit all yos.

Rnd 3: *P3, k1, yo, k1, p3, k4, k2tog; repeat from * to end.

Rnd 5: *P3, k2, yo, k1, p3, k3, k2tog; repeat from * to end.

Rnd 7: *P3, k3, yo, k1, p3, k2, k2tog; repeat from * to end.

Rnd 9: *P3, k4, yo, k1, p3, k1, k2tog; repeat from * to end.

Rnd 11: *P3, k5, yo, k1, p3, k2tog; repeat from * to end.

Rnd 13: *P3, ssk, k5, p3, k1, yo; repeat from * to end.

Rnd 15: *P3, ssk, k4, p3, k1, yo, k1; repeat from * to end.

Rnd 17: *P3, ssk, k3, p3, k1, yo, k2; repeat from * to end.

Rnd 19: *P3, ssk, k2, p3, k1, yo, k3; repeat from * to end.

Rnd 21: *P3, ssk, k1, p3, k1, yo, k4; repeat from * to end.

Rnd 23: *P3, ssk, p3, k1, yo, k5; repeat from * to end.

Rnd 24: Repeat Rnd 2.

Repeat Rnds 1–24 for Ribbons in the Round.

FLAT

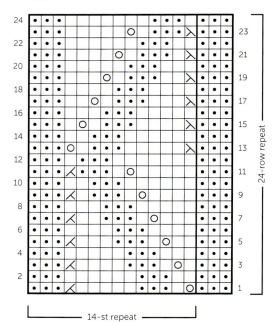

24-row repeat

14-st repeat

IN THE ROUND

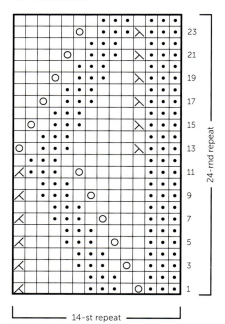

24-rnd repeat

14-st repeat

Mini Arches

FLAT

(multiple of 8 sts + 9; 24-row repeat)

Row 1 (RS): Knit.

Row 2 and all WS Rows: Purl.

Row 3: K2, k2tog, yo, k1, yo, ssk, *k3, k2tog, yo, k1, yo, ssk; repeat from * to 2 sts, k2.

Row 5: K1, *k2tog, yo, k3, yo, ssk, k1; repeat from * to end.

Row 7: K2tog, yo, k5, *yo, s2kp2, yo, k5; repeat from * to last 2 sts, yo, ssk.

Row 9: K1, *ssk, yo, k3, k2tog, k1; repeat from * to end.

Row 11: K2, ssk, yo, k1, yo, k2tog, *k3, ssk, yo, k1, yo, k2tog; repeat from * to last 2 sts, k2.

Row 13: Knit.

Row 15: K1, *yo, ssk, k3, k2tog, yo, k1; repeat from * to end.

Row 17: K2, yo, ssk, k1, k2tog, yo, *k3, yo, ssk, k1, k2tog, yo; repeat from * to last 2 sts, k2.

Row 19: K3, yo, s2kp2, yo, *k5, yo, s2kp2, yo; repeat from * to last 3 sts, k3.

Row 21: K2, yo, k2tog, k1, ssk, yo, *k3, yo, k2tog, k1, ssk, yo; repeat from * to last 2 sts, k2.

Row 23: K1, *yo, k2tog, k3, ssk, yo, k1; repeat from * to end.

Row 24: Purl.

Repeat Rows 1–24 for Mini Arches Flat.

IN THE ROUND

(multiple of 8 sts; 24-rnd repeat)

Rnds 1 and 2: Knit.

Rnd 3: K2, k2tog, yo, k1, yo, ssk, *k3, k2tog, yo, k1, yo, ssk; repeat from * to last st, k1.

Rnd 4: Knit.

Rnd 5: *K1, k2tog, yo, k3, yo, ssk; repeat from * to end.

Rnd 6: Knit to last st, reposition beginning-of-rnd marker to before last st.

Rnd 7: *S2kp2, yo, k5, yo; repeat from * to end.

Rnd 8: Knit.

Rnd 9: *K1, ssk, yo, k3, k2tog; repeat from * to end.

Rnd 10: Knit.

Rnd 11: K2, ssk, yo, k1, yo, k2tog, *k3, ssk, yo, k1, yo, k2tog; repeat from * to last st, k1.

Rnds 12–14: Knit.

Rnd 15: *K1, yo, ssk, k3, k2tog, yo; repeat from * to end.

Rnd 16: Knit.

Rnd 17: K2, yo, ssk, k1, k2tog, yo, *k3, yo, ssk, k1, k2tog, yo; repeat from * to last st, k1.

Rnd 18: Knit.

Rnd 19: K3, yo, s2kp2, yo, *k5, yo, s2kp2, yo; repeat from * to last 2 sts, k2.

Mesh

FLAT

(multiple of 3 sts + 1; 4-row repeat)

Row 1 (RS): P1, *ssk, yo, p1; repeat from * to end.

Row 2: K1, *p2, k1; repeat from * to end.

Row 3: P1, *yo, k2tog, p1; repeat from * to end.

Row 4: Repeat Row 2.

Repeat Rows 1–4 for Mesh Flat.

IN THE ROUND

(multiple of 3 sts; 4-rnd repeat)

Rnd 1: *P1, ssk, yo; repeat from * to end.

Rnd 2: P1, *k2; repeat from * to end.

Rnd 3: *P1, yo, k2tog; repeat from * to end.

Rnd 4: Repeat Rnd 2.

Repeat Rnds 1–4 for Mesh in the Round.

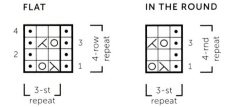

FLAT

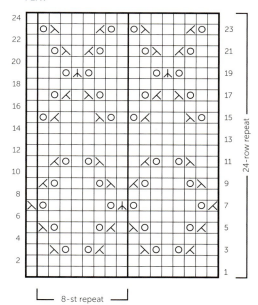

8-st repeat

24-row repeat

IN THE ROUND

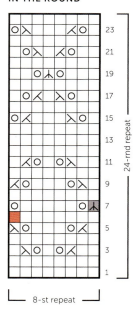

8-st repeat

24-rnd repeat

Rnd 20: Knit.

Rnd 21: K2, yo, k2tog, k1, ssk, yo, *k3, yo, k2tog, k1, ssk, yo; repeat from * to last st, k1.

Rnd 22: Knit.

Rnd 23: *K1, yo, k2tog, k3, ssk, yo; repeat from * to end.

Rnd 24: Knit.

Repeat Rnds 1–24 for Mini Arches in the Round.

On last repeat only of Rnd 6, end rnd 1 st before beginning-of-rnd marker; reposition beginning-of-rnd marker to before last st. On all preceding repeats, knit this st.

On first repeat only of Rnd 7, work s2kp2 on what was last st of Rnd 6 and first 2 sts of Rnd 7; beginning-of-rnd marker should be before this s2kp2. On all following repeats, s2kp2.

Rnd 8: Purl to last st, reposition beginning-of-rnd marker to before last st.

Rnd 9: *S2kp2, k3, yo, k1, yo, k3; repeat from * to end.

Rnd 10: Knit to last st, reposition beginning-of-rnd marker to before last st.

Rnds 11–14: Repeat Rnds 9 and 10 twice.

Rnd 15: Repeat Rnd 9.

Rnd 16: Purl.

Repeat Rnds 1–16 for Leaf Panes in the Round.

FLAT

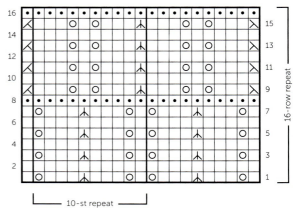

Leaf Panes

FLAT

(multiple of 10 sts + 11; 16-row repeat)

Row 1 (RS): K1, *yo, k3, s2kp2, k3, yo, k1; repeat from * to end.

Row 2: Purl.

Rows 3–6: Repeat Rows 1 and 2 twice.

Row 7: Repeat Row 1.

Row 8: Knit.

Row 9: Ssk, k3, yo, k1, yo, k3, *s2kp2, k3, yo, k1, yo, k3; repeat from * to last 2 sts, k2tog.

Row 10: Purl.

Rows 11–14: Repeat Rows 9 and 10 twice.

Row 15: Repeat Row 9.

Row 16: Knit.

Repeat Rows 1–16 for Leaf Panes Flat.

IN THE ROUND

(multiple of 10 sts; 16-rnd repeat)

Rnd 1: *K1, yo, k3, s2kp2, k3, yo; repeat from * to end.

Rnd 2: Knit.

Rnds 3–6: Repeat Rnds 1 and 2 twice.

Rnd 7: Repeat Rnd 1.

IN THE ROUND

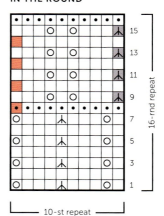

On final repeat only of Rnds 8, 10, 12, and 14, end rnd 1 st before beginning-of-rnd marker; reposition beginning-of-rnd marker to before last st. On all preceding repeats, knit or purl this st as indicated.

On first repeat only of Rnds 9, 11, 13, and 15, work s2kp2 on what was last st of Rnds 8, 10, 12, and 14 and first 2 sts of Rnds 9, 11, 13, and 15; beginning-of-rnd marker should be before this s2kp2. On all following repeats, s2kp2.

Nestled Leaves

FLAT

(multiple of 16 sts + 1; 8-row repeat)

Row 1 (RS): P1, *k3, [k2tog] twice, [yo, k1] 3 times, yo, [ssk] twice, k1, p1; repeat from * to end.

Row 2 and all WS Rows: K1, *p15, k1; repeat from * to end.

Row 3: P1, *k2, [k2tog] twice, yo, k1, yo, k3, yo, k1, yo, [ssk] twice, p1; repeat from * to end.

Row 5: P1, *k1, [k2tog] twice, [yo, k1] 3 times, yo, [ssk] twice, k3, p1; repeat from * to end.

Row 7: P1, *[k2tog] twice, yo, k1, yo, k3, yo, k1, yo, [ssk] twice, k2, p1; repeat from * to end.

Row 8: Repeat Row 2.

Repeat Rows 1–8 for Nestled Leaves Flat.

IN THE ROUND

(multiple of 16 sts; 8-rnd repeat)

Rnd 1: *P1, k3, [k2tog] twice, [yo, k1] 3 times, yo, [ssk] twice, k1; repeat from * to end.

Rnd 2 and all Even-Numbered Rnds: *P1, k15; repeat from * to end.

Rnd 3: *P1, k2, [k2tog] twice, yo, k1, yo, k3, yo, k1, yo, [ssk] twice; repeat from * to end.

Rnd 5: *P1, k1, [k2tog] twice, [yo, k1] 3 times, yo, [ssk] twice, k3; repeat from * to end.

Rnd 7: *P1, [k2tog] twice, yo, k1, yo, k3, yo, k1, yo, [ssk] twice, k2; repeat from * to end.

Rnd 8: Repeat Rnd 2.

Repeat Rnds 1–8 for Nestled Leaves in the Round.

FLAT

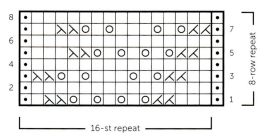

IN THE ROUND

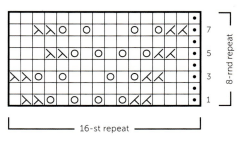

IN THE ROUND

(multiple of 10 sts; 8-rnd repeat)

Rnd 1: *K5, ssk, k3, yo; repeat from * to end.

Rnd 2: K5, ssk, k2, yo, *k6, ssk, k2, yo; repeat from * to last st, k1.

Rnd 3: P1, k4, ssk, k1, yo, k1, *p2, k4, ssk, k1, yo, k1; repeat from * to last st, p1.

Rnd 4: P1, k4, ssk, yo, k2, *p2, k4, ssk, yo, k2; repeat from * to last st, p1.

Rnd 5: P1, yo, k3, k2tog, k3, *p2, yo, k3, k2tog, k3; repeat from * to last st, p1.

Rnd 6: P1, k1, yo, k2, k2tog, k3, *p2, k1, yo, k2, k2tog, k3; repeat from * to last st, p1.

Rnd 7: K3, yo, k1, k2tog, *k7, yo, k1, k2tog; repeat from * to last 4 sts, k4.

Rnd 8: K4, yo, k2tog, *k8, yo, k2tog; repeat from * to last 4 sts, k4.

Repeat Rnds 1–8 for Serpentine Waves in the Round.

Serpentine Waves

FLAT

(multiple of 10 sts + 1; 8-row repeat)

Row 1 (RS): *K5, ssk, k3, yo; repeat from * to last st, k1.

Row 2: P2, yo, p2, ssp, *p6, yo, p2, ssp; repeat from * to last 5 sts, p5.

Row 3: P1, *k4, ssk, k1, yo, k1, p2; repeat from * to end.

Row 4: *K2, p2, yo, ssp, p4; repeat from * to last st, k1.

Row 5: P1, *yo, k3, k2tog, k3, p2; repeat from * to end.

Row 6: *K2, p3, p2tog, p2, yo, p1; repeat from * to last st, k1.

Row 7: K3, yo, k1, k2tog, *k7, yo, k1, k2tog; repeat from * to last 5 sts, k5.

Row 8: P5, p2tog, yo, *p8, p2tog, yo; repeat from * to last 4 sts, p4.

Repeat Rows 1–8 for Serpentine Waves Flat.

FLAT

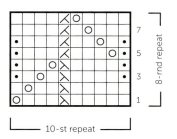

IN THE ROUND

Arches

FLAT

(multiple of 19 sts + 1; 10-row repeat)

Row 1 (RS): P1, *sk2p, k4, yo, k1, yo, p2, yo, k1, yo, k4, k3tog, p1; repeat from * to end.

Row 2 and all WS Rows: Knit the knit sts and purl the purl sts as they face you; purl all yos.

Row 3: P1, *sk2p, k3, [yo, k1] twice, p2, [k1, yo] twice, k3, k3tog, p1; repeat from * to end.

Row 5: P1, *sk2p, k2, yo, k1, yo, k2, p2, k2, yo, k1, yo, k2, k3tog, p1; repeat from * to end.

Row 7: P1, *sk2p, [k1, yo] twice, k3, p2, k3, [yo, k1] twice, k3tog, p1; repeat from * to end.

Row 9: P1, *sk2p, yo, k1, yo, k4, p2, k4, yo, k1, yo, k3tog, p1; repeat from * to end.

Row 10: Repeat Row 2.

Repeat Rows 1–10 for Arches Flat.

IN THE ROUND

(multiple of 19 sts; 10-rnd repeat)

Rnd 1: *P1, sk2p, k4, yo, k1, yo, p2, yo, k1, yo, k4, k3tog; repeat from * to end.

Rnd 2 and all Even-Numbered Rnds: Knit the knit sts and purl the purl sts as they face you; knit all yos.

Rnd 3: *P1, sk2p, k3, [yo, k1] twice, p2, [k1, yo] twice, k3, k3tog; repeat from * to end.

Rnd 5: *P1, sk2p, k2, yo, k1, yo, k2, p2, k2, yo, k1, yo, k2, k3tog; repeat from * to end.

Rnd 7: *P1, sk2p, [k1, yo] twice, k3, p2, k3, [yo, k1] twice, k3tog; repeat from * to end.

Rnd 9: *P1, sk2p, yo, k1, yo, k4, p2, k4, yo, k1, yo, k3tog; repeat from * to end.

Rnd 10: Repeat Rnd 2.

Repeat Rnds 1–10 for Arches in the Round.

FLAT

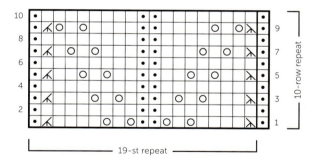

19-st repeat

10-row repeat

IN THE ROUND

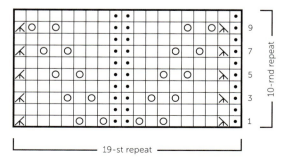

19-st repeat

10-rnd repeat

Dominoes

FLAT

(multiple of 7 sts + 3; 12-row repeat)
Row 1 (RS): K3, *yo, ssk, k2tog, yo, k3; repeat from * to end.
Row 2: K3, *p4, k3; repeat from * to end.
Rows 3–6: Repeat Rows 1 and 2 twice.
Row 7: Repeat Row 1.
Rows 8–12: Purl.
Repeat Rows 1–12 for Dominoes Flat.

IN THE ROUND

(multiple of 7 sts; 12-rnd repeat)
Rnd 1: *K3, yo, ssk, k2tog, yo; repeat from * to end.
Rnd 2: *P3, k4; repeat from * to end.
Rnds 3–6: Repeat Rnds 1 and 2 twice.
Rnd 7: Repeat Rnd 1.
Rnd 8: Knit.
Rnd 9: Purl.
Rnds 10 and 11: Repeat Rnds 8 and 9.
Rnd 12: Knit.
Repeat Rnds 1–12 for Dominoes in the Round.

FLAT

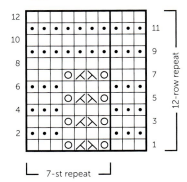

IN THE ROUND

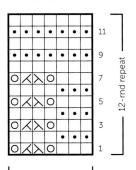

Little Shells

FLAT

(multiple of 7 sts + 2; 4-row repeat)
Row 1 (RS): Knit.
Row 2: Purl.
Row 3: K2, *yo, p1, p3tog, p1, yo, k2; repeat from * to end.
Row 4: Purl.
Repeat Rows 1–4 for Little Shells Flat.

IN THE ROUND

(multiple of 7 sts; 4-rnd repeat)
Rnds 1 and 2: Knit.
Rnd 3: K1, yo, p1, p3tog, p1, yo, *k2, yo, p1, p3tog, p1, yo; repeat from * to last st, k1.
Rnd 4: Knit.
Repeat Rnds 1–4 for Little Shells in the Round.

FLAT

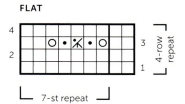

IN THE ROUND

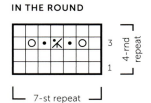

Row 5: K1, k2tog, yo, k2, *[k2tog, yo] twice, k2; repeat from * to end.

Row 7: K2tog, yo, k2, *[k2tog, yo] twice, k2; repeat from * to last st, k1.

Row 9: K3, *[k2tog, yo] twice, k2; repeat from * to last 2 sts, k2tog, yo.

Row 11: K2, *[k2tog, yo] twice, k2; repeat from * to last 3 sts, k2tog, yo, k1.

Row 12: Purl.

Repeat Rows 1–12 for Lacy Right Diagonals Flat.

IN THE ROUND

(multiple of 6 sts; 2-rnd repeat)

Note: The pattern shifts 1 st to the right with every repeat of Rnd 1.

Rnd 1: *[K2tog, yo] twice, k2; repeat from * to end.

Note: On first instance of Rnd 1, work k2tog on first 2 sts of rnd, then place removable marker on this k2tog. For all subsequent instances of Rnd 1, on first repeat only, work k2tog on marked st and what was last st of Rnd 2. Move marker up as you go.

Rnd 2: Knit to 1 st before marked st.

Repeat Rnds 1 and 2 for Lacy Right Diagonals in the Round.

Lacy Right Diagonals

FLAT

(multiple of 6 sts + 5; 12-row repeat)

Row 1 (RS): K1, *[k2tog, yo] twice, k2; repeat from * to last 4 sts, [k2tog, yo] twice.

Row 2 and all WS Rows: Purl.

Row 3: *[K2tog, yo] twice, k2; repeat from * to last 5 sts, [k2tog, yo] twice, k1.

FLAT

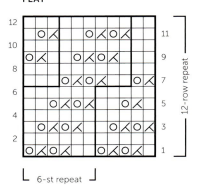

IN THE ROUND

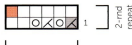

On first instance of Rnd 1, work k2tog on first 2 sts of rnd, then place removable marker on this k2tog. For all following instances of Rnd 1, on first repeat only, work k2tog on marked st and what was last st of Rnd 2. Move marker up as you go. This will shift the beginning of rnd 1 st to the right on every Rnd 1. On all following repeats, k2tog.

On final repeat only of Rnd 2, end rnd 1 st before marked st. On all preceding repeats, knit this st.

Lacy Left Diagonals

FLAT

(multiple of 6 sts + 5; 12-row repeat)

Row 1 (RS): [Yo, ssk] twice, k2; repeat from * to last 5 sts, [yo, ssk] twice, k1.

Row 2 and all WS Rows: Purl.

Row 3: K1, *[yo, ssk] twice, k2; repeat from * to last 4 sts, [yo, ssk] twice.

Row 5: K2, *[yo, ssk] twice, k2; repeat from * to last 3 sts, yo, ssk, k1.

Row 7: K3, *[yo, ssk] twice, k2; repeat from * to last 2 sts, yo, ssk.

Row 9: Yo, ssk, k2, *[yo, ssk] twice, k2; repeat from * to last st, k1.

Row 11: K1, yo, ssk, k2, *[yo, ssk] twice, k2; repeat from * to end.

Row 12: Purl.

Repeat Rows 1–12 for Lacy Left Diagonals Flat.

IN THE ROUND

(multiple of 6 sts; 2-rnd repeat)

Note: *The pattern shifts 1 st to the left with every repeat of Rnd 2.*

Rnd 1: *K2, [yo, ssk] twice; repeat from * to end.

Rnd 2: Knit to end, remove beginning-of-rnd marker, k1, pm for new beginning of rnd.

Repeat Rnds 1 and 2 for Lacy Left Diagonals in the Round.

FLAT

IN THE ROUND

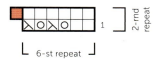

On final repeat only of Rnd 2, remove beginning-of-rnd marker, k1, pm for new beginning of rnd. This will shift the beginning of rnd 1 st to the left at the end of every Rnd 2. On all preceding repeats, omit this st.

Lacy Streamers

FLAT

(multiple of 11 sts; 32-row repeat)

Row 1 (RS): *Yo, ssk, yo, [k1, k1-tbl] 3 times, k1, k2tog; repeat from * to end.

Row 2: P2, [p1-tbl, p1] twice, p1-tbl, *p6, [p1-tbl, p1] twice, p1-tbl; repeat from * to last 4 sts, p4.

Row 3: *K1, yo, ssk, yo, [k1, k1-tbl] 3 times, k2tog; repeat from * to end.

Row 4: [P1, p1-tbl] 3 times, *p6, [p1-tbl, p1] twice, p1-tbl; repeat from * to last 5 sts, p5.

Row 5: *K2, yo, ssk, yo, [k1, k1-tbl] twice, k1, k2tog; repeat from * to end.

Row 6: P2, p1-tbl, p1, p1-tbl, *p8, p1-tbl, p1, p1-tbl; repeat from * to last 6 sts, p6.

Row 7: *K3, yo, ssk, yo, [k1, k1-tbl] twice, k2tog; repeat from * to end.

Row 8: [P1, p1-tbl] twice, *p8, p1-tbl, p1, p1-tbl; repeat from * to last 7 sts, p7.

Row 9: *K4, yo, ssk, yo, k1, k1-tbl, k1, k2tog; repeat from * to end.

Row 10: P2, p1-tbl, *p10, p1-tbl; repeat from * to last 8 sts, p8.

Row 11: *K5, yo, ssk, yo, k1, k1-tbl, k2tog; repeat from * to end.

Row 12: P1, p1-tbl, *p10, p1-tbl; repeat from * to last 9 sts, p9.

Row 13: *K6, yo, ssk, yo, k1, k2tog; repeat from * to end.

Row 14: Purl.

Row 15: *K7, yo, ssk, yo, k2tog; repeat from * to end.

Row 16: Purl.

Row 17: *Ssk, [k1, k1-tbl] 3 times, k1, yo, k2tog, yo; repeat from * to end.

Row 18: P4, [p1-tbl, p1] twice, p1-tbl, *p6, [p1-tbl, p1] twice, p1-tbl; repeat from * to last 2 sts, p2.

Row 19: *Ssk, [k1-tbl, k1] 3 times, yo, k2tog, yo, k1; repeat from * to end.

Row 20: P5, [p1-tbl, p1] twice, p1-tbl, *p6, [p1-tbl, p1] twice, p1-tbl; repeat from * to last st, p1.

Row 21: *Ssk, [k1, k1-tbl] twice, k1, yo, k2tog, yo, k2; repeat from * to end.

Row 22: P6, p1-tbl, p1, p1-tbl, *p8, p1-tbl, p1, p1-tbl; repeat from * to last 2 sts, p2.

Row 23: *Ssk, [k1-tbl, k1] twice, yo, k2tog, yo, k3; repeat from * to end.

Row 24: P7, p1-tbl, p1, p1-tbl, *p8, p1-tbl, p1, p1-tbl; repeat from * to last st, p1.

Row 25: *Ssk, k1, k1-tbl, k1, yo, k2tog, yo, k4; repeat from * to end.

Row 26: P8, p1-tbl, *p10, p1-tbl; repeat from * to last 2 sts, p2.

Row 27: *Ssk, k1-tbl, k1, yo, k2tog, yo, k5; repeat from * to end.

Row 28: P9, p1-tbl, *p10, p1-tbl; repeat from * to last st, p1.

Row 29: *Ssk, k1, yo, k2tog, yo, k6; repeat from * to end.

Row 30: Purl.

Row 31: *Ssk, yo, k2tog, yo, k7; repeat from * to end.

Row 32: Purl.

Repeat Rows 1–32 for Lacy Streamers Flat.

IN THE ROUND

(multiple of 11 sts; 32-rnd repeat)

Rnd 1: *Yo, ssk, yo, [k1, k1-tbl] 3 times, k1, k2tog; repeat from * to end.

Rnd 2: K4, [k1-tbl, k1] twice, k1-tbl, *k6, [k1-tbl, k1] twice, k1-tbl; repeat from * to last 2 sts, k2.

Rnd 3: *K1, yo, ssk, yo, [k1, k1-tbl] 3 times, k2tog; repeat from * to end.

Rnd 4: K5, [k1-tbl, k1] twice, k1-tbl, *k6, [k1-tbl, k1] twice, k1-tbl; repeat from * to last st, k1.

Rnd 5: *K2, yo, ssk, yo, [k1, k1-tbl] twice, k1, k2tog; repeat from * to end.

Rnd 6: K6, k1-tbl, k1, k1-tbl, *k8, k1-tbl, k1, k1-tbl; repeat from * to last 2 sts, k2.

Rnd 7: *K3, yo, ssk, yo, [k1, k1-tbl] twice, k2tog; repeat from * to end.

Rnd 8: K7, k1-tbl, k1, k1-tbl, *k8, k1-tbl, k1, k1-tbl; repeat from * to last st, k1.

Rnd 9: *K4, yo, ssk, yo, k1, k1-tbl, k1, k2tog; repeat from * to end.

Rnd 10: K8, k1-tbl, *k10, k1-tbl; repeat from * to last 2 sts, k2.

Rnd 11: *K5, yo, ssk, yo, k1, k1-tbl, k2tog; repeat from * to end.

Rnd 12: K9, k1-tbl, *k10, k1-tbl; repeat from * to last st, k1.

Rnd 13: *K6, yo, ssk, yo, k1, k2tog; repeat from * to end.

Rnd 14: Knit.

Rnd 15: *K7, yo, ssk, yo, k2tog; repeat from * to end.

Rnd 16: Knit.

Rnd 17: *Ssk, [k1, k1-tbl] 3 times, k1, yo, k2tog, yo; repeat from * to end.

Rnd 18: K2, [k1-tbl, k1] twice, k1-tbl, *k6, [k1-tbl, k1] twice, k1-tbl; repeat from * to last 4 sts, k4.

Rnd 19: *Ssk, [k1, k1-tbl] 3 times, yo, k2tog, yo, k1; repeat from * to end.

Rnd 20: [K1, k1-tbl] 3 times, *k6, [k1-tbl, k1] twice, k1-tbl; repeat from * to last 5 sts, k5.

Rnd 21: *Ssk, [k1, k1-tbl] twice, k1, yo, k2tog, yo, k2; repeat from * to end.

Rnd 22: K2, k1-tbl, k1, k1-tbl, *k8, k1-tbl, k1, k1-tbl; repeat from * to last 6 sts, k6.

Rnd 23: *Ssk, [k1-tbl, k1] twice, yo, k2tog, yo, k3; repeat from * to end.

Rnd 24: [K1, k1-tbl] twice, *k8, k1-tbl, k1, k1-tbl; repeat from * to last 7 sts, k7.

Rnd 25: *Ssk, k1, k1-tbl, k1, yo, k2tog, yo, k4; repeat from * to end.

Rnd 26: K2, k1-tbl, *k10, k1-tbl; repeat from * to last 8 sts, k8.

Rnd 27: *Ssk, k1-tbl, k1, yo, k2tog, yo, k5; repeat from * to end.

Rnd 28: K1, k1-tbl, *k10, k1-tbl; repeat from * to last 9 sts, k9.

Rnd 29: *Ssk, k1, yo, k2tog, yo, k6; repeat from * to end.

Rnd 30: Knit.

Rnd 31: *Ssk, yo, k2tog, yo, k7; repeat from * to end.

Rnd 32: Knit.

Repeat Rnds 1–32 for Lacy Streamers in the Round.

FLAT AND IN THE ROUND

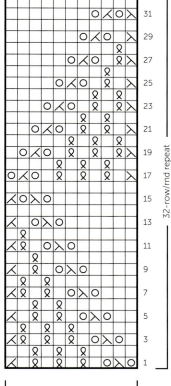

11-st repeat

32-row/rnd repeat

Right-Leaning Lace

FLAT

(multiple of 7 sts + 2; 42-row repeat)

Row 1 (RS): K3, *k2tog, yo, k2, p1, k2; repeat from * to last 6 sts, k2tog, yo, k2, p1, k1.

Row 2 and all WS Rows: Knit the knit sts and purl the purl sts as they face you; purl all yos.

Rows 3 and 5: Repeat Row 1.

Row 7: K2, *k2tog, yo, k2, p1, k2; repeat from * to end.

Rows 9 and 11: Repeat Row 7.

Row 13: K1, *k2tog, yo, k2, p1, k2; repeat from * to last st, k1.

Rows 15 and 17: Repeat Row 13.

Row 19: *K2tog, yo, k2, p1, k2; repeat from * to last 2 sts, k2tog, yo.

Rows 21 and 23: Repeat Row 19.

Row 25: K3, p1, k2, *k2tog, yo, k2, p1, k2; repeat from * to last 3 sts, k2tog, yo, k1.

Rows 27 and 29: Repeat Row 25.

Row 31: K2, p1, k2, *k2tog, yo, k2, p1, k2; repeat from * to last 4 sts, k2tog, yo, k2.

Rows 33 and 35: Repeat Row 31.

Row 37: K1, p1, k2, *k2tog, yo, k2, p1, k2; repeat from * to last 5 sts, k2tog, yo, k3.

Rows 39 and 41: Repeat Row 37.

Row 42: Repeat Row 2.

Repeat Rows 1–42 for Right-Leaning Lace Flat.

IN THE ROUND (A)

(multiple of 7 sts; 42-rnd repeat)

***Note:** Use version A if you must have a fixed location for the beginning-of-rnd marker; the only beginning-of-rnd shift occurs on Rnds 18, 20, and 22, and then it returns to its original position. Use version B if you are working a piece where the beginning-of-rnd marker can shift with every vertical repeat.*

Rnd 1: K2, *k2tog, yo, k2, p1, k2; repeat from * to last 5 sts, k2tog, yo, k2, p1.

Rnd 2: Knit the knit sts and purl the purl sts as they face you; knit all yos.

Rnds 3–6: Repeat Rnds 1 and 2 twice.

Rnd 7: K1, *k2tog, yo, k2, p1, k2; repeat from * to last 6 sts, k2tog, yo, k2, p1, k1.

Rnd 8: Repeat Rnd 2.

Rnds 9–12: Repeat Rnds 7 and 8 twice.

Rnd 13: *K2tog, yo, k2, p1, k2; repeat from * to end.

Rnd 14: Repeat Rnd 2.

Rnds 15 and 16: Repeat Rnds 13 and 14 twice.

Rnd 17: Repeat Rnd 13.

Rnd 18: Repeat Rnd 2, remove beginning-of-rnd marker, k1, pm for new beginning of rnd.

Rnd 19: *Yo, k2, p1, k2, k2tog; repeat from * to end.

Rnd 20: Repeat Rnd 18.

Rnds 21 and 22: Repeat Rnds 19 and 20.

Rnd 23: Repeat Rnd 19.

Rnd 24: Repeat Rnd 2.

Rnd 25: K2, p1, k2, *k2tog, yo, k2, p1, k2; repeat from * to last 2 sts, k2tog, yo.

Rnd 26: Repeat Rnd 2.

Rnds 27–30: Repeat Rnds 25 and 26 twice.

Rnd 31: K1, p1, k2, *k2tog, yo, k2, p1, k2; repeat from * to last 3 sts, k2tog, yo, k1.

Rnd 32: Repeat Rnd 2.

Rnds 33–36: Repeat Rnds 31 and 32 twice.

Rnd 37: P1, k2, *k2tog, yo, k2, p1, k2; repeat from * to last 4 sts, k2tog, yo, k2.

Rnd 38: Repeat Rnd 2.

Rnds 39–42: Repeat Rnds 37 and 38 twice.

Repeat Rnds 1–42 for Right-Leaning Lace in the Round (A).

IN THE ROUND (B)

(multiple of 7 sts; 6-rnd repeat)

Rnd 1: *K2tog, yo, k2, p1, k2; repeat from * to end. **Note:** On first instance of Rnd 1, work k2tog on first 2 sts of rnd, then place removable marker on this k2tog. For all subsequent instances of Rnd 1, on first repeat only, work k2tog on marked st and what was last st of Rnd 6. Move marker up as you go.

Rnd 2: Knit.

Rnds 3 and 4: Repeat Rnds 1 and 2.

Rnd 5: Repeat Rnd 1.

Rnd 6: Knit to 1 st before marked st.

Repeat Rnds 1–6 for Right-Leaning Lace in the Round (B).

FLAT

IN THE ROUND (A)

IN THE ROUND (B)

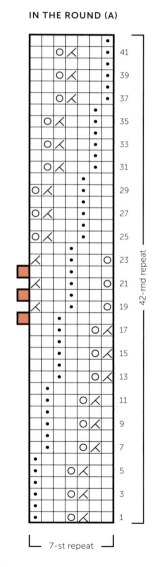

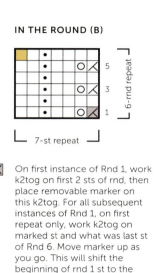

On first instance of Rnd 1, work k2tog on first 2 sts of rnd, then place removable marker on this k2tog. For all subsequent instances of Rnd 1, on first repeat only, work k2tog on marked st and what was last st of Rnd 6. Move marker up as you go. This will shift the beginning of rnd 1 st to the right on every Rnd 1.

On final repeat only of Rnd 6, end rnd 1 st before marked st. On all preceding repeats, work this st as k1.

At end of Rnds 18, 20, and 22, remove beginning-of-rnd marker, k1, pm for new beginning of rnd. On all preceding repeats, omit this st.

Left-Leaning Lace

FLAT

(multiple of 7 sts + 2; 42-row repeat)

Row 1 (RS): K1, p1, k2, *yo, ssk, k2, p1, k2; repeat from * to last 5 sts, yo, ssk, k3.

Row 2 and all WS Rows: Knit the knit sts and purl the purl sts as they face you; purl all yos.

Rows 3 and 5: Repeat Row 1.

Row 7: K2, p1, k2, *yo, ssk, k2, p1, k2; repeat from * to last 4 sts, yo, ssk, k2.

Rows 9 and 11: Repeat Row 7.

Row 13: K3, p1, k2, *yo, ssk, k2, p1, k2; repeat from * to last 3 sts, yo, ssk, k1.

Rows 15 and 17: Repeat Row 13.

Row 19: *Yo, ssk, k2, p1, k2; repeat from * to last 2 sts, yo, ssk.

Rows 21 and 23: Repeat Row 19.

Row 25: K1, *yo, ssk, k2, p1, k2; repeat from * to last st, k1.

Rows 27 and 29: Repeat Row 25.

Row 31: K2, *yo, ssk, k2, p1, k2; repeat from * to end.

Rows 33 and 35: Repeat Row 31.

Row 37: K3, *yo, ssk, k2, p1, k2; repeat from * to last 6 sts, yo, ssk, k2, p1, k1.

Rows 39 and 41: Repeat Row 37.

Row 42: Repeat Row 2.

Repeat Rows 1–42 for Left-Leaning Lace Flat.

IN THE ROUND (A)

(multiple of 7 sts; 42-rnd repeat)

Note: Use version A if you must have a fixed location for the beginning-of-rnd marker. Use version B if you are working a piece where the beginning-of-rnd marker can shift with every vertical repeat.

Rnd 1: P1, k2, *yo, ssk, k2, p1, k2; repeat from * to last 4 sts, yo, ssk, k2.

Rnd 2: Knit the knit sts and purl the purl sts as they face you; knit all yos.

Rnds 3–6: Repeat Rnds 1 and 2 twice.

Rnd 7: K1, p1, k2, *yo, ssk, k2, p1, k2; repeat from * to last 3 sts, yo, ssk, k1.

Rnd 8: Repeat Rnd 2.

Rnds 9–12: Repeat Rnds 7 and 8 twice.

Rnd 13: K2, p1, k2, *yo, ssk, k2, p1, k2; repeat from * to last 2 sts, yo, ssk.

Rnd 14: Repeat Rnd 2.

Rnds 15 and 16: Repeat Rnds 13 and 14.

Rnd 17: Repeat Rnd 13.

Rnd 18: Repeat Rnd 2 to last st, reposition beginning-of-rnd marker to before last st.

Rnd 19: Ssk, k2, p1, k2, *yo, ssk, k2, p1, k2; repeat from * to end, yo.

Rnds 20–23: Repeat Rnds 18 and 19 twice.

Rnd 24: Repeat Rnd 2.

Rnd 25: *Yo, ssk, k2, p1, k2; repeat from * to end.

Rnd 26: Repeat Rnd 2.

Rnds 27–30: Repeat Rnds 25 and 26 twice.

Rnd 31: K1, *yo, ssk, k2, p1, k2; repeat from * to last 6 sts, yo, ssk, k2, p1, k1.

Rnd 32: Repeat Rnd 2.

Rnds 33–36: Repeat Rnds 31 and 32 twice.

Rnd 37: K2, *yo, ssk, k2, p1, k2; repeat from * to last 5 sts, yo, ssk, k2, p1.

Rnd 38: Repeat Rnd 2.

Rnds 39–42: Repeat Rnds 37 and 38 twice.

Repeat Rnds 1–42 for Left-Leaning Lace in the Round (A).

IN THE ROUND (B)

Note: *Use version B if you are working a piece where the beginning-of-rnd marker can shift with every vertical repeat. Use version A if you must have a fixed location for the beginning-of-rnd marker.*

(multiple of 7 sts; 42-rnd repeat)

Rnd 1: *K2, p1, k2, yo, ssk; repeat from * to end.

Rnd 2: Knit the knit sts and purl the purl sts as they face you; knit all yos.

Rnds 3 and 4: Repeat Rnds 1 and 2.

Rnd 5: Repeat Rnd 1.

Rnd 6: Knit to end, remove beginning-of-rnd marker, k1, pm for new beginning of rnd. **Note:** *Beginning-of-rnd marker will shift 1 st to the left every 6 rnds.*

Repeat Rnds 1–6 for Left-Leaning Lace in the Round (B).

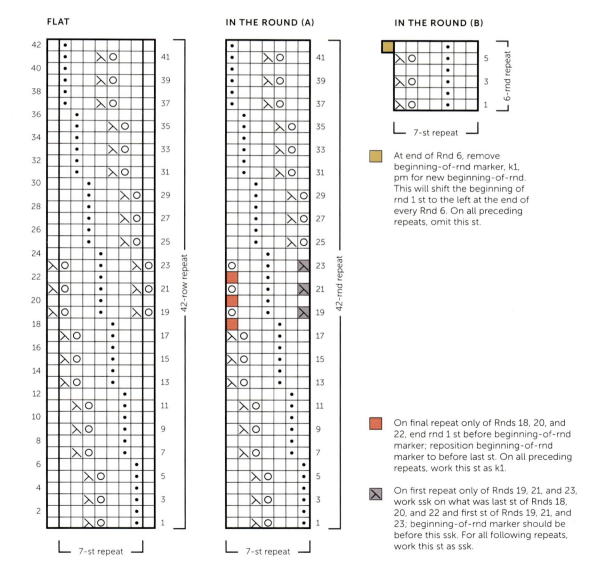

FLAT IN THE ROUND (A) IN THE ROUND (B)

At end of Rnd 6, remove beginning-of-rnd marker, k1, pm for new beginning-of-rnd. This will shift the beginning of rnd 1 st to the left at the end of every Rnd 6. On all preceding repeats, omit this st.

On final repeat only of Rnds 18, 20, and 22, end rnd 1 st before beginning-of-rnd marker; reposition beginning-of-rnd marker to before last st. On all preceding repeats, work this st as k1.

On first repeat only of Rnds 19, 21, and 23, work ssk on what was last st of Rnds 18, 20, and 22 and first st of Rnds 19, 21, and 23; beginning-of-rnd marker should be before this ssk. For all following repeats, work this st as ssk.

Open Acorns

....

FLAT

(multiple of 11 sts; 16-row repeat)
Row 1 (RS): *Yo, k1, yo, [k2tog, ssk] twice, yo, k1, yo, p1; repeat from * to end.
Row 2: K2, p8, *k3, p8; repeat from * to last st, k1.
Rows 3 and 4: Knit the knit sts and purl the purl sts as they face you.
Row 5: Repeat Row 1.
Row 6: P4, k3, *p8, k3; repeat from * to last 4 sts, p4.
Rows 7 and 8: Repeat Row 3.
Row 9: *K2tog, ssk, yo, k1, yo, p1, yo, k1, yo, k2tog, ssk; repeat from * to end.
Row 10: Repeat Row 6.
Rows 11 and 12: Repeat Row 3.
Row 13: Repeat Row 9.
Row 14: Repeat Row 2.
Rows 15 and 16: Repeat Row 3.
Repeat Rows 1–16 for Open Acorns Flat.

IN THE ROUND

(multiple of 11 sts; 16-rnd repeat)
Rnd 1: *P1, yo, k1, yo, [k2tog, ssk] twice, yo, k1, yo; repeat from * to end.
Rnds 2–4: P2, k8, *p3, k8; repeat from * to last st, p1.

Rnd 5: Repeat Rnd 1.
Rnds 6 and 7: K5, p3, *k8, p3; repeat from * to last 3 sts, k3.
Rnd 8: K5, p3, *k8, p3; repeat from * to last 3 sts, k2, reposition beginning-of-rnd marker to before last st.
Rnd 9: *Ssk, k2tog, ssk, yo, k1, yo, p1, yo, k1, yo, k2tog; repeat from * to end.
Rnds 10–12: Repeat Rnds 6–8.
Rnd 13: Repeat Rnd 9.
Rnds 14–16: Repeat Rnd 2.
Repeat Rnds 1–16 for Open Acorns in the Round.

FLAT

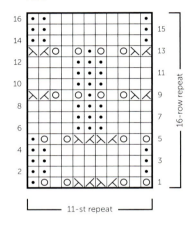

11-st repeat

IN THE ROUND

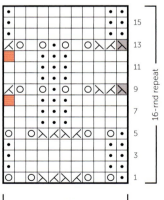

11-st repeat

On final repeat only of Rnds 8 and 12, end rnd 1 st before beginning-of-rnd marker, reposition beginning-of-rnd marker to before last st. On all preceding repeats, knit this st.

On first repeat only of Rnds 9 and 13, work ssk on what was last st of Rnds 8 and 12 and first st of Rnds 9 and 13; beginning-of-rnd marker should be before this ssk. On all following repeats, ssk.

Undulating Texture

FLAT

(multiple of 8 sts + 9; 8-row repeat)
Row 1 (RS): K1, *yo, k2, s2kp2, k2, yo, k1; repeat from
* to end.
Row 2 and all WS Rows: Purl.
Row 3: Knit.
Row 5: Ssk, k2, yo, k1, yo, k2, *s2kp2, k2, yo, k1, yo, k2;
repeat from * to last 2 sts, k2tog.
Row 7: Knit.
Row 8: Purl.
Repeat Rows 1–8 for Undulating Texture Flat.

IN THE ROUND

(multiple of 8 sts; 8-rnd repeat)
Rnd 1: *K1, yo, k2, s2kp2, k2, yo; repeat from * to end.
Rnds 2 and 3: Knit.
Rnd 4: Knit to last st, reposition beginning-of-rnd marker
to before last st.
Rnd 5: *S2kp2, k2, yo, k1, yo, k2; repeat from * to end.
Rnds 6–8: Knit.
Repeat Rnds 1–8 for Undulating Texture in the Round.

FLAT

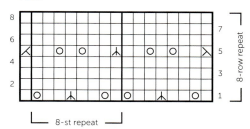

IN THE ROUND

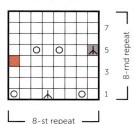

On final repeat only of Rnd 4, end rnd 1 st before
beginning-of-rnd marker; reposition beginning-of-
rnd marker to before last st. On all preceding repeats,
knit this st.

On first repeat only of Rnd 5, work s2kp2 on what
was last st of Rnd 4 and first 2 sts of Rnd 5; beginning-
of-rnd marker should be before this s2kp2. On all
following repeats, s2k2p.

Ladders and Eyelets

....

FLAT

(multiple of 18 sts + 1; 32-row repeat)

Row 1 (RS): K1, *[yo, ssk, k1] twice, yo, ssk, k10; repeat from * to end.

Row 2: K1, *p2, k1; repeat from * to end.

Row 3: K1, *[k2tog, yo, k1] twice, k2tog, yo, k10; repeat from * to end.

Row 4: Repeat Row 2.

Rows 5–16: Repeat Rows 1–4 three times.

Row 17: *K10, [yo, ssk, k1] twice, yo, ssk; repeat from * to last st, k1.

Row 18: Repeat Row 2.

Row 19: *K10, [k2tog, yo, k1] twice, k2tog, yo; repeat from * to last st, k1.

Row 20: Repeat Row 2.

Rows 21–32: Repeat Rows 17–20 three times.

Repeat Rows 1–32 for Ladders and Eyelets Flat.

IN THE ROUND

(multiple of 18 sts; 32-rnd repeat)

Rnd 1: [K1, yo, ssk] 3 times, *k10, [yo, ssk, k1] twice, yo, ssk; repeat from * to last 9 sts, k9.

Rnd 2: *P1, k2; repeat from * to end.

Rnd 3: *[K1, k2tog, yo] 3 times, *k10, [k2tog, yo, k1] twice, k2tog, yo; repeat from * to last 9 sts, k9.

Rnd 4: Repeat Rnd 2.

Rnds 5–16: Repeat Rnds 1–4 three times.

Rnd 17: *K10, [yo, ssk, k1] twice, yo, ssk; repeat from * to end.

Rnd 18: Repeat Rnd 2.

Rnd 19: *K10, [k2tog, yo, k1] twice, k2tog, yo; repeat from * to end.

Rnd 20: Repeat Rnd 2.

Rnds 21–32: Repeat Rnds 17–20 three times.

Repeat Rnds 1–32 for Ladders and Eyelets in the Round.

FLAT

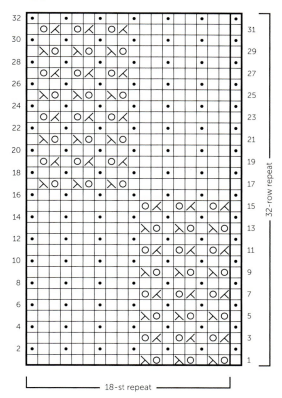

18-st repeat

32-row repeat

IN THE ROUND

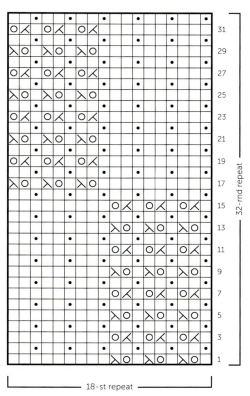

18-st repeat

32-rnd repeat

IN THE ROUND

(multiple of 14 sts; 12-rnd repeat)

Rnd 1: *Yo, ssk, k3, p3, k2tog, yo, k4; repeat from * to end.

Rnd 2 and all Even-Numbered Rnds: Knit.

Rnd 3: *K2tog, yo, k2, p3, k2tog, yo, k5; repeat from * to end.

Rnd 5: *Yo, ssk, k1, p3, k2tog, yo, k6; repeat from * to end.

Rnd 7: *K2tog, yo, k4, yo, ssk, p3, k3; repeat from * to end.

Rnd 9: *Yo, ssk, k5, yo, ssk, p3, k2; repeat from * to end.

Rnd 11: *K2tog, yo, k6, yo, ssk, p3, k1; repeat from * to end.

Rnd 12: Knit.

Repeat Rnds 1–12 for Climbing Garter Vine in the Round.

Climbing Garter Vine

FLAT

(multiple of 14 sts + 2; 12-row repeat)

Row 1 (RS): Yo, ssk, *k3, p3, k2tog, yo, k4, yo, ssk; repeat from * to end.

Row 2 and all WS Rows: Purl.

Row 3: K2tog, yo, *k2, p3, k2tog, yo, k5, k2tog, yo; repeat from * to end.

Row 5: Yo, ssk, *k1, p3, k2tog, yo, k6, yo, ssk; repeat from * to end.

Row 7: K2tog, yo, *k4, yo, ssk, p3, k3, k2tog, yo; repeat from * to end.

Row 9: Yo, ssk, *k5, yo, ssk, p3, k2, yo, ssk; repeat from * to end.

Row 11: K2tog, yo, *k6, yo, ssk, p3, k1, k2tog, yo; repeat from * to end.

Row 12: Purl.

Repeat Rows 1–12 for Climbing Garter Vine Flat.

FLAT

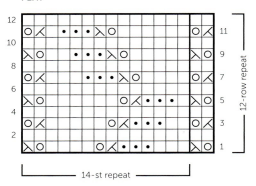

IN THE ROUND

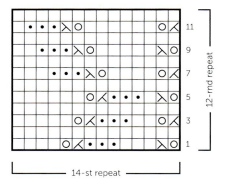

Hanging Berries

FLAT

(multiple of 10 sts + 11; 8-row repeat)

Row 1 (RS): Ssk, k3, yo, k1, yo, k3, *s2kp2, k3, yo, k1, yo, k3; repeat from * to last 2 sts, k2tog.

Row 2: P2tog, p2, yo, p3, yo, p2, *s2pp2, p2, yo, p3, yo, p2; repeat from * to last 2 sts, ssp.

Row 3: Ssk, k1, yo, k5, yo, k1, *s2kp2, k1, yo, k5, yo, k1; repeat from * to last 2 sts, k2tog.

Row 4: P2tog, yo, p7, yo, *s2pp2, yo, p7, yo; repeat from * to last 2 sts, ssp.

Row 5: K1, *yo, k3, s2kp2, k3, yo, k1; repeat from * to end.

Row 6: P2, yo, p2, s2pp2, p2, yo, *p3, yo, p2, s2pp2, p2, yo; repeat from * to last 2 sts, p2.

Row 7: K3, yo, k1, s2kp2, k1, yo, *k5, yo, k1, s2kp2, k1, yo; repeat from * to last 3 sts, k3.

Row 8: P4, yo, s2pp2, yo, *p7, yo, s2pp2, yo; repeat from * to last 4 sts, p4.

Repeat Rows 1–8 for Hanging Berries Flat.

IN THE ROUND

(multiple of 10 sts; 8-rnd repeat)

Rnd 1: *K1, yo, k3, s2kp2, k3, yo; repeat from * to end.

Rnd 2: K2, yo, k2, s2kp2, k2, yo, *k3, yo, k2, s2kp2, k2, yo; repeat from * to last st, k1.

Rnd 3: K3, yo, k1, s2kp2, k1, yo, *k5, yo, k1, s2kp2, k1, yo; repeat from * to last 2 sts, k2.

Rnd 4: K4, yo, s2kp2, yo, *k7, yo, s2kp2, yo; repeat from * to last 3 sts, k2, reposition beginning-of-rnd marker to before last st.

Rnd 5: *S2kp2, k3, yo, k1, yo, k3; repeat from * to last 10 sts, s2kp2, k3, yo, k1, yo, k2, reposition beginning-of-rnd marker to before last st.

Rnd 6: *S2kp2, k2, yo, k3, yo, k2; repeat from * to last 10 sts, s2kp2, k2, yo, k3, yo, k1, reposition beginning-of-rnd marker to before last st.

Rnd 7: *S2kp2, k1, yo, k5, yo, k1; repeat from * to last 10 sts, s2kp2, k1, yo, k5, yo, reposition beginning-of-rnd marker to before last st.

Rnd 8: *S2kp2, yo, k7, yo; repeat from * to end.

Repeat Rnds 1–8 for Hanging Berries in the Round.

FLAT

10-st repeat — 8-row repeat

IN THE ROUND

10-st repeat — 8-rnd repeat

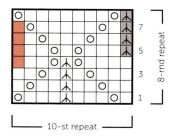 On last repeat only of Rnds 4–7, end rnd 1 st before beginning-of-rnd marker; reposition beginning-of-rnd marker to before last st. On all preceding repeats, knit this st.

On first repeat only of Rnds 5–8, work s2kp2 on what was last st of Rnds 4–7 and first 2 sts of Rnds 5–8; beginning-of-rnd marker should be before this s2kp2. On all following repeats, s2kp2.

Arrowheads and Diamonds

FLAT

(multiple of 20 sts + 21; 28-row repeat)

Row 1 (RS): K1, *k2tog, yo, k5, k2tog, yo, k1, yo, ssk, k5, yo, ssk, k1; repeat from * to end.

Row 2: P7, ssp, yo, p3, yo, p2tog, *p13, ssp, yo, p3, yo, p2tog; repeat from * to last 7 sts, p7.

Row 3: Ssk, yo, k4, [k2tog, yo] twice, k1, [yo, ssk] twice, k4, *yo, sk2p, yo, k4, [k2tog, yo] twice, k1, [yo, ssk] twice, k4; repeat from * to last 2 sts, yo, ssk.

Row 4: P5, ssp, yo, p7, yo, p2tog, *p9, ssp, yo, p7, yo, p2tog; repeat from * to last 5 sts, p5.

Row 5: K4, k2tog, yo, k1, k2tog, yo, k3, yo, ssk, k1, yo, ssk, *k7, k2tog, yo, k1, k2tog, yo, k3, yo, ssk, k1, yo, ssk; repeat from * to last 4 sts, k4.

Row 6: P3, ssp, yo, p11, yo, p2tog, *p5, ssp, yo, p11, yo, p2tog; repeat from * to last 3 sts, p3.

Row 7: [K2, k2tog, yo] twice, k5, yo, ssk, k2, yo, ssk, *k3, k2tog, yo, k2, k2tog, yo, k5, yo, ssk, k2, yo, ssk; repeat from * to last 2 sts, k2.

Row 8: P1, *ssp, yo, p15, yo, p2tog, p1; repeat from * to end.

Row 9: Ssk, yo, k3, k2tog, yo, k7, yo, ssk, k3, *yo, sk2p, yo, k3, k2tog, yo, k7, yo, ssk, k3; repeat from * to last 2 sts, yo, ssk.

Row 10: Purl.

Row 11: K4, k2tog, yo, k9, yo, ssk, *k7, k2tog, yo, k9, yo, ssk; repeat from * to last 4 sts, k4.

Row 12: Purl.

Row 13: K3, k2tog, yo, k1, yo, ssk, *k5, k2tog, yo, k1, yo, ssk; repeat from * to last 3 sts, k3.

Row 14: P7, yo, p2tog, p3, ssp, yo, *p13, yo, p2tog, p3, ssp, yo; repeat from * to last 7 sts, p7.

FLAT

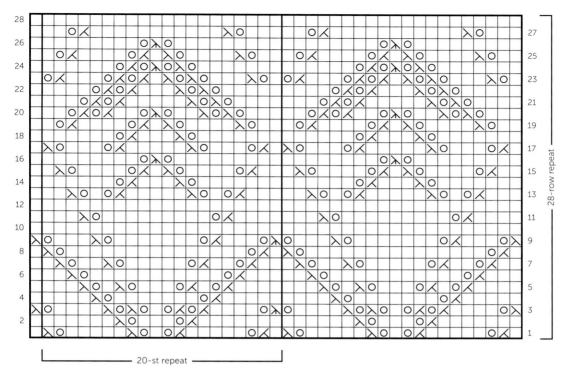

20-st repeat

28-row repeat

Row 15: K2, k2tog, yo, k4, yo, ssk, k1, k2tog, yo, k4, yo, ssk, *k3, k2tog, yo, k4, yo, ssk, k1, k2tog, yo, k4, yo, ssk; repeat from * to last 2 sts, k2.

Row 16: P9, yo, sp2p, yo, *p17, yo, sp2p, yo; repeat from * to last 9 sts, p9.

Row 17: K1, *k2tog, yo, k3, yo, ssk, k5, k2tog, yo, k3, yo, ssk, k1; repeat from * to end.

Row 18: P7, yo, p2tog, p3, ssp, yo, *p13, yo, p2tog, p3, ssp, yo; repeat from * to last 7 sts, p7.

Row 19: K2, yo, ssk, k4, yo, ssk, k1, k2tog, yo, k4, k2tog, yo, *k3, yo, ssk, k4, yo, ssk, k1, k2tog, yo, k4, k2tog, yo; repeat from * to last 2 sts, k2.

Row 20: P3, [yo, p2tog] twice, p2, yo, sp2p, yo, p2, [ssp, yo] twice, *p5, [yo, p2tog] twice, p2, yo, sp2p, yo, p2, [ssp, yo] twice; repeat from * to last 3 sts, p3.

Row 21: K4, [yo, ssk] twice, k5, [k2tog, yo] twice, *k7, [yo, ssk] twice, k5, [k2tog, yo] twice; repeat from * to last 4 sts, k4.

Row 22: P5, [yo, p2tog] twice, p3, [ssp, yo] twice, *p9, [yo, p2tog] twice, p3, [ssp, yo] twice; repeat from * to last 5 sts, p5.

Row 23: K1, *yo, ssk, k3, [yo, ssk] twice, k1, [k2tog, yo] twice, k3, k2tog, yo, k1; repeat from * to end.

Row 24: P7, yo, p2tog, yo, sp2p, yo, ssp, yo, *p13, yo, p2tog, yo, sp2p, yo, ssp, yo; repeat from * to last 7 sts, p7.

Row 25: K2, yo, ssk, k4, yo, ssk, k1, k2tog, yo, k4, k2tog, yo, *k3, yo, ssk, k4, yo, ssk, k1, k2tog, yo, k4, k2tog, yo; repeat from * to last 2 sts, k2.

Row 26: P9, yo, sp2p, yo, *p17, yo, sp2p, yo; repeat from * to last 9 sts, p9.

Row 27: K3, yo, ssk, k11, k2tog, yo, *k5, yo, ssk, k11, k2tog, yo; repeat from * to last 3 sts, k3.

Row 28: Purl.

Repeat Rows 1–28 for Arrowheads and Diamonds Flat.

IN THE ROUND

(multiple of 20 sts; 28-rnd repeat)

Rnd 1: *K1, k2tog, yo, k5, k2tog, yo, k1, yo, ssk, k5, yo, ssk; repeat from * to end.

Rnd 2: K7, k2tog, yo, k3, yo, ssk, *k13, k2tog, yo, k3, yo, ssk; repeat from * to last 6 sts, k5, reposition beginning-of-rnd marker to before last st.

Rnd 3: *Sk2p, yo, k4, [k2tog, yo] twice, k1, [yo, ssk] twice, k4, yo; repeat from * to end.

Rnd 4: K5, k2tog, yo, k7, yo, ssk, *k9, k2tog, yo, k7, yo, ssk; repeat from * to last 4 sts, k4.

Rnd 5: K4, k2tog, yo, k1, k2tog, yo, k3, yo, ssk, k1, yo, ssk, *k7, k2tog, yo, k1, k2tog, yo, k3, yo, ssk, k1, yo, ssk; repeat from * to last 3 sts, k3.

Rnd 6: K3, k2tog, yo, k11, yo, ssk, *k5, k2tog, yo, k11, yo, ssk; repeat from * to last 2 sts, k2.

Rnd 7: [K2, k2tog, yo] twice, k5, yo, ssk, k2, yo, ssk, *k3, k2tog, yo, k2, k2tog, yo, k5, yo, ssk, k2, yo, ssk; repeat from * to last st, k1.

Rnd 8: *K1, k2tog, yo, k15, yo, ssk; repeat from * to end; after final ssk of rnd, remove beginning-of-rnd marker, slip last st of rnd back to left-hand needle, place marker for new beginning of rnd.

Rnd 9: *Sk2p, yo, k3, k2tog, yo, k7, yo, ssk, k3, yo; repeat from * to end.

Rnd 10: Knit.

Rnd 11: K4, k2tog, yo, k9, yo, ssk, *k7, k2tog, yo, k9, yo, ssk; repeat from * to last 3 sts, k3.

Rnd 12: Knit.

Rnd 13: K3, k2tog, yo, k1, yo, ssk, *k5, k2tog, yo, k1, yo, ssk; repeat from * to last 2 sts, k2.

Rnd 14: K7, yo, ssk, k3, k2tog, yo, *k13, yo, ssk, k3, k2tog, yo; repeat from * to last 6 sts, k6.

Rnd 15: K2, k2tog, yo, k4, yo, ssk, k1, k2tog, yo, k4, yo, ssk, *k3, k2tog, yo, k4, yo, ssk, k1, k2tog, yo, k4, yo, ssk; repeat from * to last st, k1.

Rnd 16: K9, yo, sk2p, yo, *k17, yo, sk2p, yo; repeat from * to last 8 sts, k8.

Rnd 17: *K1, k2tog, yo, k3, yo, ssk, k5, k2tog, yo, k3, yo, ssk; repeat from * to end.

Rnd 18: K7, yo, ssk, k3, k2tog, yo, *k13, yo, ssk, k3, k2tog, yo; repeat from * to last 6 sts, k6.

Rnd 19: K2, yo, ssk, k4, yo, ssk, k1, k2tog, yo, k4, k2tog, yo, *k3, yo, ssk, k4, yo, ssk, k1, k2tog, yo, k4, k2tog, yo; repeat from * to last st, k1.

Rnd 20: K3, [yo, ssk] twice, k2, yo, sk2p, yo, k2, [k2tog, yo] twice, *k5, [yo, ssk] twice, k2, yo, sk2p, yo, k2, [k2tog, yo] twice; repeat from * to last 2 sts, k2.

Rnd 21: K4, [yo, ssk] twice, k5, [k2tog, yo] twice, *k7, [yo, ssk] twice, k5, [k2tog, yo] twice; repeat from * to last 3 sts, k3.

Rnd 22: K5, [yo, ssk] twice, k3, [k2tog, yo] twice, *k9, [yo, ssk] twice, k3, [k2tog, yo] twice; repeat from * to last 4 sts, k4.

Rnd 23: *K1, yo, ssk, k3, [yo, ssk] twice, k1, [k2tog, yo] twice, k3, k2tog, yo; repeat from * to end.

Rnd 24: K7, yo, ssk, yo, sk2p, yo, k2tog, yo, *k13, yo, ssk, yo, sk2p, yo, k2tog, yo; repeat from * to last 6 sts, k6.

Rnd 25: K2, yo, ssk, k4, yo, ssk, k1, k2tog, yo, k4, k2tog, yo, *k3, yo, ssk, k4, yo, ssk, k1, k2tog, yo, k4, k2tog, yo; repeat from * to last st, k1.

Rnd 26: K9, yo, sk2p, yo, *k17, yo, sk2p, yo; repeat from * to last 8 sts, k8.

Rnd 27: K3, yo, ssk, k11, k2tog, yo, *k5, yo, ssk, k11, k2tog, yo; repeat from * to last 2 sts, k2.

Rnd 28: Knit.

Repeat Rnds 1–28 for Arrowheads and Diamonds in the Round.

IN THE ROUND

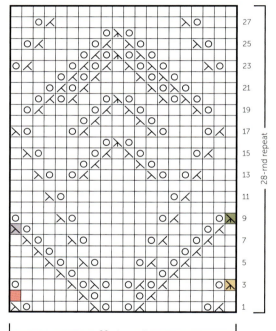

20-st repeat · 28-rnd repeat

On final repeat only of Rnd 2, end rnd 1 st before beginning-of-rnd marker; reposition beginning-of-rnd marker to before last st. On all preceding repeats, knit this st.

On first repeat only of Rnd 3, work sk2p on what was last st of Rnd 2 and first 2 sts of Rnd 3; beginning-of-rnd marker should be before this sk2p. On all following repeats, sk2p.

On final repeat only of Rnd 8, after working final ssk of rnd, remove beginning-of-rnd marker, slip last st of rnd (ssk) back to left needle, place marker for new beginning of rnd. On all preceding repeats, ssk.

On first repeat only of Rnd 9, work sk2p on what was last ssk of Rnd 8 and first 2 sts of Rnd 9; beginning-of-rnd marker should be before this sk2p. On all following repeats, sk2p.

Climbing Diamonds

FLAT

(panel of 20 sts worked on a background of St st; 16-row repeat)

Row 1: K7, k2tog, yo, k2, yo, k2tog, k7.
Row 2: P6, p2tog, yo, p4, yo, p2tog, p6.
Row 3: K5, [k2tog, yo] twice, k2, [yo, k2tog] twice, k5.
Row 4: P4, [p2tog, yo] twice, p4, [yo, p2tog] twice, p4.
Row 5: K3, [k2tog, yo] 3 times, k2, [yo, k2tog] 3 times, k3.
Row 6: P2, [p2tog, yo] 3 times, p4, [yo, p2tog] 3 times, p2.
Row 7: K1, [k2tog, yo] 3 times, k6, [yo, k2tog] 3 times, k1.
Row 8: [P2tog, yo] 3 times, p8, [yo, p2tog] 3 times.
Row 9: K1, [yo, k2tog] 3 times, k6, [k2tog, yo] 3 times, k1.
Row 10: P2, [yo, p2tog] 3 times, p4, [p2tog, yo] 3 times, p2.
Row 11: K3, [yo, k2tog] 3 times, k2, [k2tog, yo] 3 times, k3.
Row 12: P4, [yo, p2tog] 3 times, [p2tog, yo] 3 times, p4.
Row 13: K5, [yo, k2tog] twice, k2, [k2tog, yo] twice, k5.
Row 14: P6, [yo, p2tog] twice, [p2tog, yo] twice, p6.
Row 15: K7, yo, k2tog, k2, k2tog, yo, k7.
Row 16: P8, yo, [p2tog] twice, yo, p8.
Repeat Rows 1–16 for Climbing Diamonds Flat.

IN THE ROUND

(panel of 20 sts worked on a background of St st; 16-rnd repeat)

Rnd 1: K7, k2tog, yo, k2, yo, k2tog, k7.
Rnd 2: K6, k2tog, yo, k4, yo, k2tog, k6.
Rnd 3: K5, [k2tog, yo] twice, k2, [yo, k2tog] twice, k5.
Rnd 4: K4, [k2tog, yo] twice, k4, [yo, k2tog] twice, k4.
Rnd 5: K3, [k2tog, yo] 3 times, k2, [yo, k2tog] 3 times, k3.
Rnd 6: K2, [k2tog, yo] 3 times, k4, [yo, k2tog] 3 times, k2.
Rnd 7: K1, [k2tog, yo] 3 times, k6, [yo, k2tog] 3 times, k1.
Rnd 8: [K2tog, yo] 3 times, k8, [yo, k2tog] 3 times.
Rnd 9: K1, [yo, k2tog] 3 times, k6, [k2tog, yo] 3 times, k1.
Rnd 10: K2, [yo, k2tog] 3 times, k4, [k2tog, yo] 3 times, k2.
Rnd 11: K3, [yo, k2tog] 3 times, k2, [k2tog, yo] 3 times, k3.
Rnd 12: K4, [yo, k2tog] 3 times, [k2tog, yo] 3 times, k4.
Rnd 13: K5, [yo, k2tog] twice, k2, [k2tog, yo] twice, k5.
Rnd 14: K6, [yo, k2tog] twice, [k2tog, yo] twice, k6.
Rnd 15: K7, yo, k2tog, k2, k2tog, yo, k7.
Rnd 16: K8, yo, [k2tog] twice, yo, k8.
Repeat Rnds 1–16 for Climbing Diamonds in the Round.

FLAT AND IN THE ROUND

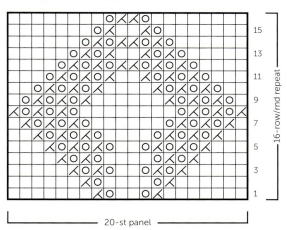

IN THE ROUND

(multiple of 11 sts; 12-rnd repeat)

Rnd 1: *Yo, k3, ssk, k2tog, k3, yo, k1; repeat from * to end.

Rnd 2: Knit.

Rnd 3: *K1, yo, k3, ssk, k2tog, k3, yo; repeat from * to end.

Rnd 4: Knit.

Rnd 5: Repeat Rnd 1.

Rnds 6 and 7: Knit.

Rnd 8: Purl.

Rnds 9 and 10: Repeat Rnds 7 and 8.

Rnds 11 and 12: Knit.

Repeat Rnds 1–12 for Waves and Welts in the Round.

Waves and Welts

···

FLAT

(multiple of 11 sts + 2; 12-row repeat)

Row 1 (RS): K1, *yo, k3, ssk, k2tog, k3, yo, k1; repeat from * to last st, k1.

Row 2: Purl.

Row 3: K2, *yo, k3, ssk, k2tog, k3, yo, k1; repeat from * to end.

Row 4: Purl.

Row 5: Repeat Row 1.

Row 6: Purl.

Rows 7–11: Knit.

Row 12: Purl.

Repeat Rows 1–12 for Waves and Welts Flat.

FLAT

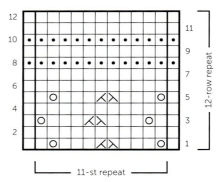

IN THE ROUND

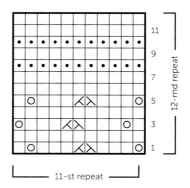

Welted Herringbone

FLAT

(multiple of 15 sts; 10-row repeat)

Row 1 (RS): K1, yo, k5, s2kp2, k5, yo, *k2, yo, k5, s2kp2, k5, yo; repeat from * to last st, k1.

Row 2: Purl.

Rows 3–6: Repeat Rows 1 and 2 twice.

Rows 7–10: Knit.

Repeat Rows 1–10 for Welted Herringbone Flat.

IN THE ROUND

(multiple of 15 sts; 10-rnd repeat)

Rnd 1: K1, yo, k5, s2kp2, k5, yo, *k2, yo, k5, s2kp2, k5, yo; repeat from * to last st, k1.

Rnd 2: Knit.

Rnds 3–6: Repeat Rnds 1 and 2 twice.

Rnd 7: Knit.

Rnd 8: Purl.

Rnds 9 and 10: Repeat Rnds 7 and 8.

Repeat Rnds 1–10 for Welted Herringbone in the Round.

FLAT AND IN THE ROUND

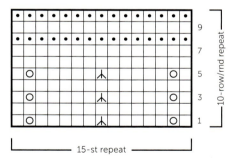

FINISHED MEASUREMENTS
Approximately 7" (18 cm) wide × 60"
(152.5 cm) long, not including fringe

YARN
Blue Sky Fibers Bulky [50% alpaca,
50% wool; 45 yards (42 meters) /
3½ ounces (100 grams)]: 3 hanks
#1219 Atlantis

NEEDLES
One pair straight needles size US 19
(15 mm)
Change needle size if necessary to
obtain correct gauge.

NOTIONS
Crochet hook size US P/Q (15 mm),
for Fringe

GAUGE
6 sts and 8 rows = 4" (10 cm) in
Little Berries, washed and blocked,
unstretched

Little Berries Bulky Scarf

I'm the type of knitter who prefers that both sides of a scarf or stole look the same or similar. This bulky scarf looks good on both sides and despite its length, it is a super-fast knit. Most lace patterns look good on both sides, so if you want to swap out the Little Berries pattern for another, work up a quick swatch, then cast on and go!

STITCH PATTERN

LITTLE BERRIES

(panel of 9 sts; 4-row repeat)
Row 1 (RS): Yo, s2kp2, yo, p3, yo, s2kp2, yo.
Row 2: K3, p3, k3.
Row 3: P3, yo, s2kp2, yo, p3.
Row 4: P3, k3, p3.
Repeat Rows 1–4 for Little Berries.

LITTLE BERRIES

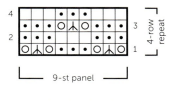

Scarf

CO 11 sts.
Set-Up Row (RS): K1 (edge st, knit every row), work Little Berries to last st, k1 (edge st, knit every row).
Work even, knitting first and last st of every row, until you have completed 30 vertical repeats of Little Berries. BO all sts.

Finishing

Block as desired.

Fringe

Cut 20 strands of yarn 12" (30.5 cm) long. Work 5 fringes each along CO and BO edges, as follows: Using 2 strands of yarn held together, fold in half; with RS of piece facing, insert crochet hook just above edge to receive fringe, from back to front; catch the folded strands of yarn with the hook and pull through work to form a loop, insert ends of yarn through loop and pull to tighten.

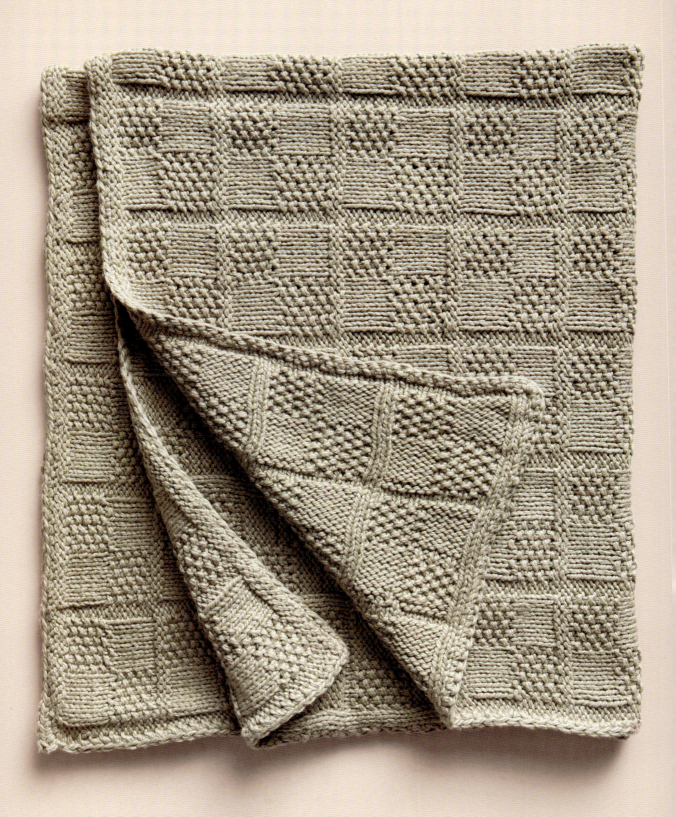

From-Scratch Projects

MAKE-IT-YOUR-OWN BLANKET

COCOON SHRUG

OVERSIZED COWL

These three "From-Scratch" projects will get you well on your way to designing on your own. Incorporating stitch patterns into these basic designs is fun and easy—all you have to do is find stitch patterns that strike your fancy, follow a few guidelines, and you'll have a personalized design of your own making.

Make-It-Your-Own Blanket

For many of us, a handknit blanket offers the height of contentment. It's something you'll find in nearly every home. Many times, they're given as gifts (my grandmas both knit afghans for me that I cherish), or knit to welcome a new baby. They can also pull a room together and make it feel complete. They're used as forts for children during playtime, and they provide comfort when it is needed.

When you knit a blanket as a gift or for yourself, there are so many ways to make it your own. Your choice of stitch pattern or a blend of stitch patterns, the yarn and the color, the size, and the embellishments all come together to represent the time you put into it, your style, and your hope that it will keep someone warm.

The Stacked Boxes stitch pattern is a perfect choice for this baby blanket–sized throw. When selecting yarn, be sure to swatch first to see if your selected stitch pattern "pops." If you want to make a different size blanket with different yarn, check out Calculating How Much Yarn You Need on page 15. The tutorial follows. To knit the sample blanket, see the pattern on the opposite page.

TUTORIAL

SIZES
See sidebar opposite page.

YARN
See Calculating How Much Yarn You Need on page 15.

NEEDLES
One circular needle in size needed to obtain desired gauge; choose a needle length that will fit the width of your blanket. You might be able to work a small blanket on straight needles, but a circular needle is recommended when working with a large number of stitches.

NOTIONS
Stitch markers; crochet hook one size larger than needle size (optional)

Getting Started

Knit a gauge swatch in your stitch pattern and block it the same way you will be blocking your blanket. Fill in the blanks below.

Stitches per inch (centimeter) (from your swatch): _____ (A).

Goal width: _____ (B).

Approximate stitches to cast on: (A × B) = _____ (C).
Note: *You will most likely have to adjust the number of stitches to accommodate your stitch pattern.*

Before moving on, decide if you want to add a non-rolling edge to your blanket. You can simply use Garter stitch (knit every row) or something more decorative such as Seed or Moss stitch.

Total stitches for edging for each side: _____ (D).

Cast on in this order: The number of stitches for (D), pm, the adjusted number of stitches for (C), pm, the number of stitches for (D). If desired, work several rows in a non-rolling stitch pattern before starting your chosen stitch pattern. Work even in pattern until just short of your desired length, ending with a row that finishes a complete stitch repeat or that makes your pattern mirror the rows at the beginning of the blanket. Work the same number of rows in the non-rolling stitch pattern that you worked at the beginning. Bind off all stitches.

Work an edging if desired, then block.

INSTRUCTIONS

Here are the directions for the Make-It-Your-Blanket shown on page 264.

FINISHED MEASUREMENTS
35" × 33¾" (89 × 85.5 cm)

YARN
Blue Sky Fibers Organic Cotton Worsted [100% certified organic cotton; 150 yards (140 meters) / 3½ ounces (100 grams)]: 6 hanks #626 Stone

NEEDLES
One 24" (60 cm) long or longer circular needle size US 7 (4.5 mm)

Change needle size if necessary to obtain correct gauge.

NOTIONS
Stitch markers; crochet hook size I-9 (5.5 mm) (optional)

GAUGE
18 sts and 24 rows = 4" (10 cm) in Stacked Boxes, washed and blocked, unstretched

. . . .

STITCH PATTERN

STACKED BOXES

(multiple of 14 sts + 2; 20-row repeat)
Row 1 (RS): Purl.
Row 2: Knit.
Row 3: P2, *k7, [p1, k1] twice, p3; repeat from * to end.
Row 4: K2, *[p1, k1] 3 times, p6, k2; repeat from * to end.
Rows 5–10: Repeat Rows 3 and 4 three times.
Row 11: Repeat Row 3.
Row 12: K2, *[p1, k1] 5 times, p1, k3; repeat from * to end.
Row 13: P2, *[k1, p1] 3 times, k6, p2; repeat from * to end.
Row 14: K2, *p7, [k1, p1] twice, k3; repeat from * to end.
Rows 15–20: Repeat Rows 13 and 14 three times.
Repeat Rows 1–20 for Stacked Boxes (see chart for Stacked Boxes Flat, page 25).

. . . .

Blanket

CO 158 sts.
Set-Up Row (RS): K1, pm, work in Stacked Boxes to last st, pm, k1. Work even, knitting first and last st of every row, and working sts between markers in Stacked Boxes, until piece measures approximately 33¾" (85.5 cm) from the beginning, ending with Row 2 of pattern. BO all sts.

Finishing

Crocheted Edging (optional)
With RS of Blanket facing, using a crochet hook, join yarn at corner and work single crochet around entire piece, working 2 single crochets in each corner; join with a slip st in first single crochet. Fasten off.

Block as desired.

Typical Knit Blanket Sizing

Receiving Blanket: 24 × 24" (61 × 61 cm)
Stroller Blanket: 30 × 40" (76 × 101.5 cm)
Cradle Blanket: 18 × 36" (45.5 × 91.5 cm)
Baby Blanket: 36 × 36" (91.5 × 91.5 cm)
Lapghan: 36 × 48" (91.5 × 122 cm)
Throw Blanket: 48 × 48"–60" (122 × 122–152.5 cm)
Twin Top of Mattress: 39 × 75" (99 × 190.5 cm)
Twin with Drape: 66 × 90" (167.5 × 228.5 cm)
Full/Double Top of Mattress: 54 × 75" (137 × 190.5 cm)
Full/Double with Drape: 80 × 100" (203 × 254 cm)
Queen Top of Mattress: 60 × 80" (152.5 × 203 cm)
Queen with Drape: 90 × 100" (228.5 × 254 cm)
King Top of Mattress: 76 × 80" (193 × 203 cm)
King with Drape: 108 × 100" (274.5 × 254 cm)

Ideas for Sprucing Up Your Custom Blanket

Add an applied I-cord to finish all four edges of your blanket. Typical cast-on numbers are three or four stitches. See Special Techniques, page 278.

Using contrasting-colored yarn, embroider flowers or other motifs over the surface of the blanket.

Employ more than one motif for your blanket— use stitch markers to separate the areas and consider using stitches like Seed stitch or simple Stockinette to separate the stitch patterns.

Instead of making one large square or rectangle, knit squares the size you desire and stitch them together.

Consider working stitch patterns in strips and changing colors for each.

Begin and end with a few inches' (centimeters') worth of ribbing.

Don't shy away from cables! Cables make for lovely, luxurious blankets.

Choose bulky yarn for a quicker knit.

Cocoon Shrug

Here's a simple shrug pattern with a twist. Normally, this type of shrug is made by knitting a long rectangle, folding it in half, and seaming together the short ends from the selvedge edge, leaving a gap for armholes. If an edging is to be added, stitches are picked up and knit around the edge in the round.

This iteration is very different and completely seamless. Although this Cocoon Shrug does start with a rectangle, there's a twist: Instead of binding off and sewing up the sides to create sleeve openings, you begin with a provisional cast-on (this is optional, but to keep it completely seamless, it's the best way to start). Once you've knit the rectangle, you place the provisional stitches on the other side of the circular needle and begin knitting in rounds to finish off the body of the shrug. Although the body of this shrug is worked in Stockinette stitch, you can customize your version with a knit-purl stitch pattern from this book—or if you really want to change it up, choose some lace. The tutorial follows. To reproduce the Cocoon Shrug shown here, find the pattern on page 270.

TUTORIAL

SIZES
X-Small (Small, Medium, Large, X-Large, 2X-Large, 3X-Large)

FINISHED MEASUREMENTS
See Women's Sizes table on page 270.

YARN
See Calculating How Much Yarn You Need on page 15.

NEEDLES
Two 24" (60 cm) long or longer circular needles and one set of five double-pointed needles in size needed to obtain desired gauge.

NOTIONS
Stitch marker

Getting Started
Note: *Choose a unit of measurement (either inches or centimeters) and work only in the chosen unit of measurement (for both gauge and finished measurements).* Make a gauge swatch in each stitch pattern you'd like to use in your project and block it the same way you will be blocking your shrug. Determine the number of stitches per inch (centimeter) in the stitch pattern you're using for the body.

Stitches per inch (centimeter) (from your body swatch): _____ (A).

Stitches per inch (centimeter) (from your sleeve/edging pattern swatch): _____ (B).

You will start with a body rectangle that is approximately two times as wide as your crossback measurement.

Goal Body Width: _____ (C) (Choose body width from the table on the next page in your chosen unit of measurement.)

Goal Body Stitches: (A × C) = _____ (D) (Adjust count for stitch pattern if different from Stockinette or Garter).

Selecting Stitch Patterns
This project requires at least two different stitch patterns. One stitch pattern will be used in the body in both its flat and in-the-round versions, and the second stitch pattern will be used in the sleeves and body edging in its in-the-round version.

Since the body is worked both flat and in the round, Stockinette stitch and Garter stitch are good choices. This way, when you change from flat to in-the-round knitting, you won't have to make any adjustments so that motifs line up.

When selecting an in-the-round stitch pattern, the sky's the limit. Ribs, lace, even cables are all good choices. It really depends upon the look that you're after.

Body

Using a circular needle, provisionally cast on (optional) the adjusted stitches for (D). Work your stitch pattern flat for Length #1 in the table below, ending with a wrong-side row. Set piece aside, leaving stitches on the needle; don't cut the yarn (see Figure 1).

Carefully unravel the provisional cast-on and place these stitches on a second circular needle, picking up one additional stitch if necessary so that you have the same number of stitches on both needles (see Figure 2). Return to the stitches on the first needle and knit across them, then with the right side of the stitches on the second needle facing, knit across these stitches (see illustrations below). **Note:** *If no provisional cast-on was used, pick up and knit the original number of stitches (D) along the cast-on edge, picking up with the right side facing you. You will now have double the number of stitches on your needle that you started with.* Place a marker for the beginning of the round and continue working in rounds for Length #2 (see table below).

Work one last round, and make any stitch-count adjustments to accommodate your second stitch pattern's multiple. On the following round, begin your new stitch pattern and work to the desired length.

Bind off using your preferred stretchy bind-off method. Or, you could simply bind off loosely.

Sleeves

Using double-pointed needles, pick up and knit approximately 3 stitches for every 4 rows around the sleeve opening, being sure to pick up the correct multiple for your chosen stitch pattern. **Note:** *Since the gauge of your sleeve stitch pattern may differ from that of your body stitch pattern, you may need to experiment with the number of stitches you pick up to get the fit that you want.* Place a marker and work in rounds to the desired length. Bind off loosely. Repeat for the other sleeve.

FIGURE 1

provisional cast-on

FIGURE 2

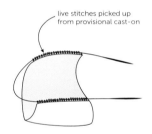

live stitches picked up from provisional cast-on

Womens' Sizes *(For a looser fit, size up)*

IN INCHES

	X-SMALL	SMALL	MEDIUM	LARGE	X-LARGE	2X-LARGE	3X-LARGE
BUST	28–30	32–34	36–38	40–42	44–46	48–50	52–54
CROSSBACK	14	15	16	17	17½	18	18½
BODY WIDTH	28	30	32	34	35	36	37
LENGTH #1	10	11	11	12	13	13	13
LENGTH #2	3	3	3½	4	4½	4½	4½

IN CENTIMETERS

	X-SMALL	SMALL	MEDIUM	LARGE	X-LARGE	2X-LARGE	3X-LARGE
BUST	71–76	81.5–86.5	91.5–96.5	101.5–106.5	112–117	122–127	132–137
CROSSBACK	36.5	38	40.5	43	44.5	45.5	47
BODY WIDTH	73	76	81	86	89	91	94
LENGTH #1	25.5	28	28	30.5	33	33	33
LENGTH #2	7.5	7.5	9	10	11.5	11.5	11.5

Provisional Cast-Ons

A provisional cast-on is used whenever you need to create a starting point in your knitting from which you may want to:

- knit in a different direction;

- add an edging later because you haven't yet decided what you want;

- create a symmetrical or two-directional piece of knitting.

Here are three ways to work a provisional cast-on:

LONG-TAIL PROVISIONAL CAST-ON

Using your working yarn and a slippery piece of waste yarn in a contrasting color and similar weight, make a slipknot with both strands and place it on your needle. Set up for Long-Tail Cast-On (see Special Techniques, page 278), but put the waste yarn over your thumb and the working yarn over your index finger.

Cast on as usual, and notice that the waste yarn creates a chain at the bottom of your needle. Cast on the number of stitches required in the pattern, but don't count or knit the original slipknot.

Cut your waste yarn, turn your work, and begin working stitches using the working yarn. Allow the original slipknot to hang there while you knit; it will mark the end from which you unravel the stitches.

Getting Your Stitches Back on Your Needles

Recall that you made a slipknot with your waste yarn and working yarn. Place your knitting right side up with the slipknot on your right.

Carefully untie the slipknot and begin to unravel the stitches. As you do this, you will see a loop of working yarn. This is your first stitch. Pluck out the waste yarn and place the working yarn loop on the needle, being careful not to twist the stitch. Continue across the remaining stitches. Have a sharp pair of scissors and a tapestry needle available in case you need to trim the waste yarn to remove it easily. Because there will be one fewer loop than the original number of stitches cast on, you will need to pick up or increase one stitch to match the number of cast-on stitches.

CROCHET HOOK PROVISIONAL CAST-ON

Using a slippery piece of waste yarn in a contrasting color and similar weight to your working yarn, and a crochet hook approximately the same size as your knitting needle, make a slipknot and place it on the crochet hook. Hold the knitting needle in your left hand and the hook in your right hand above the needle. Take the waste yarn under the needle and hold it over your left index finger.

Take the crochet hook over the needle and behind the working yarn from left to right, then draw the yarn back over the needle and through the st on the crochet hook; 1 st has been cast on. Bring the working yarn under the needle and to the back again. Repeat this process until the correct number of stitches are on the needle. Note that you will be casting on from left to right, rather than from right to left.

Cut your waste yarn and fasten off. With working yarn, work directly into the cast-on waste yarn stitches.

How to Remove the Crochet Hook Provisional Cast-On

Beginning with the fastened-off end of the crocheted cast-on, unravel the end from the last loop.

Pull the end carefully and begin to unravel the stitches. As you do this, you will see a loop of working yarn. This is your first stitch. Pluck out the waste yarn and place the working yarn on the needle, being careful not to twist the stitch. Continue across the remaining stitches. Because there will be one fewer loop than the original number of stitches cast on, you will need to pick up or increase one stitch to match the number of cast-on stitches.

CROCHET CHAIN PROVISIONAL CAST-ON

Using a slippery piece of waste yarn in a contrast color and similar weight to your working yarn, and a crochet hook approximately the same size as your knitting needle, make a slipknot and place it on the crochet hook.

Crochet a chain that is several chain stitches longer than the number of cast-on stitches required. Fasten off the last stitch and cut the yarn. Tie a knot in the fastened-off end so you will know which end to unzip.

Looking at the crochet chain, note that one side is smooth and the other side has bumps. Using your knitting needle, pick up and knit a stitch directly into the first bump. Repeat this process, being careful to pick up and knit only into the bumps, until the correct number of stitches is on the needle.

How to Remove the Crochet Chain Provisional Cast-On

Look for the knot tied into one end of the crocheted chain. Untie the knot and unfasten the end.

Pull the end carefully and begin to unzip the stitches. As you do this, you will see a loop of working yarn. This is your first stitch. Pluck out the waste yarn and place the working yarn on the needle, being careful not to twist the stitch. Continue across the remaining stitches. Because there will be one fewer loop than the original number of stitches cast on, you will need to pick up or increase one stitch to match the number of cast-on stitches.

INSTRUCTIONS

Here are the directions for the size Medium Shrug shown on page 268 and opposite.

FINISHED MEASUREMENTS
31" (78.5 cm) Body width; 36" (91.5 cm) cuff-to-cuff width; 11" (28 cm) long

YARN
Blue Sky Fibers Woolstok [100% fine highland wool; 123 yards (113 meters) / 2 ounces (50 grams)]: 5 hanks #1320 Spring Ice

NEEDLES
Two 29" (70 cm) long or longer circular needles and one set of five double-pointed needles size US 7 (4.5 mm)
Change needle size if necessary to obtain correct gauge.

NOTIONS
Stitch markers

GAUGES
13¼ sts and 22 rnds = 4" (10 cm) in St st, washed and blocked
13 sts and 24 rnds = 4" (10 cm) in Single Lace Rib, washed and blocked, unstretched

....

STITCH PATTERN

SINGLE LACE RIB

(multiple of 4 sts; 2-rnd repeat)
Rnd 1: *K1, yo, k2tog, p1; repeat from * to end.
Rnd 2: *K1, p1, k2tog, yo; repeat from * to end.
Repeat Rnds 1 and 2 for Single Lace Rib.

SINGLE LACE RIB

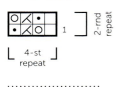

....

Body
Using Provisional CO of your choice (see sidebar page 271), CO 103 sts. Do not join; work back and forth in rows. Change to working yarn. Begin St st; work even until piece measures 11" (28 cm) from the beginning, ending with a WS row. Set aside, leaving sts on needle; do not cut yarn.

Carefully unravel Provisional CO and place sts on second circular needle, picking up 1 additional st if necessary so that you have 103 sts on this needle.

Next Row (RS): Returning to sts on first circular needle, knit to end of needle, then with RS of sts on second circular needle facing, knit across these sts—206 sts. Join for working in the rnd; pm for beginning of rnd.

Work in St st (knit every rnd) for 3" (7.5 cm), decreasing 2 sts evenly on last rnd—204 sts remain.

Change to Single Lace Rib; work even for 2½" (6.5 cm).

Bind-Off Rnd: *K2tog-tbl, slip st back to left-hand needle; repeat from * until 1 st remains. Fasten off.

Sleeves
With RS of Body facing, using dpns, pick up and knit 48 sts around sleeve opening. Join for working in the rnd; pm for beginning of rnd. Begin Single Lace rib; work even until piece measures 2½" (6.5 cm) from pick-up rnd. BO all sts as for Body.

Finishing
Block as desired.

Oversized Cowl

....

This from-scratch pattern, as written, can be worn as a hood or a cowl. Worked from the bottom up and in the round, it has front and back panels in a lacy stitch pattern and side panels of Seed stitch where all the shaping happens. To customize, select another stitch pattern for the front and back and keep the Seed stitch sides that are outlined in the tutorial. Another option would be to swap out the side panels with a plain stitch like Stockinette. The tutorial follows. To make the Oversized Cowl pictured here, the pattern can be found on page 277.

TUTORIAL

SIZES
Small/Medium (Large/X-Large, 2X/3X-Large)

FINISHED MEASUREMENTS
See Measurements table.

YARN
See Calculating How Much Yarn You Need on page 15.

NEEDLES
One 29" (70 cm) long or longer circular needle in size needed to obtain desired gauge.

NOTIONS
Stitch markers

Getting Started
Note: Choose a unit of measurement (either inches or centimeters) and work only in the chosen unit of measurement (for both gauge and finished measurements). Take a look at the table below and decide what size you'd like to make. Remember, these are guidelines only and depending upon the main stitch pattern you choose and your gauge, you will end up making adjustments to stitch count, which might slightly change the final measurements.

Make two gauge swatches, one in your chosen main stitch pattern and one in your side panel pattern, and block them the same way you'll be blocking your cowl, then fill in the blanks below. Note that your chosen stitch patterns should have the same or similar row gauge to keep the top and bottom edges even across the patterns.

Gauges
Main Panel Pattern:
Stitches per inch (centimeter) (from your swatch): _____ (A).

Rows per inch (centimeter): _____ (B).

Side Panel Pattern:
Stitches per inch (centimeter) (from your swatch): _____ (C).

Rows per inch (centimeter): _____ (D).

Measurements
Goal Bottom Circumference (see table on page 276): _____ (E).

Your side panels will each be approximately $\frac{1}{6}$ of the total bottom circumference; the main pattern panels will each be approximately $\frac{1}{3}$ of the total bottom circumference.

Goal Bottom Main Panel Width: $0.33 \times E =$ _____ (F).

Goal Bottom Side Panel Width: $0.165 \times E =$ _____ (G).

Goal Top Circumference (see Table): _____ (H).

Goal Top Side Panel Width: $(H - (2 \times F)) / 2 =$ _____ (I).
Note: Your main panel will stay the same throughout the piece; all of the shaping will be worked within the side panels.

Stitch Counts
Main Panel Stitches to cast on: $A \times F =$ _____ (J). (Round this number up or down to accommodate your chosen stitch pattern.)

Side Panel Stitches to cast on: $C \times G =$ _____ (K). (Round this number up or down to accommodate your chosen stitch pattern.)

Side Panel Stitches at Top: $C \times I =$ _____ (L). (In order to make the decreases work, adjust this number so that when you subtract it from G, the remainder is evenly divisible by 4.)

Number of 4-stitch Decrease Rounds in Shaping Section: $(K - L) / 4 =$ _____ (M).

Shaping
You will begin shaping your cowl at 4" (10 cm) from the cast-on edge, and you will end shaping approximately 2" (5 cm) before binding off.

Total Cowl Length (see Table): _____ (N).

Goal Shaping Length: $N - 6$" (15 cm) = _____ (O).

Number of Rounds in Shaping Section: $(O \times B) - 1$ round = _____ (P).

Frequency of Decrease Rounds: $P / M - 1 =$ _____ (Q).
Note: You will work the decrease round every Q rounds.

Using your working yarn and needles that you used for your gauge swatch, cast on stitches in the following order: (K), pm, (J), pm, (K), pm, (J). Join for working in the round, being careful not to twist your stitches, and place a unique marker for the beginning of the round.

Purl one round, then begin working Seed stitch (see page 277) or Stockinette stitch in the side panels and your main stitch pattern in the front and back panels.

Work approximately 4" (10 cm) of your cowl. After that, it will be time to shape it. On your first decrease round, [work 3 stitches together (sssk if the first stitch should be a knit stitch to keep in pattern or sssp if the first stitch should be a purl stitch), work in Seed or Stockinette stitch

to 3 stitches before the first center panel, work 3 stitches together (k3tog if the first stitch should be a knit stitch to keep in pattern or p3tog if the first stitch should be a purl stitch), slip your marker, then work across the center panel to the next marker, slip that marker] twice. You will now have worked one decrease round, decreasing a total of 8 stitches. Repeat the decrease round at the frequency you have determined (Q) the number of times you have determined, minus the first decrease round that you have already worked (M − 1).

Once you've finished all your decreases, measure your cowl (or try it on), and continue working until it is the length in the Sizes table below, then work one purl round. Bind off loosely in pattern.

Sizes

IN INCHES	SMALL/MEDIUM	LARGE/X-LARGE	2X-LARGE/3X-LARGE
WOMAN'S BUST	32–38	40–46	48–54
BOTTOM CIRCUMFERENCE	44	52	60
TOP CIRCUMFERENCE	34	36	38
LENGTH	17	18	19
IN CENTIMETERS	SMALL	LARGE	3X-LARGE
WOMAN'S BUST	81.5–96.5	101.5–117	122–137
BOTTOM CIRCUMFERENCE	112	132	152.5
TOP CIRCUMFERENCE	86.5	91.5	96.5
LENGTH	43	45.5	48.5

INSTRUCTIONS

If you want to dive in and make a 44" (112 cm) oversized cowl like the one shown on page 274 and opposite, here are the instructions:

FINISHED MEASUREMENTS
42" (106.5 cm) bottom circumference; 34" (86.5 cm) top circumference; 17" (43 cm) long

YARN
Blue Sky Fibers Woolstok [100% fine highland wool; 123 yards (113 meters) / 2 ounces (50 grams)]: 5 hanks #1307 Pressed Grapes

NEEDLES
One circular needle 24" (60 cm) long size US 7 (4.5 mm)
Change needle size if necessary to obtain correct gauge.

· ·

STITCH PATTERNS

SEED STITCH

(even number of sts; 2-rnd repeat)
Rnd 1: *P1, k1; repeat from * to end.
Rnd 2: Knit the purl sts and purl the knit sts as they face you.
Repeat Rnd 2 for Seed Stitch.

LACE AND SEED STITCH

(multiple of 8 sts; 14-rnd repeat)
Rnd 1: *P1, k1; repeat from * to end.
Rnds 2–8: Knit the purl sts and purl the knit sts as they face you.
Rnd 9: *K1, yo, ssk, k3, k2tog, yo; repeat from * to end.
Rnd 10: Knit.
Rnd 11: K2, yo, ssk, k1, k2tog, yo, *k3, yo, ssk, k1, k2tog, yo; repeat from * to last st, k1.
Rnd 12: Knit.
Rnd 13: K3, yo, sk2p, yo, *k5, yo, sk2p, yo; repeat from * to last 2 sts, k2.
Rnd 14: Knit.
Repeat Rnds 1–14 for Lace and Seed Stitch.

· ·

NOTIONS
Stitch markers

GAUGES
15 sts and 25 rnds = 4" (10 cm) in Lace and Seed Stitch, washed and blocked, unstretched
16 sts and 25 rnds = 4" (10 cm) in Seed Stitch, washed and blocked, unstretched

Cowl

CO 160 sts as follows: 24 sts for left side, pm, 56 sts for Front, pm, 24 sts for right side, 56 sts for Back, place unique marker for beginning of rnd.

Knit 2 rnds.
Purl 1 rnd.

Set-Up Rnd: [Work Seed st to marker, sm, work Lace and Seed Stitch to marker, sm] twice.
Work Rnds 2–14 of Lace and Seed Stitch once, then Rnds 1–14 once.

Shape Cowl

Decrease Rnd: [Sssp, work to 3 sts before marker, k3tog, sm, work to next marker, sm] twice—8 sts decreased.
Work 27 rnds even, ending with Rnd 14 of pattern.
Repeat Decrease Rnd once—144 sts remain.
Work 27 rnds even, ending with Rnd 14 of pattern.
Repeat Decrease Rnd once—136 sts remain.
Work 13 rnds even, ending with Rnd 14 of pattern.
Repeat Decrease Rnd once—128 sts remain.
Work 11 rnds even, ending with Rnd 12 of pattern.
Repeat Decrease Rnd once—120 sts remain.
Work 1 rnd even (Rnd 14 of pattern).
Change to Seed st across all sts, removing all markers except beginning-of-rnd marker; work 8 rnds even.
Purl 1 rnd. Knit 2 rnds. Bind off all sts.

Finishing
Block as desired.

LACE AND SEED STITCH

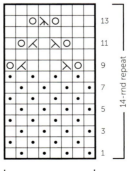

Special Techniques

APPLIED I-CORD: Using a double-pointed needle, cast on the desired number of sts; the working yarn will be at the left-hand side of the needle. *Transfer the needle with the sts to your left hand, bring the yarn around behind the work to the right-hand side; insert right-hand tip of same needle under st at edge to which I-cord will be applied; using a second double-pointed needle, work across the sts as follows: k2tog, k2, pulling the yarn from left to right for the first st; do not turn. Slide the sts to the opposite end of the needle; repeat from * around the entire edge to which the I-cord is to be applied, working even rows between pick-up rows if necessary so that I-cord is smooth. When working around a corner, work 2 or more rows at each corner without picking up a st to allow the I-cord to turn the corner smoothly.

BACKWARD-LOOP CO: Make a loop (using a slip knot) with the working yarn and place it on the right-hand needle (first st CO), *wind yarn around thumb clockwise, insert right-hand needle into the front of the loop on thumb, remove thumb and tighten st on needle; repeat from * for remaining sts to be CO, or for casting on at the end of a row in progress.

KITCHENER STITCH: Using a blunt tapestry needle, thread a length of yarn approximately four times the length of the section to be joined. Hold the pieces to be joined with wrong sides together, with the needles holding the sts parallel, both ends pointing to the right. Working from right to left, insert tapestry needle into first st on front needle as if to purl, pull yarn through, leaving st on needle; insert tapestry needle into first st on back needle as if to knit, pull yarn through, leaving st on needle; *insert tapestry needle into first st on front needle as if to knit, pull yarn through,

remove st from needle; insert tapestry needle into next st on front needle as if to purl, pull yarn through, leave st on needle; insert tapestry needle into first st on back needle as if to purl, pull yarn through, remove st from needle; insert tapestry needle into next st on back needle as if to knit, pull yarn through, leave st on needle. Repeat from *, working 3 or 4 sts at a time, then go back and adjust tension to match the pieces being joined. When 1 st remains on each needle, cut yarn and pass through last 2 sts to fasten off.

LONG-TAIL CO: Leaving tail with about 1" (2.5 cm) of yarn for each st to be cast on, make a slipknot in the yarn and place it on the right-hand needle, with the tail to the front and the working end to the back. Insert the thumb and forefinger of your left hand between the strands of yarn so that the working end is around your forefinger, and the tail end is around your thumb "slingshot" fashion; *insert the tip of the right-hand needle into the front loop on the thumb, hook the strand of yarn coming from the forefinger from back to front, and draw it through the loop on your thumb; remove your thumb from the loop and pull on the working yarn to tighten the new st on the right-hand needle; return your thumb and forefinger to their original positions, and repeat from * for remaining sts to be CO.

PROVISIONAL CO: See sidebar page 271.

Symbol Key

....

☐ Knit on RS, purl on WS.

▪ Purl on RS, knit on WS.

Ⓠ K1-tbl on RS, p1-tbl on WS.

● **MB: Make Bobble.** (K1, p1, k1, p1) into same st to increase to 4 sts, pass second, third, then fourth sts one at a time over first st and off needle.

Ⓞ Yo

Ⓥ Slip 1 purlwise wyib on RS, slip 1 purlwise wyif on WS.

⩔ Slip 1 purlwise wyif on RS, slip 1 purlwise wyib on WS.

⩘ LLI: Left lifted increase.

⩗ RLIL Right lifted increase.

⧅ K2tog on RS, p2tog on WS.

⧄ Ssk on RS, ssp on WS.

⧅ P2tog on RS, k2tog on WS.

⧄ Ssp on RS, ssk on WS.

⧅ K3tog on RS, p3tog on WS.

⧄ Sk2p on RS, sp2p on WS.

⧅ P3tog on RS.

⧄ S2kp2 on RS, s2pp2 on WS.

RC: Right Cross. On RS rows, insert tip of right-hand needle into front of second st, bringing tip to front of work between second and first sts, knit st, knit first st through front loop, slip both sts from left-hand needle together. On WS rows, purl into front of second st, then purl into front of first st, slip both sts from left-hand needle together.

LC: Left Cross. Insert needle from back to front between first and second sts on left-hand needle and knit the second st through the front loop. Knit first st; slip both sts from left-hand needle together.

RPC: Right Purl Cross. Slip 1 st to cable needle, hold to back, k1, p1 from cable needle.

LPC: Left Purl Cross. Slip 1 st to cable needle, hold to front, p1, k1 from cable needle.

1/2 RC: 1 over 2 Right Cross. Slip 2 sts to cable needle, hold to back, k1, k2 from cable needle.

1/2 LC: 1 over 2 Left Cross. Slip 1 st to cable needle, hold to front, k2, k1 from cable needle

2/1 RC: 2 over 1 Right Cross. Slip 1 st to cable needle, hold to back, k2, k1 from cable needle.

2/1 LC: 2 over 1 Left Cross. Slip 2 sts to cable needle, hold to front, k1, k2 from cable needle.

2/1 RPC: 2 over 1 Right Purl Cross. Slip 1 st to cable needle, hold to back, k2, p1 from cable needle.

2/1 LPC: 2 over 1 Left Purl Cross. Slip 2 sts to cable needle, hold to front, p1, k2 from cable needle.

C4B: Cable 4 Back. Slip 2 sts to cable needle, hold to back, k2, k2 from cable needle.

C4F: Cable 4 Front. Slip 2 sts to cable needle, hold to front, k2, k2 from cable needle.

C4B-p: Cable 4 Back, purled. Slip 2 sts to cable needle, hold to back, k2, p2 from cable needle.

C4F-p: Cable 4 Front, purled. Slip 2 sts to cable needle, hold to front, p2, k2 from cable needle.

3/1 RC: 3 over 1 Right Cross. Slip 1 st to cable needle, hold to back, k3, k1 from cable needle.

3/1 LC: 3 over 1 Left Cross. Slip 3 sts to cable needle, hold to front, k1, k3 from cable needle.

2/3 LC: 2 over 3 Left Cross. Slip 2 sts to cable needle, hold to front, k3, k2 from cable needle.

C6B: Cable 6 Back. Slip 3 sts to cable needle, hold to back, k3, k3 from cable needle.

C6F: Cable 6 Front. Slip 3 sts to cable needle, hold to front, k3, k3 from cable needle.

Abbreviations

....

1/2 LC: 1 over 2 Left Cross. Slip 1 stitch to cable needle, hold to front, k2, k1 from cable needle.

1/2 RC: 1 over 2 Right Cross. Slip 2 stitches to cable needle, hold to back, k1, k2 from cable needle.

2/1 LC: 2 over 1 Left Cross. Slip 2 stitches to cable needle, hold to front, k1, k2 from cable needle.

2/1 LPC: 2 over 1 Left Purl Cross. Slip 2 stitches to cable needle, hold to front, p1, k2 from cable needle.

2/1 RC: 2 over 1 Right Cross. Slip 1 stitch to cable needle, hold to back, k2, k1 from cable needle.

2/1 RPC: 2 over 1 Right Purl Cross. Slip 1 stitch to cable needle, hold to back, k2, p1 from cable needle.

2/3 LC: 2 over 3 Left Cross. Slip 2 stitches to cable needle, hold to front, k3, k2 from cable needle.

3/1 LC: 3 over 1 Left Cross. Slip 3 stitches to cable needle, hold to front, k1, k3 from cable needle.

3/1 RC: 3 over 1 Right Cross. Slip 1 stitch to cable needle, hold to back, k3, k1 from cable needle.

BO: Bind off.

C4B: Cable 4 Back. Slip 2 stitches to cable needle, hold to back, k2, k2 from cable needle.

C4B-p: Cable 4 Back, purled. Slip 2 stitches to cable needle, hold to back, k2, p2 from cable needle.

C4F: Cable 4 Front. Slip 2 stitches to cable needle, hold to front, k2, k2 from cable needle.

C4F-p: Cable 4 Front, purled. Slip 2 stitches to cable needle, hold to front, p2, k2 from cable needle.

C6B: Cable 6 Back. Slip 3 stitches to cable needle, hold to back, k3, k3 from cable needle.

C6F: Cable 6 Front. Slip 3 stitches to cable needle, hold to front, k3, k3 from cable needle.

CN: Cable needle

CO: Cast on.

dpn: Double-pointed needle(s)

k1b: Knit into stitch below next stitch on left-hand needle, dropping stitch from left-hand needle.

k1-tbl: Knit 1 stitch through back loop.

k2tog: Knit 2 stitches together—1 stitch decreased, right-slanting.

k2tog-tbl: Knit 2 stitches together through back loops—1 stitch decreased, left-slanting.

k3tog: Knit 3 stitches together—2 stitches decreased, right-slanting.

k4tog: Knit 4 stitches together—3 stitches decreased, right-slanting.

k: Knit.

LC: Left Cross. Insert needle from back to front between first and second stitches on left-hand needle and knit the second stitch through the front loop. Knit first stitch; slip both stitches from left-hand needle together.

LLI: Left Lifted Increase. With left-hand needle, pick up left leg of stitch 2 stitches below stitch just knit; knit picked-up stitch through back loop—1 stitch increased, left-slanting.

LPC: Left Purl Cross. Slip 1 stitch to cable needle, hold to front, p1, k1 from cable needle.

M1-L: Make 1 left-slanting. With tip of left-hand needle inserted from front to back, lift strand between 2 needles onto left-hand needle; knit strand through back loop—1 stitch increased.

M1-R: Make 1 right-slanting. With tip of left-hand needle inserted from back to front, lift strand between 2 needles onto left-hand needle; knit strand through front loop—1 stitch increased.

MB: Make Bobble. (K1, p1, k1, p1) into same stitch to increase to 4 stitches, pass second, third, then fourth stitches one at a time over first stitch and off needle.

p1b: Purl into stitch below next stitch on left-hand needle, dropping stitch from left-hand needle.

p1-tbl: Purl 1 stitch through back loop.

p2tog: Purl 2 stitches together—1 stitch decreased, right-slanting.

p3tog: Purl 3 stitches together—2 stitches decreased, right-slanting.

p: Purl.

pm: Place marker.

RC: Right Cross. On right-side rows, insert tip of right-hand needle into front of second stitch, bringing tip to front of work between second and first stitches, knit stitch, knit first stitch through front loop, slip both stitches from left-hand needle together. On wrong-side rows, purl into front of second stitch, then purl into front of first stitch, slip both stitches from left-hand needle together.

Rev St st: Reverse Stockinette stitch. When working flat, purl on right-side rows, knit on wrong-side rows. When working in the round, purl all sts.

RLI: Right Lifted Increase. With right-hand needle, pick up right side of stitch below next stitch on left-hand needle, and place it on left-hand needle; knit picked-up stitch through front loop—1 stitch increased, right-slanting.

RPC: Right Purl Cross. Slip 1 stitch to cable needle, hold to back, k1, p1 from cable needle.

Rnd(s): Round(s)

RS: Right side

s2kp2: Slip next 2 stitches together to right-hand needle as if to knit 2 together, k1, pass the 2 slipped stitches over—2 stitches decreased, centered.

s2pp2: Slip next 2 stitches knitwise one at a time to right-hand needle, then slip them back to left-hand needle in their new orientation. Slip the same 2 stitches together to right-hand needle as if to purl 2 together through the back loops, p1, pass the 2 slipped stitches over—2 stitches decreased, centered.

sk2p: Slip next stitch knitwise to the right-hand needle, k2tog, pass slipped stitch over stitch from k2tog—2 stitches decreased, left-slanting.

sm: Slip marker

sp2p: Purl 2 stitches together, then slip resulting stitch back to left-hand needle. Slip second stitch on left-hand needle over last stitch, then slip resulting stitch to right-hand needle—2 stitches decreased, left-slanting.

ssk: Slip next 2 stitches to right-hand needle one at a time as if to knit; return them to left-hand needle one at a time in their new orientation; knit them together through back loops—1 stitch decreased, left-slanting.

ssp: Slip next 2 stitches to right-hand needle one at a time as if to knit; return them to left-hand needle one at a time in their new orientation; purl them together through back loops—1 stitch decreased, left-slanting.

sssp: Slip next 3 stitches to right-hand needle one at a time as if to knit; return them to left-hand needle one at a time in their new orientation; purl them together through back loops—2 stitches decreased, left-slanting.

ssssk: Slip next 4 stitches to right-hand needle one at a time as if to knit; return them to left-hand needle one at a time in their new orientation; knit them together through back loops—3 stitches decreased, left-slanting.

st(s): Stitch(es)

tbl: Through the back loop

tog: Together

WS: Wrong side

wyib: With yarn in back

wyif: With yarn in front

yo: Yarnover

Stitch Multiple Index

Index

Acknowledgments

As I look back to the year I began to knit again—around 2001—I was expecting my first child. I made her a tiny strawberry cap that I planned for her to wear when she came home. Although a series of events intervened and she never wore that cap, her sister, who came a year later, did. Despite all that happened, I will forever cherish the cap and its history. There was love and hope woven into each and every stitch of that tiny cap.

Knitting is more than just making fabric with yarn and needles. When we knit a fabric, we knit into it hopes and dreams. We knit for solidarity or for protest. We knit for comfort or stress relief or for utilitarian purposes—but even the utilitarian projects bear memories and marks of our personal history.

My hope is that you will use the patterns within this book to add your own personal history to items you use, give away, or knit "just because."

This book would not have been possible without the support and understanding of my husband and daughter, nor my friends both personal and virtual. Thanks to Cristina Garces and Shawna Mullen, my editors, and to Darilyn Carnes, whose design brought this book together. I owe Sue McCain, my technical editor, so much gratitude. Her expertise and ability to spot my errors and shed light on my many knitting conundrums are valuable beyond words. Thank you to Robin Melanson for refining the text.

One of my very favorite yarn companies, Blue Sky Fibers, generously provided all of the yarn for this book. I am grateful for their vast palette of colors and the exquisite quality of their yarns. Knitting the many swatches and projects for this book with their yarn was, and still is, a pleasure.

About the Author

Wendy Bernard is a knitwear designer–author based in Southern California. She is the author of the *Custom Knits* series, *Up, Down, All-Around Stitch Dictionary,* and *The Knitting All Around Stitch Dictionary*. Her knitwear patterns have been published in several magazines such as *Interweave Knits* and *Knitscene* and in several edited volumes.

Editor: Cristina Garces
Designer: Darilyn Lowe Carnes
Production Manager: Katie Gaffney

Library of Congress Control Number: 2013945660

ISBN: 978-1-4197-2906-5
eISBN: 978-1-68335-218-1

Printed and bound in China
10 9 8 7 6 5 4 3 2

Abrams books are available at special discounts when purchased in quantity for premiums and
promotions as well as fundraising or educational use. Special editions can also be created to
specification. For details, contact specialsales@abramsbooks.com or the address below.

ABRAMS The Art of Books
195 Broadway, New York, NY 10007
abramsbooks.com